Compliments of
The Reynolds and Reynolds Company
NADA 2008

Stay legal! Tom

CARLAW® II
STREET LEGAL

CARLAW® II
STREET LEGAL

THOMAS B. HUDSON

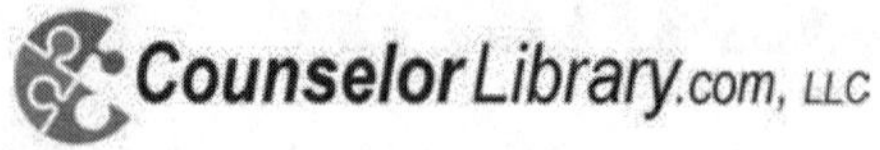

ISBN: 978-0-9779501-2-6

Printed in the United States of America

Project Director: Patricia A. Fitzpatrick
Production Manager: Marlene K. Locke
Editor: Janet A. Martin
Cover and Jacket Design: Christopher A. Pearl
Book Design: Lisa A. Allen
Printer: Victor Graphics

DEDICATIONS

To Lily Grace, my best critic,
and loving and supportive wife,
and to
Teresa Rohwedder, our colleague,
who lost a long fight with breast cancer.
She is in our thoughts daily.

CONTENTS

ACKNOWLEDGEMENTS

Again, the list is long, and to our loyal readers, it's also familiar. First and foremost, our clients and friends in the car business continue to educate me and keep me honest.

Our Hudson Cook, LLP, lawyers, all 39 of them, constitute an invaluable resource. On the one hand, I often swipe case summaries that they have done for our monthly reporting service and build articles on them. On the other hand, I have ready access to some of the best brains in the consumer financial services legal field. They help insure that what I write is actually correct (mostly). A special thanks to my pal, Emily Beck, who proofs nearly everything I do, often catching glitches, and always improving my work.

Marlene Locke and Pat Fitzpatrick are, after three books, a veritable publishing company themselves. On three separate outings in the book ballpark, they have had to learn new publishing approaches, techniques, and operational methods on their own and on the fly. They are a super team.

Janet Martin does her third stint as editor and, in the interim, has finished her own book, *The Christmas Swap*. She's one of those people who actually gets things done rather than just talks about them.

Lisa Allen again made our word processing text look like a book, and served as a valuable second editor. The cover to this newest edition, like that of *The F&I Desk Book*, is the work of the imaginative Chris Pearl. The hot rod appearing on the cover is owned by Brian Ecker, who kindly let us use photos of his mean machine.

All of the above helped with the hits and runs in this volume. The errors, small and large, and the typos, substantive or not, well, they are mine.

INTRODUCTION

Coming up with a book name can be a challenge. My first book, which was a collection of nine years of articles, was simply ***CARLAW®***, which is also the name of our Internet-based monthly reporting service. We did that just to confuse everyone.

The second book was a reference volume, and we titled it ***CARLAW®*** *F&I Legal Desk Book.* No pizzazz, but it got the job done.

When we started the third book, which, like ***CARLAW®***, was a collection of articles, our working title was *Son of* ***CARLAW®***. As we approached press time, Pat Fitzpatrick and Marlene Locke of our team began to frown. "Too much like 'Son of Sam' or 'SOB,'" they said.

So, we had a contest, and asked all hands to submit suggestions. The only rule was that the title had to contain either "CARLAW" or "CARLAWYER" to maintain the brand. Other than that, people were free to submit as many names as they wished.

Within minutes, Tim Naughton proffered ***CARLAW®*** *II, On the Road Again*, which I liked, but which I thought might draw some copyright fire from Willie Nelson. Other suggestions with copyright problems were Liz Huber's ***CARLAW®*** *for Idiots* and Hattie Stewart's *Mamas Don't Let Your Babies Grow Up To Be CARLAWYERS.*

Because I lost a thumb in a shotgun accident when I was 13, and because this place (which also doubles as a legal office) is often like a fraternity or sorority house when it comes to people ragging on each other, I expected at least a couple of "thumb" entries. It took 40 minutes for the first one, Jeremy Sausser's ***CARLAW® II: Rules of Thumb by Tom Hudson.*** A couple more like that came in, so I decided to shut them up by submitting my own: *Thumbthings You Need to Know About* ***CARLAW®***. That worked. They still gagged, but silently.

We got a couple of variations on *Cruising with* ***CARLAW®***, some references to Bruce Willis movies, Homer Simpson, Posh Spice, Paris Hilton, and my second favorite, from son Brian, ***CARLAW®*** *Reloaded.* We got puns, some of them (especially the ones from David Darland) very bad, and one suggestion that we name it *The* ***CARLAW®*** *Diet Book*, because diet books always sell well. Clara Alvarado must have felt personally challenged by the contest—she ended up getting a prize for most entries, with 28.

I knew we had our winner, though, when Dan Laudicina offered ***CARLAW®*** *II: Street Legal.* We figured that most half-way serious motorheads would know that the term "street legal" refers to a hot rod or racing car that is tame enough, or appropriately equipped, to drive on the street. Laura Slusher had just shown me a bunch of photos of her dad's newly restored hot rod, so we put the two together and came up with a title and a cover!

So, that's the story on the title. The book is a collection of my articles together with some articles from the fine lawyers I'm privileged to work with. The collection is drawn from material published since our first book, ***CARLAW®***. We hope you enjoy the ride, er, read!

Tom Hudson
November 2007

NOT JUST A BOOK

Books are cool. Books are really useful. You can haul one to the beach with you, or read it on an airplane.

Of course, with today's electronics, you can often get the same sort of content from computer and phone devices, if you are into that sort of thing, and if you are willing to put up with their limitations. But for many of us, there is nothing like a book.

But books, once printed, are immediately dated. If something happens after printing, you're out of luck until the next edition, if there is one.

Because laws change, we thought that it would be helpful to you, our readers, to have a resource that would permit us to let you know if we wanted to communicate with you about events that occurred after printing, and that would permit you to communicate with us. To that end, we have established www.carlawstreetlegal.com.

So, we invite you to come visit us. Check for important updates. Give us your feedback on the articles in the book. Any pitches are fair game—slow balls, fastballs, curves. Just, please, no "thumb" slurs. Those are out of the ballpark.

MEET THE AUTHORS

Here are the authors and editors who wrote the articles featured in this book. They are among the 39 attorneys at the law firm of Hudson Cook, LLP, and represent over 450 years' experience in consumer finance.

Thomas B. Hudson
Phone: 410.865.5411
E-mail: thudson@hudco.com

Teresa Rohwedder
1963–2006

Emily Marlow Beck
Phone: 410.865.5438
E-mail: ebeck@hudco.com

C. Carter Berkeley
Phone: 410.782.2346
E-mail: cberkeley@hudco.com

Catherine M. Brennan
Phone: 410.865.5405
E-mail: cbrennan@hudco.com

James Chareq
Phone: 202.327.9711
E-mail: jchareq@hudco.com

Charles F. Dodge, Jr.
Phone: 410.865.5427
E-mail: cdodge@hudco.com

Patricia E.M. Covington
Phone: 410.865.5409
E-mail: pcovington@hudco.com

Rochelle B. (Shelley) Fowler
Phone: 410.865.5406
E-mail: rfowler@hudco.com

Michael A. Goodman
Phone: 202.327.9704
E-mail: mgoodman@hudco.com

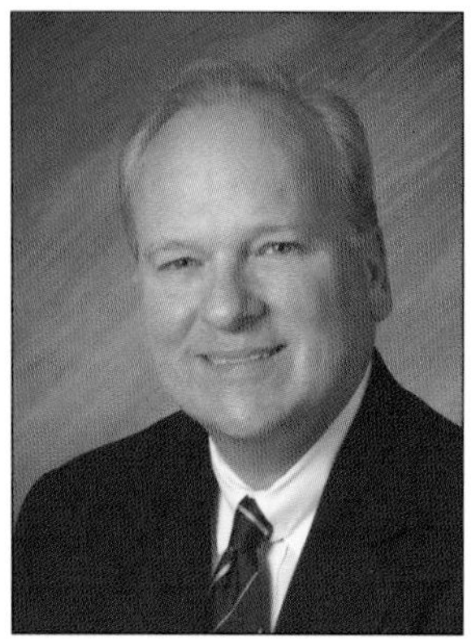

D. Brent Gunsalus
Phone: 434.220.9310
E-mail: dbgunsalus@hudco.com

Maya P. Hill
Phone: 410.782.2356
E-mail: mhill@hudco.com

Daniel J. Laudicina
Phone: 410.865.5435
E-mail: dlaudicina@hudco.com

Wingrove S. Lynton
Phone: 410.865.5408
E-mail: wslynton@hudco.com

Nicole Frush Munro
Phone: 410.865.5430
E-mail: nmunro@hudco.com

Meghan S. Musselman
Phone: 410.865.5403
E-mail: mmusselman@hudco.com

Timothy O. Naughton
Phone: 410.782.2353
E-mail: tnaughton@hudco.com

L. Jean Noonan
Phone: 202.327.9700
E-mail: jnoonan@hudco.com

Clayton C. Swears
Phone: 410.865.5419
E-mail: cswears@hudco.com

David K. Tomar
Phone: 410.865.5407
E-mail: dtomar@hudco.com

Alicia H. Tortarolo
Phone: 310.536.9099
E-mail: atortarolo@hudco.com

Catherine C. Worthington
Phone: 410.782.2349
E-mail: cworthington@hudco.com

Chapter 1

Basics

You've heard the phrase, "Jailhouse Lawyer"? That's a prison denizen who has used his stretch of time to read and absorb all the law he can lay his hands on. Some of these folks get to be pretty fair lawyers, but most just know enough to be dangerous.

There are "Dealership Lawyers" as well—people who have been in the car business since the invention of the wheel, and who, over time, have picked up bits of this and that legal knowledge. Some of these folks get to be pretty fair car sale, lease, and F&I experts, but many, if not most, understand just enough to sound like they know what they are talking about, but not enough to stay out of trouble.

There are dozens of state and federal laws that regulate the credit, sale, and lease of cars by dealers, and dealers must navigate them every day for every deal. Dealer personnel seldom get any significant amount of legal training, and they have very few resources to help them understand what all those regulatory laws require and prohibit. How can a dedicated car dealer learn what he needs to know to do his job effectively when the bulk of information he needs could easily require three years of concentrated study and a law degree?

In this chapter, we discuss, in no particular order, a number of basic concepts that dealers need to know. Bankruptcy, corporate buyers, negative equity, different prices for cash and credit customers—it is all here, and more. Our intent is to arm you, not with a "jailhouse degree," but rather with a handy guide to specific cases, conclusions, and practical concepts to draw on. There are useful signposts within these stories that highlight the everyday conundrums we all encounter in the world of cars and the law.

Most of us (thankfully) don't have time to burn behind bars. So, instead we offer a timely reference, which, along with the

Web site, www.carlawstreetlegal.com, should provide specific answers to further questions you may have.

Happy reading!

Understanding Vehicle Finance

October 2005

By Thomas B. Hudson

Would you, Mr. and Ms. Dealer, be interested in a helpful training aid that you could use to educate your dealership personnel (and, quite likely, yourself) about one of the basic things you do for a living—selling and financing cars?

And would you be interested in having a booklet you could give to every customer that accurately and in detail explains the basics of buying a car on credit in language pitched at about the tenth grade level?

And how about a booklet with your dealer's name and address stamped on it that you could take to the local high school for distribution to seniors, to hand out to the teacher of "personal finance" or "life skills" (or whatever they are calling the course these days)? And would you be impressed if you knew that the booklet had been prepared by the National Automobile Dealers Association and the American Financial Services Association at a cost (I'm guessing) of many, many thousands of dollars?

And would you be even more impressed if you knew that the booklet had been reviewed by the Federal Trade Commission and had that agency's stamp of approval on it?

And how about if the booklet were available in Spanish as well as English?

And, finally—the icing on the cake—what if this little gem were free? That's "free" as in "doesn't cost anything," as in ziperoo.

Well, all of the above is true. The name of the booklet is *Understanding Vehicle Finance*. For a copy, go to www.nada.org, click on "NADA Guides" at the top of the screen and choose "Consumer," and then click on "Finance" on the left side of the screen. This booklet can also be found on the FTC's Web site at www.ftc.gov/bcp/conline/pubs/autos/vehfine.htm. I've read through it, and I see nothing that would prohibit you from downloading it and printing it (in fact, I confirmed that NADA intends for it to be downloaded and used by the general public). It's not often that you get something this good, and this useful, free for nothing. (OK, so you have to print it—quit your griping).

If I were a dealer, I'd be all over this one. I'd have copies spread around my dealership (again, with the dealership's name emblazoned on them). I'd give copies to each customer who bought and financed a car from my dealership. I'd provide them to the local high school (emphasizing that the FTC has approved them), send them to newspaper and TV reporters who cover consumer matters, and to my state legislative representatives and consumer protection agencies. Basically, I'd paper the town with the things.

If you agree and decide to do this, I will bet that your dealership will begin to get a reputation as a progressive and consumer-friendly place of business—not a bad reputation to have in the community. And if you did happen to be sued by some plaintiff's lawyer who claims that you tried to pull the wool over his client's eyes about the basics of auto sales and financing, you would end up with a very strong retort for the charge.

Best of all, you would have obtained this code of commandments from the people who inscribe and enforce them for the princely cost of nothing; that is, for free.

Remember, you heard it here.

News Flash—There's No Crime in Ohio

April 2005

By Thomas B. Hudson

Stop the presses! We have an announcement!

Ohio is crime-free. No robbers, no murderers, no arsonists, no child molesters. No kidnappers, no tax evaders, no car thieves.

How do we know this? Because Ohio Attorney General Jim Petro just sued GMAC after GMAC reported to the AG that a dealer had defrauded the company in connection with the dealer's sale of leased cars. Listen to GMAC's travails...

Midway Motors Sales, Inc., leased a fleet of cars to its customer and assigned the lease contracts to GMAC. The two-year lease agreements Midway assigned to GMAC allowed for 30,000 miles, but apparently, Midway entered into separate lease agreements with its customers—agreements that provided two-year mileage allowances of 60,000 to 80,000 miles. According to the AG, when the cars were returned to Midway, Midway rolled back the odometers to reflect the typical 30,000 mileage for vehicles leased for two years. The AG says that Midway, or GMAC, or both, sold the vehicles with the incorrect odometer readings.

That doesn't sound like particularly bad AG behavior, until you read GMAC's press release in response to the AG's announcement of the lawsuit.

GMAC announced that it was "deeply disappointed" at the AG's suit, "particularly since GMAC discovered the problem, put a stop to it, corrected the harm, and brought it to the Attorney General's attention in the first place."

Say what?

GMAC's press release recounts that it discovered the rollbacks and notified the AG of the problem. Then, on its own initiative, GMAC identified the new owners of the cars, 23 of whom were in Ohio, and either bought the cars back from the new owners or paid them a monetary adjustment for the odometer discrepancy. The AG's office expressly endorsed and encouraged GMAC's remediation efforts.

In the process of cleaning up the mess, GMAC spent more than $1.2 million. GMAC stated that it was the victim of the dealer's actions, and that it expected a commendation from the AG's office for its "exemplary" handling of the matter.

Instead, GMAC got hit with the AG's suit. Talk about "no good deed goes unpunished!"

GMAC discovered a mess, voluntarily cleaned it up, made sure no one got hurt financially, reported the wrongdoing to the AG, and gave the AG evidence to use against Midway. What else could a responsible and ethical corporate citizen have done? How many corporations would have taken such a "high road" approach? What will other Ohio corporate citizens think of the idea of reporting bad acts like these in the future?

The only explanation that fits this thoroughly bizarre action by the AG is that there is no criminal activity in Ohio to occupy the AG's time and resources. No healthcare fraud, no organized crime, no bribery, no extortion.

We think maybe we'll move to Ohio where, evidently, the only crime is the way the AG wastes his time and the taxpayers' money.

'Predatory Lending' Comes to the Auto Side

September 2005

By Thomas B. Hudson

Our law firm does consumer financial services work. About 40% of our work is housing finance, and another 40% deals with auto sales, financing, and leasing. Those of us on the car side call the real estate crowd "Dirt Lawyers." They call us, with equal affection, "Motorheads."

For the greater part of the last decade, real estate lenders have been doing battle with plaintiffs' lawyers, consumer advocates, Attorneys General, and legislatures over so-called "predatory lending."

The practices that were labeled "predatory" by those seeking to curb what they saw as abuses included high up-front points and fees, high rates, "single premium" credit insurance, balloon payment provisions, and the use of arbitration agreements. Some lenders engaging in these practices were, in fact, bad guys intent on ripping off unsuspecting and unsophisticated consumers. Others were legitimately trying to design and price their loan products in a way that would permit them to make a (gasp!) profit when lending to a pool of customers comprised of many who were unlikely to repay their loans.

A lot of litigation by borrowers ensued, AGs attacked some of the practices, and, as a result, federal and state legislation addressing these practices was enacted. Even local governments got in on the action, enacting their own laws to address "predatory lending." In short, the real estate lending world has been swamped with "predatory lending" and the myriad of compliance nightmares fostered by that concept for years.

It wasn't surprising then, that the Motorhead lawyers in our firm began to hear questions from our car clients close to home and from those at various industry conferences asking, essentially, "When will the car world begin to see predatory lending attacks?"

The auto side of the consumer financing business has been under attack for years, with plaintiffs' lawyers, AGs, and regulators focusing on rate participation, rate discrimination, spot deliveries, and other areas, but usually the phrase "predatory lending" hasn't been used extensively in connection with these initiatives.

Now, the Iowa Attorney General, Tom Miller, has accused an Iowa car dealer of predatory practices. The AG alleged that the dealer, the Dan Nelson Auto Group, "targets vulnerable customers with marginal credit histories by promising them reliable and safe transportation and the chance to build or rebuild their credit." According to a lawsuit filed by the AG, "Customers often find themselves much worse off, with more debt, worse credit and no working vehicle."

Getting to specifics, the AG said: "We allege the defendants use misleading advertising to induce customers to come to their lot, where the defendants hide the extremely high price of their cars." The suit claimed that in a typical transaction, the defendants charged purchase prices far exceeding the value of the vehicles, arranged typical interest rates of over 24%, and provided loan terms that were likely to exceed the mechanical life of the vehicle.

"We allege that this is a predatory system," says the AG, "aggravated by the poor condition of the vehicles, in-house warranties offered by the defendants that often are not honored in a timely manner, and repair work that is substandard."

In a final volley, the AG alleged that "the defendants used illegal and harassing debt collection techniques designed to intimidate and embarrass consumers, and that many consumers ultimately default on these predatory loans, resulting in high repossession rates."

The AG's technique here is familiar. Note that many of the dealer's alleged practices, if true, would violate various parts of Iowa's consumer protection laws. Other so-called "predatory" actions are not necessarily illegal—the "over 24%" rate would be legal for certain older cars in Iowa, and selling cars for high prices has not heretofore been a sin in Iowa, of which we are aware.

But rather than announcing a lawsuit alleging violations of this section and that section of various parts of Iowa law, the AG has rolled up all of the specific violations he has uncovered, lumping them with practices that are either expressly permitted or that at least are not clearly illegal, and has claimed that, taken together, the dealer's activities constitute "predatory lending." Much sexier, and more likely to get headlines.

The AG employs this tactic because "predatory" is a loaded word, guaranteed to elicit a knee-jerk response on the part of newspapers, judges and juries. It is, essentially, a marketing effort for the AG's actual case.

And, back to the case for a moment, I'm sure that if you are in the subprime car business, and especially in the buy here, pay here business, you swallowed hard when you read the Iowa AG's allegations, because at least some of this dealer's actions (charging high prices and rates, and advertising that the customer can build or rebuild credit, for example) are pretty common.

So, it's time to assess your operation with attacks like this one in mind. If you actually are doing what the Iowa AG claimed Dan Nelson Auto Group was doing, then you ought to be wearing stripes and making license plates. But if you're trying to run an honest business, but some of these targeted activities are ones you engage in, perhaps it's time to reassess how close to the legal/illegal line you are, and, if you are close, to assess whether, perhaps, you are too close.

Yep, for those who asked when, the answer is—now. Predatory lending attacks have come to the car side of our business.

The Rent-A-Bling is Mine, Says the Car's Lienholder

November 2005

By David K. Tomar

The aftermarket car parts industry is booming. It has been growing an average of 8% per year for the last 10 years, with 9% growth in 2004. This $31 billion business includes custom accessories like aftermarket radios, wheels and tires, and even television sets. But not everybody can afford to buy these goodies outright or has the option to buy them on credit.

So why not rent the parts rather than purchasing them? Better still, why not rent-to-own?

A growing segment of the aftermarket car parts industry offers just that—motorists have the option of renting aftermarket parts, rather than buying them outright. The motorists pay for them in weekly, biweekly or monthly payments. They need only show a steady paycheck to qualify. At the end of the payment plan, the motorists own the aftermarket parts. The customers can also walk away at any time without further obligation, provided they return the aftermarket parts.

Interesting, but so what, right? Well, imagine that you have financed a car, that the buyer is in default, and you want to repossess. Imagine the buyer has rented custom wheels and tires for the vehicle. You have a security interest in the vehicle, but what about those freaky, funky, cool rented custom wheels and tires? The seller/renter of the custom wheels and tires has notified you that he wants the custom wheels and tires back, or fair market value, upon repossession.

What should you do? First, consider the type of transaction you're dealing with—a financed sale or a lease; this is not necessarily easy to determine. And while you are figuring this out, start hoping that if the guy rented the custom wheels and tires, it created a lease with a security interest because that's the only way you, as the vehicle-secured party, are going to end up with priority over those rented custom wheels and tires.

A Wheel is a Wheel, Unless it's Before July 1, 2001

Before July 1, 2001, Article 9 of the Uniform Commercial Code (Old Article 9) governed "accessions." Accessions were defined by case law as something that was an integral part of the original collateral and not easily detached.

Under Old Article 9, the priority of accessions followed the common law, providing that a "security interest in goods which attaches before they are installed in or affixed to other goods takes priority as to the goods installed or affixed (called in this section 'accessions') over the claims of all persons to the whole." So, under Old Article 9, radios, wheels and tires were not considered accessions to a motor vehicle, and the party with the security interest in the tires or wheels had higher lien priority than the party holding a lien on the vehicle. The case *Goodrich Silvertown Stores v. Caesar*, 197 S.E. 698 (N.C. 1938), is typical of how courts dealt with the issue.

In *Goodrich Silvertown Stores*, the North Carolina Supreme Court held that the seller of automobile tires and tubes who possessed a chattel mortgage on those items was entitled to recover the tires and tubes, or their value, even though they had been placed on a truck later repossessed by the seller of the truck under a conditional sales contract containing an after-acquired property clause. The North Carolina high court set forth the oft-followed reasoning on why the tires and tubes were not accessions: "The doctrine of accession is inapplicable in cases where the personal property is placed upon the other personal property if the property so placed had not become an integral part of the property to which it was attached and could be conveniently detached."

The majority of courts followed the rationale that wheels and tires were not an integral part of and could be conveniently detached from the vehicle. See, e.g., *Bank of America v. J & S Auto Repairs*, 143 Ariz. 416, 694 P.2d 246 (1985), (Old Article 9 did not control because parts such as tires, engine, and transmission were not accessions if they could be removed without damaging the vehicle); *Paccar Fin. Corp. v. Les Schwab Tire Centers of Montana*, 277 Mont. 171, 920 P.2d 977 (1996), (Old Article 9 did not control because tires, rims, and lug nuts were not integral parts of a motor vehicle or trailer that one would have to cause damage in order to remove items). Prior to July 1, 2001, the seller/renter would have had priority over those fabulous custom wheels and tires in purchase money security interest transactions.

Fortunately, common sense struck.

'Tires, We Don't Need No Stinking Tires'

On July 1, 2001, Revised Article 9 of the Uniform Commercial Code entered the picture. Revised Article 9 includes a special priority rule that gives the holder of a lien noted on a certificate of title priority over other lienholders.

Specifically, Revised Article 9 provides: "A security interest in an accession is subordinate to a security interest in the whole which is perfected by compliance with the requirements of a certificate-of-title statute." Although this special priority rule cuts against the notion of purchase money priority, Revised Article 9 justifies it on the ground that secured parties should be able to rely on a notation of a lien on a certificate of title without having to check the UCC files to determine whether accessions to the vehicle may be encumbered. The new rule imposes corresponding risks on financers of accessions affixed to titled motor vehicles.

Unlike Old Article 9, which relied on case law to define "accession," Revised Article 9 includes a definition of the term. Under Revised Article 9, an accession is defined as a good that is "physically united" with other goods to become one good in such a manner that the identity of the original goods is not lost. It no longer matters how much it costs to remove the accession, or how difficult it is to remove the accession, or whether the original goods have come to form an integral part of the other goods. Goods only become accessions if the identity of the original goods is preserved in spite of the union. Goods whose identity has been lost are "commingled goods" and not accessions.

Thus, Old Article 9 is no longer good law. Revised Article 9 reverses the lien priority that appeared to be reasonable to most courts prior to its inception.

Save the champagne. Unfortunately, Revised Article 9 does not control in a lease or a rent-to-own transaction. Instead, UCC Article 2A controls.

Last But Not Lease

Any transaction, regardless of form, that creates a lease is subject to the provisions of Article 2A. Determining if a transaction is a lease for Article 2A purposes can be complicated—a lease can operate as a sale, a financing transaction, or simply as a lease. Article 2A defines a "lease" as "a transfer of right to possession and use of goods for a term in return for consideration, but a sale, including a sale on approval or a sale or return, or retention or creation of a security interest is not a lease." Therefore, a lease intended to create a security interest is not subject to Article 2A and may be re-characterized as a retail installment sale subject to Revised Article 9.

Courts in the majority of states deem a rent-to-own transaction as a true lease and not as an installment sale or a lease intending to create a security interest.

If the rental agreement creates a lease intended as a security, the analysis and result above would govern, and the security interest in the custom wheels and tires would be inferior to the security interest in the car. However, the holder of the security interest in the vehicle would be stuck with a less favorable result if the transaction is a true lease or a rent-to-own transaction, as the transaction would be governed by Article 2A.

Note that a transaction does not create a security interest merely because it provides that the lessee has an option to renew the lease. Nor does a transaction create a security interest merely because it provides that the lessee can become the owner of the goods. This is not an exhaustive analysis of all the possible permutations; one must look at Article 2A for guidance.

If a lessor structures the rental agreement as a rent-to-own transaction or a true lease that allows the customer to terminate the agreement and return the custom wheels and tires at any point, a court would likely consider the transaction as *not* creating a security interest; thus, the transaction would be subject to Article 2A.

Under Article 2A, goods are accessions when they are installed in or affixed to other goods. Where the lease contract is entered into before the goods became accessions, the interest of a lessor or a lessee is superior to the interest in the whole (i.e., a sales finance company with a security interest in the vehicle). This Article 2A superiority rule is subject to certain narrow exceptions.

Conclusion—The Good, the Bad, and the Ugly

So, we are back where we began—you have financed a car, the buyer installed custom wheels and tires and is now in default, and you want to repossess. Is the transaction involving those custom wheels and tires a financed sale or a lease?

If the transaction falls under Revised Article 9, a security interest in the vehicle will have priority over a purchase money security interest in custom wheels and tires. You will not have to notify the seller/renter of the custom wheels before you repossess or sell the car, provided the car was used primarily for personal, family, or household purposes.

You would have to give notice to the seller/renter of the custom wheels in the case of a car used primarily for business purposes. Of course, even though not required, the prudent course would be to give notice prior to selling the repossessed vehicle if you have been made aware of a purchase money security interest in custom wheels and tires.

After the sale of the car, the money should be applied first to any sale expenses, second to the money owed to you, the vehicle-secured party, and third, in certain circumstances, to other subordinate interests.

So, after you receive a letter from a seller/renter claiming they have a purchase money security interest in aftermarket parts, think of Revised Article 9 and smile.

However, if the transaction is a true lease or rent-to-own transaction, the lessor of the custom wheels and tires will be entitled to "remove the goods from the whole, free and clear of all interests in the whole," and could do so based on default, expiration, termination or cancellation of the lease agreement, or when removal is "necessary to enforce other rights and remedies under" Article 2A. The lessor would be required to reimburse you only for "the cost of repair of any physical injury but not for any diminution of value of the whole caused by the absence of the goods removed or by any necessity for replacing them."

Under UCC Article 2A, if you repossesses a vehicle that has rented custom wheels and tires, you must permit the lessor to remove the tires. However, there is nothing in the UCC that requires you to remove the custom wheels and tires and send them to the lessor or to return the vehicle to the lessor so it can remove the custom wheels and tires. Rather, you must simply allow the lessor to come to where the vehicle is being held to remove the wheels and tires.

If neither the lessor nor the customer returns the original wheels and tires to you, you may install new tires on the vehicle and include the cost of the wheels and tires and their installation in the cost of disposition charged to the borrower.

So, the good news is that if it's a financed sale or lease intended as security, you have priority. The bad news is, if it's a true lease or a rent-to-own transaction, the lessor has priority and can remove the custom wheels and tires. And what you are left with is a bling-less, ugly car, without those custom wheels and tires.

End-of-Year Thoughts

January/February 2006

By Thomas B. Hudson

This month, I have a bit of this and a bit of that in reflection on recent end-of-year events. I want to share with you some fan mail I received, note the death and accomplishments of Senator William Proxmire, and muse over a recent release from the Federal Reserve Board.

Fan Mail

When you write articles, you occasionally get some feedback from your readers. Here's a missive I received, just before Christmas, from a devoted fan in response to an article in which I made reference to a "shyster lawyer":

> *I am often called upon to advise my many dealer contacts about insurance matters. In doing so, I try to present myself as a scrupulous practitioner of the law. I believe I am viewed by them as a highly ethical and honest attorney. I truly believe not one of them would refer to me as their "friendly local shyster." It isn't bad enough that the general public perceives lawyers as "shysters," but to hear a lawyer call other lawyers "shysters" does a serious disservice to those of us who have to combat that image every day. Obviously, you consider yourself a shyster and therefore I must conclude you are both unethical and unscrupulous in your day-to-day practice of the law. I think it is sad you have assumed the role of the "friendly local shyster" to your clients.*
>
> *Whenever I read one of your future articles, I will do so with the suspicion you are promoting skullduggery among your readers.*

Well! I guess he told me!

I e-mailed him back and told him that I hoped Santa would bring him a sense of humor. Meanwhile, you readers go out and do some of that skullduggery stuff, OK?

Senator William Proxmire

Some readers may be old enough to remember a time when there was no federal Truth in Lending Act. If you were in this business in the mid-1960s, you didn't have to worry about any federal laws that required the disclosure of finance charges, interest rates, and other terms of credit.

That changed in the late sixties, when Wisconsin Senator William Proxmire successfully pushed for the enactment of TILA. He later championed other consumer protection measures, including the Fair Credit Reporting Act, which my partner, Anne Fortney, credits with giving U.S. citizens a bargain on credit rates compared to the rest of the world. In addition, I have little doubt that his efforts on behalf of consumers inspired consumer advocates to press for a variety of state law measures for which he doesn't get credit. I'm a fellow of the American College of Consumer Financial Services Lawyers, and last year the ACCFSL awarded Senator Proxmire its Lifetime Achievement Award for his many contributions to the protection of consumers.

The Senator died in mid-December. He changed the face of consumer credit in America forever, benefiting consumers and providing a framework for all creditors to compete fairly for business. We should thank him for all he has done for us as consumers and as business people.

The Truth in Lending Act

When the Truth in Lending Act was passed, Congress was concentrating on protecting ordinary citizens engaging in consumer credit transactions. The general consensus among the lawmakers was that business credit to individuals, credit extended to corporations and partnerships and credit extended to the well-to-do were not in need of regulation. Congress's answer to the carve-out of credit extended to the well-to-do was to limit the application of TILA (in other than residential credit) to transactions in which the amount financed exceeded $25,000. But Congress didn't provide that the $25,000 cap would be adjusted for inflation.

Oops.

In the car world, there were precious few cars that cost anywhere near $25,000 in 1968. I recall buying a brand new 1964 Ford Falcon for $1,964 (clever, huh), and paying under $1,800 for a new 1967 VW Beetle. I can't recall what a Mercedes-Benz went for, but I'll bet you could buy a new one for $5,000 or so. It's probably safe to say that in 1968, and the years immediately following, nearly 100% of car credit transactions were subject to TILA.

All of this came to mind a couple of weeks back when the Federal Reserve Board released a batch of credit statistics showing that the average amount financed in car credit transactions was just a few hundred dollars shy of the $25,000 mark. Now, I have taken statistics courses, and I know the difference between an average and a median, but it still looks like some significant percentage of car deals—some percentage a bit under 50%—are no longer covered by TILA.

What is the practical implication of this bit of trivia, you ask? Well, it shouldn't change the way you do business, that's for sure. You should go right on using those contracts containing TILA disclosures, even when those disclosures aren't required. Why? For starters, it's hard enough for dealers to get this compliance stuff right without having two sets of documents, one for TILA deals and one for non-TILA deals. Many states have disclosure requirements, too, and most retail installment sale contracts are set up to combine many of the required state disclosures with the federal itemization of amount financed, the federally-required payment schedule, and federally-required disclosures. And some states, like California, require as a matter of *state* law that creditors make federal TILA disclosures even when federal law does not require them.

It is helpful in defending TILA cases against dealerships to keep the $25,000 figure in mind. The fact that the amount financed in a car finance transaction exceeds $25,000 should be a complete defense to a TILA claim.

That's it for this month. Keep those cards, letters, and hate mail coming. Happy New Year!

Eight Things Dealers and Finance Companies Should Know About the New Bankruptcy Law

January/February 2006

By Thomas B. Hudson and Charles F. Dodge, Jr.

The Bankruptcy Abuse Prevention and Consumer Protection Act of 2005, effective October 17, 2005, is a big overhaul to existing bankruptcy law. Many of the changes will affect the way dealers and finance companies conduct themselves with respect to consumer bankruptcies. For example, the new Act eliminates "lien stripping" on motor vehicles bought within two and one-half years before a bankruptcy filing, and eliminates "ride-through." It is now more difficult for debtors who are able to pay certain amounts to receive Chapter 7 protection. Reaffirmation agreements now have to comply with certain disclosure requirements.

There's much more to know about the changes implemented by the new Act. Here is a rundown of eight things dealers and finance companies should know about the new bankruptcy Act:

1. Debtors must receive credit counseling before filing.

An individual does not qualify as a "debtor" under the new Act unless he has received group or individual credit counseling from an "approved nonprofit budget and credit counseling agency" within 180 days prior to filing bankruptcy. 11 U.S.C. § 109(h).

2. Debtors must pass a means-test before filing; this is a new concept.

If the debtor's income is sufficient to pay $100 per month for 60 months, there is a presumption that granting the debtor relief under Chapter 7 is an abuse of the bankruptcy process. As a result, the debtor's case may be dismissed or converted into a Chapter 11 case. If the debtor's income is higher than the median income for his state, he must enter a 5-year (as opposed to 3-year) repayment plan or obtain no bankruptcy relief at all. The debtor has an opportunity to present special circumstances and rebut the presumption of abuse. 11 U.S.C. § 707.

3. "Ride-through" is no longer an option for debtors.

Before the Act was effective, debtors in certain federal circuits could continue making payments on secured debts included in the bankruptcy and keep the collateral. The new Act requires the debtor to reaffirm the underlying debt or redeem the property within 45 days of the first creditor meeting under section 341(a). 11 U.S.C. § 521(a)(6). If the debtor does not take this action, the creditor may go forward without regard to the automatic stay. 11 U.S.C. § 362(h).

4. Lien stripping is no longer a problem in certain Chapter 13 cases.

A creditor with motor vehicle collateral will not have its lien stripped in Chapter 13 cases, as long as the purchase occurred within 910 days (two and one-half years) of the date the debtor filed his petition. 11 U.S.C. § 1325. This is, arguably, the best news in the Act for motor vehicle finance companies.

5. The "ordinary course of business" exception to the preferential transfer rule is extended.

You are probably used to completing and filing title work with the state or local authorities within 20 days of a financed sale to ensure perfection of the security interest and exemption from the trustee's preferential transfer avoidance claims. The new Act extends that 20-day "ordinary course of business" perfection period to 30 days. 11 U.S.C. §§ 547(c)(2) and (3). Note that state law might still require you to file paperwork within some period less than 30 days.

6. The Truth in Lending Act is revised, but the changes will not affect typical motor vehicle financing transactions.

The new Act revised some TILA disclosures for open-end and closed-end transactions, but the revisions do not affect transaction documents executed in connection with a typical credit sale. 15 U.S.C. §§ 1637, 1637A and 1638.

7. Reaffirmation agreements are subject to form requirements.

Your reaffirmation agreements will now look more like loan documents. The new Act prescribes disclosure and content requirements, including amount reaffirmed, applicable APR information, payment schedule, etc. 11 U.S.C. § 524(k). You need to revise these reaffirmation agreements.

8. ***Help is out there.***

There are many more changes as a result of the new Act that do not appear in this article, and these changes may affect your business. We have a pretty good feel for the law, but we aren't bankruptcy lawyers. If you need a good bankruptcy lawyer who can explain nuances of the new Act, contact Lawrence A. Young, Esq., a partner at Hughes Watters Askanase, LLP, 333 Clay, 29th Floor, Houston, TX; 713.328.2805 (phone); lyoung@hwallp.com (e-mail).

This article is based on Larry's recent article titled *The Bankruptcy Pond Six Months From Now—More Stepping Stones for Lenders; Less Float for Debtors.*

Why Look For Hard Answers When There Are Easy Ones?

March 2006

By Thomas B. Hudson

A couple of months back, I screamed and shouted about a plaintiff's lawyer who sued a dealer for violation of the Truth in Lending Act. The dealer defended the TILA claim, and the court concluded that the dealer's practices did not violate the federal Act. The problem with the decision was that the amount financed in the transaction exceeded $25,000, making the transaction exempt from TILA.

The "amount financed" exemption isn't the only exemption available. Transactions that are "primarily" (over 50%) for business or commercial purposes are also exempt from TILA. However, TILA isn't the only consumer protection law where you'll find such exemptions. Other federal laws sometimes carve out business and commercial transactions as exempt, as do some state laws. Let's look at a state law example—this one from Ohio.

Madeline Lecso bought a vehicle from Motorcars of Toyota. Lecso used the vehicle primarily for business purposes and reported the vehicle as a deduction on her business tax returns.

Lecso took the car to Motorcars on several occasions for service under her warranty. She later claimed that Motorcars overfilled the oil on one occasion and, on another occasion, charged her for brake repairs that should have been covered by her warranty. Lecso eventually sold the vehicle, but she claimed it sold for less than NADA book value due to the oil overfill. She sued Motorcars for violating the Ohio Consumer Sales Practices Act, and for negligence and fraudulent misrepresentation.

The trial court granted Motorcars' motion for summary judgment on all three of Lecso's claims. The Ohio Court of Appeals affirmed the trial court's decision. The appellate court concluded that, because Lecso bought and used the vehicle primarily for business purposes, she could not maintain a claim under the Ohio CSPA, which applies only to the sale of goods or services for primarily personal, family, or household purposes.

The appellate court also affirmed summary judgment on the negligence and misrepresentation claims based on lack of proof that Motorcars' actions injured Lecso and that Motorcars misrepresented the nature of the brake repairs.

I frequently get calls from dealers who have been sued, asking me to come up with some brilliant, intricate, and stunningly technical theory of defense. I'm not that smart, so I ask a few quick questions:

- Is the buyer a corporation or partnership?
- Is the buyer an individual who bought the vehicle for business or commercial purposes? (Some hints are usually

available here, such as lettering of a business name on the truck, repair payments by a business credit card or checking account, occupation statements on a credit application, and other documents in the credit file, etc.)

- Is the buyer claiming the vehicle expense as a business tax deduction?
- Did the amount financed exceed $25,000?
- Did the buyer sign an arbitration agreement?

You'd be amazed how often the answers to these questions will knock the plaintiff out of court. And that's a whole lot easier than having to think hard.

Lecso v. Toyota of Bedford, 2005 WL 3475769 (Ohio App. December 20, 2005).

Law 101: Plaintiffs' Bar Favorites

June 2006

By Thomas B. Hudson

When I was a first-year law student (before the wheel was invented), the required classes were criminal law, civil procedure, contracts and something they called "torts." When I grew up to be a car lawyer, I found that I didn't do litigation, so I didn't have much use for civil procedure. I also found that my clients tended not to commit crimes, so the criminal law stuff sort of fell by the boards, too. However, contract law and tort law turned out to be two subjects with legs.

Contract law is a subject most folks generally understand. Car dealers are especially familiar with contract law, because their business consists in large part of trading cars for contractual promises by car buyers to pay. The buyers promise to pay, but the dealers also have obligations under those contracts. When a dealer fails to deliver a vehicle in accordance with the terms of the buyers order or the retail installment contract, a buyer will often bring a lawsuit alleging breach of contract.

When plaintiffs' lawyers sue dealers, their standard practice is to throw all the stuff they can against the wall and see what sticks. For that reason, plaintiffs' lawyers often include breach of contract claims in lawsuits against dealers. These types of claims aren't favorites of the plaintiffs' bar, however.

Why not? Two reasons. Unless the contract or some statute says differently, in most states, the plaintiff in a breach of contract action can recover his actual damages, but cannot recover his costs or attorneys' fees. In addition, in most states, punitive damages aren't available in a breach of contract action.

Tort claims are a completely different kettle of fish. What is a "tort," anyway? My *Black's Law Dictionary* defines a tort as "a civil wrong, other than a breach of contract, for which a civil remedy may be obtained, usually in the form of damages." Some common torts are fraud, negligence, and defamation. A driver who runs a red light and hits someone has committed a tort. One of the most common tort claims against dealers is fraud.

Why do plaintiffs' lawyers like fraud claims? Because fraud is one of the so-called "intentional" torts, which, in many states, gives rise to a claim for "punitive" or "exemplary" damages; that is, damages above and beyond the plaintiff's "actual" damages that are awarded to punish perceived bad behavior.

Although the U.S. Supreme Court has ruled that there must be some reasonable relationship between a plaintiff's actual damages and the amount of punitive damages assessed against the defendant, the permissible ratio of actual damages to punitive damages is pretty high. A car buyer with a claim for $30,000 in actual damages could still be awarded hundreds of thousands of dollars in punitive damages. The plaintiff who has a successful tort claim doesn't get attorneys' fees (because fraud claims are based on common law, not on a statute), but there is often plenty of extra cash in a punitive damages award to pay the blood-sucking lawyer.

So, plaintiffs' lawyers like contract claims well enough, and they like fraud claims a lot. But do you know what they really, really like?

What they drool over is an "unfair and deceptive act or practice," or "UDAP" claim. Most states have a UDAP law, and these laws are powerful weapons in the hands of a plaintiff's lawyer. UDAP laws generally prohibit practices that are unfair or deceptive and use very general terms, permitting plaintiffs' lawyers to argue that any number of practices fall within the scope of these statutes. State UDAP laws have been used, for example, to attack dealer advertising, provisions in buyers orders, spot delivery procedures, and other dealer actions and forms. State UDAP laws often permit a plaintiff to recover some amount of statutory damages and his attorneys' fees even when the plaintiff shows no injury. When a plaintiff has been injured, many state UDAP laws permit the plaintiff to recover some multiple (usually two or three times) of the plaintiff's actual damages, plus attorneys' fees. No wonder UDAP laws are favorites of the plaintiffs' bar!

These distinctions between and among contract, fraud and UDAP claims are interesting, but they are a bit academic. If a plaintiff's lawyer can do so, he'll hit your dealership with all three counts, and will probably throw in a couple more to boot. Usually a single fact pattern will support several different claims like this, and plaintiffs' lawyers can be fairly creative.

So buckle your chin strap, and keep using those arbitration agreements.

Vermont Votes 'Yes' to Negative Equity

July 2006

By Emily Marlow Beck

On May 15, 2006, Vermont enacted Public Act 143, expressly permitting motor vehicle dealers to include amounts for negative equity in their retail installment sale contracts. In addition, the Act expressly exempts dealers that include amounts for negative equity from licensure as lenders under the Vermont Licensed Lender Provisions.

While this is good news for the Vermont dealers, the new law does impose a few hoops and hurdles. Effective July 1, 2006, dealers must provide a new form of disclosure for all sales subject to the Vermont Motor Vehicle Retail Installment Sales Financing Act. The disclosure is required in connection with every motor vehicle retail installment contract, regardless of whether or not the transaction involves negative equity.

The Vermont Department of Banking, Insurance, Securities and Health Care Administration issued the new disclosure form on June 26, 2006, in "Department Banking Bulletin #28." The new disclosure must be provided on a single sheet of paper prior to consummation of the transaction and requires the dealer to disclose specific information, such as the cash price of the vehicle, and whether the amount financed in the transaction exceeds the cash price of the vehicle sold.

Easy enough, right? Well, there's more...

Guidance issued by the department about how dealers should calculate the "cash price" for this new disclosure will ultimately require changes to some Vermont retail installment sale contracts. Specifically, Bulletin #28 provides instructions about the calculation of "cash price" on the disclosure form and the retail installment sale contract to avoid situations where the "cash price" would vary from dealer to dealer based upon the dealer's particular contract or software program.

Pursuant to Bulletin #28, the "cash price" on the disclosure form and the DMV dealer's vehicle record log must be the "minimum price of the vehicle including any accessories that have been attached to the vehicle and reductions for rebates." In addition, the "cash price" does not include any service contracts, insurance, warranty contracts, debt cancellation agreements, or similar agreements or contracts, and does not include the purchase and use tax.

Fortunately, the department recognized that change doesn't happen over night. In its "Implementation of Department Banking Bulletin #28," the department recognized that some dealerships might not be able to modify their platform automation software to remove the purchase and use tax from the "cash price" and include it in "official fees" on the retail installment sale contract by the effective date of the new law on July 1, 2006. However, the department expects that dealerships will make any changes necessary to bring their retail installment sale contracts and platform automation systems into compliance by November 1, 2006.

So, for all you Vermont dealers out there, it's time to sharpen your pencils and make sure your paperwork is up to speed with the new changes. Stock up on the new disclosure form, and make sure your retail installment sale contracts and platform provide the proper "cash price." In the meantime, Banking Bulletin #28, along with the new disclosure, is available at www.bishca.state.vt.us/RegsBulls/bnkbulls/bul28-rev.pdf.

Sales to Business Entities—The LLC and the LLP

August 2006

By Timothy O. Naughton

Most of the vehicle sales you make are to individuals, and the vehicles are purchased for personal, family, or household purposes. But some of your sales are to businesses. You are probably familiar with sole proprietors, partnerships, and corporations. For the latter two, you pay attention to the contracting risks associated with such entities.

These same risks are present with other "entity buyers," the limited liability corporation, or "LLC" and the limited liability partnership, or "LLP." What are LLCs and LLPs, and what contracting risks do they present?

First, maybe we should explain the "Why." Why do people do business in these forms? The short answers are double income taxation and unlimited liability.

Double Tax

Corporate income is subject to tax. As corporations pay dividends, shareholders also are taxed on those dividends—double taxation. But partnership income is passed through to the partners, who then pay income tax. The partners may not like taxes, but at least the entity's revenue is subject to tax only once—single taxation.

Unlimited Liability

Partners generally are responsible for acts of the entity and of one another. When someone is damaged by the entity, the partner may be at risk, especially if the entity itself has no money to pay damages. The LLC or LLP investor, on the other hand, generally is not responsible for acts of the entity. He may lose his entire investment, but he is not at risk if someone is hurt by the entity.

False Start—"S Corp"

Many states' first solution was to allow "S Corporations" to form. Investors enjoyed limits on liability, and income was taxed only at the shareholder level, but the rules for these entities were very limiting. "S Corp" rules limited the number of members and permitted only one class of ownership. Very democratic, but if you needed different ownership classes (or income streams), the "S Corp" was not for you.

LLC and LLP to the Rescue

The LLC and the LLP are two forms of entity, now available in all fifty states, which offer single taxation and limits to investor liability. But cautions apply:

- Limited liability entities are creatures of state law; while the statutes borrow heavily from one another state-to-state, there are differences. "There are rules," as they say.
- When you are dealing with someone making the purchase, you need a comfort level that he or she has authority to act on the entity's behalf. But how do you know? The long answer is to obtain the Certificate of Limited Liability Partnership, or the LLC Operating Agreement and the LLC Articles of Organization, confirm who may enter into contracts on the entity's behalf, and seek assurance that the relevant organizational documents remain in effect. This way, you have confirmed who has the actual authority to act on the entity's behalf.
- But maybe the entity has bought other cars from you. Or other documentation leads you to conclude that the

person making the purchase has been sent to do so. Each business sets its own tolerance for risk, but you might be comfortable pursuing something less. Can you confirm (by reviewing correspondence or calling the entity's offices) that the entity's senior manager dispatched this person to buy a car? You may anger some people by going behind their backs, but the entity's senior manager will appreciate that you've got his or her back.

Fraud risks are the same as sales to other entities. If you accept a company check to buy a car that is then titled in a person's name, you may well have to answer for that. And remember, these entities are creatures of state law. A quick call to your compliance counsel can yield the necessary form for the entity's signature, confirming that the purchase is *bona fide.*

And, like all of the other areas of your dealership that are driven by compliance-related requirements, you need a written policy to guide your employees in dealing with these entities, and you need to train those employees so they will know your policy and implement it properly.

So cancel those vacation plans and get to work.

New Rules for Oklahoma Used Car Dealers

September 2006

By D. Brent Gunsalus

The Oklahoma Used Motor Vehicle and Parts Commission has been busy recently issuing new regulations. The regulations became effective on June 25, 2006, and all Oklahoma used motor vehicle dealers will need to comply with them. Some of the highlights are discussed below, but dealers should review the regulations in their entirety.

Separate Location

Among the new rules are a couple that make clear that the vehicle sales business must be physically separate from any other business conducted at the same location. The rules always required used vehicle dealers to maintain an established place of business, but now they make clear that the display area must make vehicles that are for sale readily distinguishable from vehicles parked on the premises for any other purpose.

This appears to mean that spaces for employee and customer parking and for vehicles waiting for repairs should be clearly separated from the sale display area. It may be a good idea to mark the various parking areas with "Customer Parking" and "Service Shop Parking" or similar signs. In addition, the new rules make clear that the vehicle sales office must be "devoted exclusively to the operation of the used motor vehicle business." Dealers who share space with another business or conduct multiple businesses from the same location must make sure that their vehicle dealership office is completely separate from any room in which other business is conducted.

Recordkeeping

The new rules specify that among the records required to be maintained for at least three years from the sale of a vehicle are bills of purchase, bills of sale, odometer statements, invoices of repairs or other expenses, certificates of title, and accounting records for the operation of the business including checking accounts, checks, drafts, and inventory financing agreements. All of these records are subject to review by the Used Motor Vehicle and Parts Commission upon request.

Payments for Referrals

The new rules prohibit a used motor vehicle dealer from soliciting or offering compensation for referrals of prospective buyers from a used motor vehicle salesperson employed by another used motor vehicle dealer.

Advertising Disclosures

The rules always required that certain disclosures be made in advertising if a price is listed for a vehicle. The new rules also require that the disclosures be made if the advertising states the payment amount or makes a claim about savings. The regulations now state that the required disclosures of make, model year, and other information must be located adjacent to the price or in an area clearly marked with reference symbols, and must be in 5-point type in capital letters. So while the required disclosures may be made in a footnote, they must be in the proper type size and clearly referenced immediately next to the vehicle price.

In audio advertising, the disclosures must appear at the end of the advertisement. In television advertising, the disclosure must be in visual form, "so that the average viewer may easily read and understand it," and must be at least 20 scan lines and appear continuously on the screen for at least 10 seconds. A voice-over announcement alone of the required disclosures in a television ad is not sufficient. While it is not so clear what is required to make the disclosure easily readable and understandable, dealers should make sure that any TV ads that mention price, payments or savings contain the required disclosures in the proper size in type that contrasts with the background and that the disclosures stay on the screen for a minimum of 10 seconds.

Going Out of Business Sales

A dealer may not use terms such as "liquidation" or "going out of business" unless the dealer is actually going out of business and ceasing operations at its licensed location, and the terms may only be used from the time the dealer has executed a sale agreement with the buyer of the business until the effective date of the sale.

Pay-Offs on Trade-Ins

A dealer may not use a phrase such as, "we pay off your trade no matter how much you owe," unless it is accompanied by a disclaimer indicating that pay off is dependent on approved credit. In addition, trade-in amounts or a range of amounts may not be advertised.

Buy Down Rates

An offer of a buy down rate is prohibited unless the following disclaimer is made: "This is a buy down rate. The amount of the buy down may affect the price of the vehicle."

Dealer Name

All advertising must conspicuously display the licensed name of the used motor vehicle dealership.

Copies of the regulations may be obtained from the Oklahoma Used Motor Vehicle and Parts Commission, 2401 N.W. 23rd St., Suite 57, Oklahoma City, Oklahoma 73107; 405.949.2626 (phone).

We Get Letters...

September 2006

By Thomas B. Hudson

Another correspondent sent this story:

I run a special finance department for a dealership with two locations. Recently the question was presented to me, "What is the policy for advertised vehicles versus acquisition fees for sub-prime customers?" The inquiry stemmed from a letter to the Better Business Bureau about a customer who was sub-prime that paid a different price than what was advertised on our Web site.

In the past, it has been my practice to inform these customers that they may not qualify for the Internet price due to the fees imposed by banks. In saying that, most accept the fact and move on through the process. When I answered the question that way, the owner then proceeded to remind me of the old "cash vs. finance pricing" that is illegal in the state of Texas. Our next decision was to, instead of telling the customer that he may have to pay more for the car, that we will not sell them that car for the advertised price. Well, as you know, there goes "discriminatory practices." What would be a good compromise to this situation to alleviate all of the potential law suits that you just read through in this letter? I am sure that we are not the only dealer that is confronted with this situation on a daily basis.

My reply was as follows:

If you charge a higher price to a credit-challenged customer than you charge to a good credit customer (or a cash customer), the increase in the price becomes a finance charge for federal Truth in Lending purposes, and may be a finance charge for state law purposes, as well; such a situation requires special treatment, or may be subject to limits. Also, the practice may violate other state laws. We advise dealers to operate their special finance operations as separate lots and to price all the cars on that lot at one price for all customers—cash customers, "good credits," and "bad credits." The discounts imposed by those who buy paper from the dealer should be treated as general overhead like the light bill and not ever attributed to a particular deal.

Many dealers consider this advice to be impractical, and I'd have to agree, but it is the only way I can come up with that avoids pricing cars higher for credit-challenged customers and having the extra price treated as a finance charge.

That's the mailbag for this month. I'm hoping Spot will stay awake next month so I won't have to write this column. Meanwhile, I trust regular readers of our legal newsletter, ***Spot Delivery***®, know of whom I'm talking...our trusty Dalmatian, our mascot, the faithful companion known to sniff out compliance issues and bite (occasionally) crooks, the mailman, and subscribers who don't pay on time. In his spare hours between naps, he's an occasional writer, too. And not a bad one...not bad at all...

CHAPTER 1

Focus on the 'Pay Here' of 'Buy Here, Pay Here'

September 2006

By Emily Marlow Beck

Running a compliant shop is a difficult task for any dealer. I'd strongly argue that it's even more difficult for buy here, pay here dealers. That's because the buy here, pay here dealership is a hybrid, of sorts—part dealer, part finance company (quite literally so, if the dealership has a related finance company). The "pay here" part of a "buy here, pay here" facility creates special compliance challenges, which dealers who sell all their paper are able to avoid.

Buy here, pay here dealers know that they are, at times, subject to different laws than are other types of dealers. Some of these laws include state collection laws and sales finance licensing laws. But, often, obligations imposed on buy here, pay here dealers are different—*not* because the laws are different—but because the undertakings of the buy here, pay here dealers require a different response to the same laws that are applicable to all dealers. In other words, the "pay here," or financing arm, triggers different sorts of obligations from, and responses to, the same old laws that apply to all types of dealers.

What do I mean?

Take, for example, your dealership's obligation to check the Office of Foreign Assets Control "bad guy" list. By now, you know that under federal law, you are prohibited from doing business with anyone on the list. For most dealers, this means that, among other things, you must check the OFAC list prior to selling or leasing a vehicle to a customer.

For buy here, pay here dealers, however, the sale or lease of the vehicle signals the beginning of the OFAC obligation.

Because the buy here, pay here dealership (or its related finance company) will be accepting payments and thus "doing business" with customers until their obligations are satisfied, it must screen the OFAC "bad guy" list regularly to make sure that none of its customers has been added to the list. (After all, you never know when one of your customers might go out and join a terrorist organization.)

Another example is a dealer's obligation under the federal Safeguards Rule. If you've been keeping up with your compliance duties, you know that the federal Safeguards Rule requires dealerships to have, among other things, a written safeguards policy.

But, what about buy here, pay here dealers with related finance companies? After all, a related finance company would certainly be a "financial institution" for purposes of the Safeguards Rule, wouldn't it? Of course! If your dealership has a related finance company, it, too, must be Safeguards Rule compliant. In most cases, this means that the related finance company must have, among other things, a written policy and a designated safeguards coordinator.

Failure to comply with the federal Safeguards Rule can result in an FTC enforcement action. If the Federal Trade Commission pays you a visit and neither your dealership nor your related finance company is Safeguards Rule compliant, you could be in really hot water.

In addition, although the laws governing credit discrimination apply to all dealers, the "pay here" financing arm can arguably put dealers at a higher risk of claims of credit discrimination. Buy here, pay here dealers are often able to set their own creative underwriting criteria to best serve the types of customers they work with and allow dealers to finance customers that would otherwise be off-limits. However, this flexibility can put buy here, pay here dealers at risk of inadvertently running afoul of state and federal law.

Specifically, federal laws and some state laws restrict the types of information creditors can request or consider in connection with a credit transaction. For example, the Equal Credit Opportunity Act places certain restrictions on when and how a creditor can ask about an applicant's marital status and restricts the situations in which a creditor can request information about a spouse. The Act provides that a creditor can't request information about the spouse (or former spouse) of an applicant unless the spouse will be permitted to use the account, the spouse will be contractually liable on the account, the applicant is relying on the spouse's income as a basis for repayment, the applicant resides in a community property state or is relying on property located in a community property state as a basis for repayment, or the applicant is relying on alimony, child support, or separate maintenance payment from a spouse or former spouse as a basis for repayment of the credit requested.

Perhaps more important for the buy here, pay here dealer is that federal law limits situations in which a creditor can require a spouse to co-sign a credit obligation. Many buy here, pay here dealers always require a spouse to co-sign on a contract. However, under the Equal Credit Opportunity Act, with a few exceptions, a creditor may not require the signature of another person unless the creditor has first determined that the applicant alone does not qualify for the credit requested. When an applicant requests individual credit but cannot, on his or her own, meet a creditor's standards, the creditor may require a cosigner, guarantor, endorser, or the like, but, with few exceptions, the creditor cannot require that such additional signers be a spouse. Some state laws have similar restrictions.

This is certainly not an exhaustive list of the unique

challenges facing buy here, pay here dealers. Many federal laws effectively impose requirements on buy here, pay here dealers and/or their related finance companies. These requirements differ from those imposed on other types of dealers. Consider the Fair Credit Reporting Act, the federal Privacy Rule, the Truth in Lending Act, federal cash reporting requirements, and state and federal collection requirements, for starters. And that's not mentioning the complex tax and accounting rules that only the most knowledgeable accountants and tax lawyers should handle.

So, for all you buy here, pay here folks out there, recognize the additional legal challenges posed by your dual-purpose dealership operations, and educate yourselves as to the steps you need to take to make sure that the finance arm of your dealership operation complies with applicable state and federal laws.

If that means you're uncomfortable with what you may not know, a compliance review of your operation by legal counsel with specific knowledge of buy here, pay here operations would be a great place to start to put your mind at ease.

We Get Letters...

October 2006

By Thomas B. Hudson

There's a new book out about a dog that supposedly is the worst dog that ever lived. It's called *Marley and Me*, and it's a good read. Marley is really a problem dog, but I'm not ready to vote him "Worst Dog in the World" as long as Spot is around.

Most days, Spot has just one lousy, stinkin' job. He's supposed to bite the mailman so mail won't get delivered and so I don't have to write this column every month. Once again, he fell asleep on the job, and a letter got through. Steve Eisenberg writes:

I just finished reading your article. It was very informative. I've been a Finance & Insurance Manager for a long, long time. I feel that I do a very good job when it comes to "compliance." I would like to get your response to an issue that comes up very, very often. The issue is this. A customer comes in looking to buy. The sales process is started. A customer statement (credit application) is completed and a credit report(s) is obtained through Equifax, Experian, and/or TransUnion. Upon the review of the credit bureau report(s) and the credit application, the opinion is reached (by us) that the customer (based on PTI, DTI, lack of credit, low or no FICO score, etc.) will not get approved/financed. If we do not submit the application to any lender(s), is that an "adverse action"? All lenders have minimum requirements. What can a dealer do if someone does not meet the minimum lender requirements? Do we still have to send the application in? Do we have to send it to a "conventional lender" and a "secondary lender," or is it OK to only send it to one of them? And, last but not least, if we elect not to send it at all, what is the "proper" notification we should use? Thanks so very much.

I replied:

Steve,

Thanks for the kind words about the article. As for a reply to your question, my first response, since I don't represent you, is to ask your lawyer the question and rely upon his or her advice.

When you do talk with your lawyer, however, you can share with him/her my thoughts on this topic, and I'll be glad to talk with him/her about it.

If a buyer fills out an application and upon your review you determine that the buyer does not meet the minimum credit requirements of any of the banks or sales finance companies you sell contracts to, and you elect not to submit the application to any of them, you have engaged in adverse action under the federal Fair Credit Reporting Act (if you have pulled a bureau) and under the federal Equal Credit Opportunity Act (whether you pull a bureau or not). For that reason, you are required to give the buyer an adverse action notice. The Federal Reserve Board provides sample form adverse action notices, and you can use a single form to comply with the ECOA and FCRA requirements. You should not use the model forms without having them reviewed by your counsel, however, because they may need to be modified for your situation.

One of the sources of confusion in connection with dealer financing is that dealers believe that they just sell cars, and they don't realize that they also extend credit. In a typical dealer financed transaction, the buyer signs a "retail installment contract" under which he promises to pay the dealer, over time, for the car. The dealer then sells the contract to a sales finance company. In such a transaction, the dealer is a credit seller; he extends credit when he gives the buyer the keys to the car and lets him drive off the lot. There is no "loan" and there is no "lender," even though dealers and those who buy contracts from dealers use those terms (incorrectly) every day! The customer has applied for credit to the dealer, not to GMAC, Chase, or Americredit, and if the dealer doesn't extend credit, he has engaged in adverse action.

Anybody want a dog? Free to a good home, or even to an average home.

Is Your Lawyer a 'Top Gun' Fan?

November 2006

By Thomas B. Hudson and Meghan Musselman

In the movie "Top Gun," Maverick and Goose are engaging in a dogfight when the other plane gets the drop on them and is about to fire a missile. Goose, who is in the back and sweating BBs, calls on Maverick, saying, "OK, Mav, do some of that pilot s--t."

Pilots have their pilot s--t, and lawyers have their lawyer s--t. This article shows how effective lawyer s--t can be.

In 2001, Harry Drinkwine leased a car (don't quit reading—this same concept would apply to a financed deal) from Leasing Professionals, Inc. That lease included a provision allowing for early termination on 30 days' notice, after eight monthly payments and a payment of $250, plus any monthly payment then due and the amount by which the lease balance exceeded the realized value. Drinkwine claimed that Leasing Professionals offered oral assurances that he could terminate the lease after eight monthly payments by simply paying the $250 fee; he also claimed that he exercised that option.

Drinkwine later entered into a second vehicle lease with Leasing Professionals, containing an early termination provision similar to the first lease. Again, Drinkwine claimed Leasing Professionals offered oral assurances that he could terminate the lease after eight monthly payments by paying a $250 termination fee.

Shortly after Drinkwine entered into the second lease agreement, Royal Oakland Community Credit Union acquired his lease from Leasing Professionals. After eight monthly payments, Drinkwine sought early termination under the terms of Leasing Professionals' oral assurances, but Royal Oakland refused to honor those terms. Drinkwine sought specific performance of the oral promise—the equivalent of saying, "Judge make them do what they promised they'd do." The trial court rejected Drinkwine's argument and granted Royal Oakland's motion for summary judgment. Drinkwine appealed.

The Michigan Court of Appeals noted that Drinkwine's lease agreement contained an "integration clause." An integration clause is genuine "lawyer s--t." It is a provision stating that the written lease contains the entire agreement between the parties and can be amended only by a writing signed by the party to be bound. Drinkwine argued that the integration clause wasn't effective because it was contained in a preprinted contract. The appellate court concluded that the integration clause was valid, despite the fact that the contract was preprinted. The court went on to note that the existence of the integration clause rendered Drinkwine's reliance on Leasing Professionals' oral assurances unreasonable. Thus, the appellate court upheld the trial court's grant of summary judgment in favor of Royal Oakland.

Integration clauses can be tricky. In most states, the Uniform Commercial Code (Section 2-209) provides that "[a] signed agreement which excludes modification or rescission except by a signed writing cannot be otherwise modified or rescinded, but except as between merchants such a requirement on a form supplied by the merchant must be separately signed by the other party." It isn't clear from the court's decision whether Drinkwine had separately signed the provision. If not, and if Michigan's UCC has such a provision, Drinkwine's lawyer failed to do his "lawyer s--t."

If you look through the retail installment contracts, leases and buyers orders you are using, you are likely to find versions of an integration clause. If you do, and they are done correctly, it's because some lawyer was doing some of his "lawyer s--t" to keep you out of trouble.

Drinkwine v. Royal Oakland Community Credit Union, 2006 WL 2787980 (Mich. App. September 28, 2006).

I Reserve the Right to Get Smarter

December 2006

By Thomas B. Hudson

I screwed up. Ever happen to you? Happened to me. As a matter of fact, if they gave merit badges for dumb, I'd be an Eagle Scout.

During the course of the last year, I got three things wrong. At least, three things that I know about. There were probably other things I got wrong, but nobody's taken out the 2x4 to correct me on them yet.

Since we're coming up to the end of the year, I thought it would be a good time to 'fess up and correct the mistakes that I know I made.

Here goes.

Mistake No. 1—Truth in Lending Act

This one's embarrassing. I've been doing Truth in Lending stuff since before fire was invented. When a Florida dealer asked me at a conference early this year whether he could use a Spanish-language retail installment sale contract, I told him I thought he could, but that he'd need to give his Truth in Lending disclosures separately in English, because TILA required English-language disclosures.

Wrong.

For years, TILA said that you were required to give TILA

disclosures in English, except in Puerto Rico, where Spanish-language disclosures were permitted provided that creditors gave English-language disclosures on request. That was the rule until the Federal Reserve Board changed it while I wasn't looking.

Now, TILA disclosures may be made in a language other than English, provided that English-language disclosures are given on request.

Actually, no one challenged me on this one; we fell over it when we were doing our most recent book.

Mistake No. 2—Dealer Tent Sales

In at least one article, I warned dealers to beware of the FTC's Door-to-Door Sales Rule when they conducted sales away from the dealership. An alert reader pointed out that the FTC provided an express exemption from the Rule for dealers when they hold tent sales or when they sell cars from some other temporary place of business. The exemption says,

> The requirements of this part do not apply for sellers of automobiles, vans, trucks, or other motor vehicles sold at auctions, tent sales or other temporary places of business, provided that the seller is a seller of vehicles with a permanent place of business.

It would be nice if I could *read*. I'm red-faced, but my warnings might have been somewhat useful since they pointed out that some *states* had door-to-door sales laws, and just because the FTC has provided an exemption doesn't mean there's a state law exemption. The possible application of the FTC's rule to Internet sales is also something with which dealers still need to be concerned.

Still, I was wrong, any way you slice it.

Mistake No. 3—FTC's Penalty for Privacy Violations

In articles and in talks to dealerships, I've said for several years that dealers who don't meet their Gramm-Leach-Bliley Privacy Act requirements run the risk of a visit by the FTC and an $11,000 penalty for noncompliance.

Wrong (well, mostly wrong).

The FTC can impose an $11,000 penalty for violating some, but not all, of its rules. The Privacy Rule is not the type that carries the $11,000 penalty. The FTC can still bring an enforcement action against a dealer and ruin the dealer's day. My learned and patient partner, Jean Noonan, used to work for the FTC. She straightened me out thusly:

> *The FTC does not have civil penalty authority for violations of the GLB Safeguards Rule. Violations of the Rule are deemed to be unfair or deceptive acts or practices, in violation of the FTC Act. Violations of the FTC Act, alone, are punishable only by a cease and desist (C&D) order. Civil penalties can be assessed for violations of a C&D order, in the amount of $11,000 per violation. Thus, a violator of the Safeguards Rule would be put under C&D order by the FTC (through litigation or, more often, by consent). Any subsequent violation of the Rule would be a violation of the order and subject to a monetary penalty of $11,000 per violation.*

I wish she'd used smaller words, but you get the idea.

So there you go. My three mistakes for the year. I've shown you why my motto has always been, "I reserve the right to get smarter."

I Reserve the Right to Get Smarter, Part Two

January/February 2007

By Thomas B. Hudson

In last issue's Commentary, I was 'fessing up to some mistakes I made during the year. One of them was my frequent assertion that there was an $11,000 FTC fine for privacy violations. I said:

> *The FTC can impose an $11,000 penalty for violating some, but not all, of its rules. The Privacy Rule is not the type that carries the $11,000 penalty. The FTC can still bring an enforcement action against a dealer and ruin the dealer's day.*

My learned and patient partner, Jean Noonan, used to work for the FTC. She straightened me out thusly:

> *The FTC does not have civil penalty authority for violations of the GLB Safeguards Rule. Violations of the Rule are deemed to be unfair or deceptive acts or practices, in violation of the FTC Act. Violations of the FTC Act, alone, are punishable only by a cease and desist order (C&D). Civil penalties can be assessed for violations of a C&D order, in the amount of $11,000 per violation. Thus, a violator of the Safeguards Rule would be put under C&D order by the FTC (through litigation or, more often, by consent). Any subsequent violation of the Rule would be a violation of the order and subject to a monetary penalty of $11,000 per violation.*

I replied, "I wish she'd used smaller words, but you get the idea." That seems to have gotten Ms. Noonan's shorts in a twist. Here's her reply:

> *Harrumph! Here's my re-write: The FTC can't nail you for 11,000 smackers for violating the GLB Safeguards Rule.*

But it can sue your ass anyway, because violating the Safeguards Rule gets your John Hancock on a Cease & Desist order. So you get a free kiss at the pig. But if you screw up a second time and violate the order, that pucker is gonna cost you 11,000 big ones.

Her rewrite is written in "Oklahoman," a language not frequently used in most of the country, and may not be understandable by all, so I had it translated. The rough translation is, "...what I said the first time."

Fort Confusion and the Puzzle Palace

January/February 2007

By Thomas B. Hudson

When I tell people that I am from the suburban Washington, D.C., area, I'm often asked about national political issues, as if living 25 miles from Fort Confusion (the Capitol) and the Puzzle Palace (the White House) gives me some special insight into what's going on with our federal government. While I subscribe to the *Washington Post*, which offers great coverage of our federal government, I generally don't know any more about what's going on in the District than anyone who stays reasonably informed.

The operative word in that last sentence, however, is "generally." When it comes to consumer credit matters, including dealer sales and finance issues, I have a pretty good ear to the ground about events, and likely events, in the District that are likely to affect dealers.

I think that there are at least three things that are likely to occur, or not occur, as the case may be, now that the resurgent

Democrats control Congress. Here are my (somewhat educated) guesses about the Democrats' agenda for consumer credit and dealer sales and finance.

Forget Tort Reform

The half-hearted class action measure that the Republicans managed to pass wasn't much help to dealers facing potential class action risks, and while I don't think the Democrats will be successful in repealing what the Republicans did, they certainly aren't going to try to help business interests. Remember that the "trial lawyers" (in Washington-speak, this means plaintiffs' lawyers who sue businesses) are solidly in the Democrats' corner, and they are not about to support a measure that would have an impact on their collective wallets.

The Federal Arbitration Act Has a Bulls-Eye Drawn On It

Dealers and sales finance companies have increasingly turned to arbitration agreements as a means of blunting class actions and reducing the risks that accompany any courtroom appearance with a consumer on the other side. The fact that the FAA is a federal law, thus preempting state laws that prohibit arbitration, has stymied efforts by consumer advocates and trial lawyers in many states to bar dealers and finance companies from using arbitration agreements. Look for consumer advocates and the trial lawyers to try to convince Congress to amend the FAA so that it will not apply to consumer transactions, or to urge some other way to eliminate businesses' ability to use arbitration.

The Truth in Lending Act Will Be Amended

TILA, enacted in 1968, applies to transactions in which the amount financed does not exceed $25,000. That dollar limit in 1968 would have meant that virtually all car credit transactions were covered by TILA. Every year, though, car prices have climbed, and the concept of "1/3 down" has gone the way of the dodo bird. Last year, the Federal Reserve Board announced that the average amount financed in car credit transactions exceeded $25,000. That means that something like half of all car credit transactions are not subject to TILA. If the trial lawyers and consumer advocates can get someone to drop a bill in the hopper raising the $25,000 cap, industry will have a very hard time resisting such a measure.

So, those are my thoughts about the things that a Democratically-controlled Congress is likely to do or avoid doing. Dealers need to keep a wary eye on Washington as a New York judge noted in 1866, "No man's life, liberty or property is safe while the legislature is in session."

Rogue Waves

January/February 2007

By Thomas B. Hudson

Once upon a time, I was a sail boater. I plied the Chesapeake Bay, where winds and waters were generally calm, but I subscribed to sailing magazines that told tales of deep-water and rough weather sailing. Some of the stories dealt with so-called "rogue waves," those waves that suddenly came at the mariners from an unexpected quarter and could be deadly.

I thought of rogue waves recently while reading of two developments in real estate financing. (I know you thought I was only an ignorant car lawyer, but about half our firm's practice is in residential real estate financing.) Residential real estate financing legal concepts are similar in many ways to auto financing concepts, and they sometimes migrate to the car side of our business. These two developments have migrating potential.

The first development is the spike in real estate foreclosures, which the experts attribute in large part to innovative mortgage products that make it easier for new buyers to buy their first houses, and to relaxed underwriting standards that make residential mortgage loans available to people whose credit histories would not have permitted them to qualify for financing in years past. The innovative mortgage products include new spins on variable rate mortgages, "interest-only" mortgages that begin amortizing after an introductory period, and very low or no down payment mortgage loans. Most of these loan products result in borrowers with less equity than would have been the case with more conventional financing.

When delinquencies and foreclosures rise, plaintiffs' lawyers will not be far behind. You can expect lawsuits challenging the foreclosures, and, on the theory that the best defense is a good offense, alleging various lender misdeeds in making the loans. Some of these lawsuits will assert novel theories, and at least some of the theories will find their way into the auto finance and lease litigation arena. Ahoy, mate: *Rogue wave Number 1.*

The other development comes from a new decision by the Ninth Circuit Court of Appeals in a housing litigation matter. A federal "Court of Appeals" is the court that litigants appeal to if they don't like the results that they get in trial court. The only higher federal court is the U.S. Supreme Court. In this case, the Ninth Circuit held that an investment bank that merely loaned money to a lender could be held responsible for the misdeeds of the lender, under certain circumstances.

The case involved a non-prime mortgage lender, First Alliance Mortgage Company, which had been driven to seek bankruptcy protection after suits and investigations dealing with alleged unfair and deceptive practices by FAMC. A class action lawsuit alleged that Lehman Brothers, Inc., a lender to FAMC, was aware of and assisted FAMC's bad acts. Lehman argued that it was not an active participant in the allegedly fraudulent practices, and that while it assisted FAMC generally, it did not do so with respect to the specific practices. The court did not buy Lehman's defenses, and, after a jury verdict, Lehman was socked with a $5 million verdict, which it appealed. The Ninth Circuit opinion affirmed the trial court's judgment.

The theory that an investment bank that merely loaned money to a lender could be held responsible for the misdeeds of the lender, under certain circumstances could work as well in the car financing business as it did in the housing financing business. The subprime automotive finance sector is not exactly awash with capital at the moment, and you can bet that the companies who lend to subprime finance companies are going to take a long, hard look at this decision to see whether they might be held liable under similar circumstances. If they conclude that the theory poses significant additional risk, they will either charge more for that risk, reduce their subprime financing activities, or both. That won't bode well for dealers with special financing departments and buy here, pay here dealers. Ahoy! *Rogue wave Number 2.*

Whatcha think, mates? It might be time to shorten sail a bit.

'Rip-Off Nation' Revisited

March 2007

By Thomas B. Hudson

Several years ago, I wrote an article in response to a so-called "report" by Public Citizen, an organization founded in 1971 by Ralph Nader to represent consumer interests in the Congress, the executive branch, and the courts. A national, nonprofit entity, according to its Web site, www.citizen.org, the group is described as a public-interest watchdog that is frequently critical of organizations. The report to which I responded a few years ago dealt with "fraud" by car dealers. If you don't recall the article, this is part of what I said:

An organization called "Public Citizen" has issued a report titled "Rip-Off Nation: Auto Dealers' Swindling of America." If the report were a product, it would be recalled immediately. And if any other organization had issued the report, Public Citizen would be screaming that it was a fraud.

Long on bald accusations, short on fact, based on misunderstandings of the auto finance business so profound that they leave you wondering whether the report was written by college students or first-year law students interning for the summer, the report is a criminally reckless indictment of the entire car industry based on the undeniable wrongdoing of some dealers and dealer personnel.

That should give you some notion of my opinion of the report, which was based, at least in part, on the revelations of Duane Overholt (whose Web page, www.stopautofraud.com, contains the amazing statement: "...for 22 years I had been an active participant in...deceptive sales practices"), and which relied upon a relatively few legal cases, Attorney General investigations, and anecdotes.

Research, it wasn't. It's as if I went looking for 100 satisfied car purchase customers and found them, then issued a report saying that the car sales and finance business was squeaky clean. Pure garbage. I still get steamed every time I think about it.

All of this came to mind when I saw that the Federal Trade Commission had recently issued a press release reporting the

"Top 10 Consumer Complaint Categories in 2006." Auto sales, financing and leasing, once again, didn't make the FTC's Top 10 list, which sort of makes you wonder what the folks at Public Citizen have been smoking.

My point is not that all car dealers are honest, or that there are no consumer abuses in the car business. There are bad apples in our basket, no doubt. But Public Citizen, and all of the other organizations that paint the entire car dealership population with that defamatory "rip-off" accusation, should be called to task by the overwhelming percentage of car dealers trying to run honest and ethical businesses in one of the thorniest legal environments in the marketplace.

Honest dealers don't deserve to be tarred with Public Citizen's brush. "Rip-Off Nation" is a "rip-off report."

I Needed a Laugh

May 2007

By Thomas B. Hudson

I needed a laugh.

I mean, with Iran, North Korea, Democrats, Republicans, global warming, Don Imus, and the Washington Nationals, I needed a laugh. With a court in Arkansas holding that a dealer was engaged in the unauthorized practice of law when he charged a doc fee for, among other things, filling in the blanks of a retail installment contract, I needed a laugh. And when the South Carolina Supreme Court issued an opinion on the arbitration of Magnuson-Moss warranty claims that would make a law school freshman blush, I needed a laugh.

And just when I needed it most, Duane Overholt supplies it.

One of our lawyers, Maya Hill, was trying to locate a copy

of a complaint filed in a Nevada court alleging various misdeeds by a dealer. She hoped to get a copy so that she could discuss the case in our upcoming compliance workshop.

Usually, trying to run down a document like this is no big deal; you just call up the plaintiff's lawyer and ask for it. Most lawyers, when asked, will do you the courtesy of supplying what is, after all, a public document.

So that's what Maya did. She explained to the plaintiff's lawyer what she was looking for, and he said he would send it over. Two hours later, the documents hadn't turned up, but someone had called her.

That someone turned out to be Duane Overholt. I won't bother to try to characterize Duane. You can go to his Web site, www.stopautofraud.com, where he does it himself. You can check out his resume and see his collection of trophies as an expert witness in cases against car dealerships in the form of a long list of dealership names.

Now, I hadn't run into Ol' Duane in several years. As a matter of fact, the last time we spoke was when he called me to object to an article I had written criticizing a so-called "study" by a D.C.-based outfit called "Public Citizen" titled "Rip-Off Nation." The reason I call it a "so-called" study is that is was long on conclusions but woefully short of anything that you could remotely call evidence. I wrote then that dealer fraud might, or might not, be rampant, but that the Public Citizen study certainly didn't support its conclusion.

But I digress. As I said, Duane shows up again, this time responding to Maya's request to the plaintiff's lawyer for a copy of a complaint. After some back and forth, Duane refuses to provide the requested copy on the grounds that we were intending to use it to "teach car dealers how to violate the law." Now, we spend a lot of time educating dealers and finance companies about the thicket of laws and regulations that govern the F&I process—and the lawsuits they face if they don't comply with them. We write books, we put out a monthly legal newsletter, we hold workshops, and we regularly speak before industry groups—always trying to teach dealers how to get it right and how to stay out of trouble. We huff and we puff, giving the best compliance advice we know how to give.

But "teaching dealers to violate the law?" I really hope Duane knows more about the car business than he knows about our legal business.

Like I said, I needed a laugh.

The Devil is in the Details

May 2007

By Nicole F. Munro

My husband and I just had our second child last month. With the addition to our family, we thought it might be a good idea to invest in a family car.

Being your typical soccer mom, I looked at the minivans available and decided to buy a Honda Odyssey. It's stylish and practical, with room for the appropriate number of car seats, grandparents, and pieces of sporting equipment.

Being a dealer lawyer, I found the best price for the minivan via the Internet. Being a credit lawyer, I reviewed my financing alternatives before heading to the dealership. I called the dealership, confirmed the pricing, and drove to the dealership to look at the van. Knowing that I was going to buy, I braced myself for a long evening of negotiation with the F&I guy/gal.

Let me preface this story by commenting that the dealership, my salesperson, and the F&I manager were very professional, knowledgeable, and honest (I think). I did tell them when I arrived that I was an attorney, that I represent car dealers, and that my industry experience related to retail installment sales situations and contract drafting. I also told them I've done a dealer audit or two. With that said, I'm fairly certain they just wanted to sell me a car and get me out of their dealership or, maybe, just get me out of the dealership.

My husband took the van I chose on a test drive, and then we sat down with the salesman to discuss our purchase and financing options. After refusing to respond to the monthly payment question, that is, "Where do you want to keep your monthly payments?", we waited five minutes for a visit from the F&I guy, who offered us a less than stellar annual percentage rate.

Doing the numbers in my head, I asked about dealer participation when I realized that the dealer had just raised the rate over my estimated buy rate by about the amount I saved on the cash price of the vehicle. When I asked for a lower rate, the gentleman responded that it wouldn't change my monthly payment significantly. I recall telling him something to the effect that I was not concerned about the amount of the monthly payment, but about the amount of interest charged over the life of the installment contract. I was certain we had "A" credit and we wanted an "A" credit rate. Flustered, the F&I manager left for a few minutes and came back with an acceptable rate.

I asked him to put the rate in the contract so that I could take it with me, review it, and consider my purchase overnight. I did this for three reasons: (1) to find out if he would give me a copy of the contract to take with me; (2) to review the federal Truth in Lending Disclosures and the Itemization of Amount Financed without my three-year-old trying to jump in and out of cars at the dealership; and (3) to find out if the dealer was using a contract I had written or helped write.

Again flustered, the F&I manager said that he couldn't give me a copy of the contract to take with me. I pleasantly reminded him that the Truth in Lending Act disclosures must be given prior to consummation and in a form the buyer can keep. The Federal Reserve Board Staff has stated in the Commentary to Regulation Z, implementing the Truth in Lending Act, that this can be accomplished by having the dealer hand the completely filled in, but unexecuted, retail installment sale contract to the buyer, relinquishing control of it. I asked for nothing less.

Moreover, the Truth in Lending Act is a disclosure law meant to inform the buyer of the cost of his credit and allow the buyer to "shop" for the best deal.

Finally relenting, the F&I manager gave me a completely filled in copy of the contract to take with me. I smiled and left the dealership. The F&I manager may have smiled, too.

Maybe not.

My review of the contract revealed that the dealer properly made the Truth in Lending disclosures; the Itemization did not include any additional charges other than required VSI; and the contract was one I had helped write. I contacted my salesperson and let him know that I would be in the next day to buy the minivan.

The next evening we went to the dealership, signed the papers, and drove off in our brand new family car.

Because the dealership eventually gave me the copy of the contract the previous night, I gave them a freshly printed contract to replace the one that I took, and a copy of the *F&I Legal Desk Book*, written by Tom Hudson and the attorneys at Hudson Cook.

Two months later, after I had made at least one payment (maybe two) to the bank that bought my contract, I received a telephone call from the F&I manager.

Apparently, my contract contained the incorrect VIN number. Consequently, the wrong car was registered in my name.

The F&I manager asked if I would come back in and re-contract. Not wanting two contractual obligations for two different vehicles, only one of which I was driving, I asked whether we would be able to modify the current contract to correct the VIN number. A week or two later, I received a call from the F&I manager stating that the bank would only accept a new contract with the correct VIN number. While I was tempted to call the bank to confirm or to request a modification from the bank, I didn't.

Instead, I gathered my family together in my recently used minivan, and went back to the dealership to re-contract. I asked the F&I manager to void my current contract and return it to me. He said he would just shred it. Knowing that there were three more copies of the first contract I signed still somewhere out there in dealer and finance land, I refused to turn over my copy to be shredded. He reluctantly voided and initialed my contract, a copy of which I dutifully placed in my file, just in case.

It has been almost four months since I bought my minivan. I've made payments to the bank, driven my car up to the point of the first oil change, and carried the required number of car seats, grandparents, and pieces of sporting equipment. However, I don't have the correct certificate of title, and I still have some outstanding issues to address with the dealership. Yet, despite the nettling inconvenience, I have a practical and stylish car that carries almost anything.

Is there a moral to this story? Actually, there are two:

First, don't mess up the retail installment sale contract of a finance lawyer because you may have an article written about you in ***Spot Delivery***®.

Second, there are a lot of things that can go wrong when completing a retail installment sale contract, so pay attention, cross every "T" and dot every "I," and fix any issues as fast as you can. Your finance company will appreciate it. Your customer will appreciate it. And, you won't get stuck buying back a contract that was an easy sell in the first place.

By the way, if you are really nice to me, I promise I won't buy a car at your dealership any time soon.

Double Drivel

June 2007

By Thomas B. Hudson

Recently, a couple of friends of mine in the subprime car business sent around by e-mail an article by Mark Huffman of www.consumeraffairs.com titled, "Road to Ruin: Subprime Lending in the Car Industry." The e-mail from one said, "Have you seen this drivel?"

I did not need to read further than the second paragraph to conclude that the piece was another Duane Overholt attack on the auto sales and finance business. The article, after noting that Duane had "swindled consumers out of $33 million," went on to quote Overholt's by-now-familiar accusations against car dealers.

Now I know that there are dishonest dealers who believe that every dollar of profit justifies another fraud on consumers, and that the auto business is no stranger to sharp practices. I differ with Overholt in two major areas.

First, I believe that most dealers work hard to run honest businesses, and that they do not countenance having their employees lie, cheat, and steal in the car purchase and finance process. Perhaps Overholt has never had the experience of working for one of these dealers, so he cannot fathom the possibility that every dealer isn't crooked.

Second, and more important, however, is my belief that when you make accusations, you have a responsibility to back them up with facts. When Overholt accuses dealers of falsifying documents, inflating length of employment and income, and claiming to finance sources that cars have equipment that they don't have in order to justify higher advances, he admits that it is hard to know for sure how many dealers engage in such practices. Up to that point, I agree with him. Not happy with these bald allegations, though, he then claims that as many as 60% of dealers engage in such practices.

What is the basis for such a sweeping allegation? Who has done the research to determine that such a claim is remotely accurate? I have never seen such research, and, frankly, I really doubt that it exists.

A couple of years ago, a D.C.-based, so-called "public interest" organization put out a "study" titled "Rip-Off Nation" that made similar wild and unsupported accusations against car dealers. But "Rip-Off Nation" was nothing more than a collection of consumer complaints, lawsuits, and enforcement actions selected by Public Citizen because they supported the study's conclusion. It would be as if I went out and located 30 people who were thrilled with their car buying and financing experiences and "concluded" from their reports that there were no abuses in the marketplace. Such a conclusion would be ridiculous, and the conclusions by "Rip-Off Nation" were just as ridiculous. It won't surprise you to learn that Overholt was instrumental in preparing "Rip-Off Nation."

Overholt is reported later in the article as saying, "The American public should realize the federal government is not protecting them any more." And, "Most states have abandoned, abolished, or modified their deceptive trade practice laws."

The folks over at the Federal Reserve Board who make the Truth in Lending and Equal Credit Opportunity Act rules, the folks at the Federal Trade Commission who enforce those rules, the plaintiffs' lawyers who use the rules in suing car dealers, and the dealers who spend a lot of money every year trying to comply with the rules—all will be surprised to learn that the federal government isn't protecting car buyers any more. And I know of no recent instance in which any state has abandoned or abolished its unfair and deceptive trade practices laws. Needless to say, Overholt doesn't bother actually giving us any examples to support these wild accusations.

The article also quotes a fellow named William Cunningham, identified as an investment advisor at the Washington, D.C.-based organization, Creative Investment Research. He's also identified as having an expertise in mortgage lending. Cunningham is quoted as saying that the predatory lending practices showing up in the housing sector started in the auto finance sector, that the practices originated in "communities of color," and that subprime credit has an inherent racial and gender bias. Cunningham doesn't offer a shred of evidence to support these sweeping statements. Maybe that's why his organization is named "Creative" Investment Research.

I have no idea whether Cunningham's statements are true or not. What I am certain of is that he doesn't proffer anything remotely resembling a fact to back up his statements. I checked Creative Investment Research's Web site at www.creativeinvest.com and clicked on the "Research" button. None of the listed research reports bear on this topic.

By the way, my favorite quote attributed to Cunningham (appearing immediately after a paragraph on dealers embracing subprime lending) is, "What the financial institutions have decided to do in order to get some of that revenue is to defraud customers." That one really left me scratching my head. What financial institution buying retail installment contracts from a dealer would countenance for a split second any dealer activity that would falsely increase the amount of the customer's obligation?

None that I've ever heard of. The financial institutions have to collect that paper, and if it turns out that the dealer has loaded the customer up with phony extra profit or fake equipment, the finance company will take a bath. Maybe Cunningham ought to stick to mortgage lending.

The article's author, Mark Huffman, deserves a comment here, as well. I believe that a reporter has the obligation to ask hard questions when his subject—in this case Overholt and Cunningham—make such claims. In my opinion, the author needs to say, "Show me the facts." If facts are not forthcoming, a reporter should identify his data as unsupported statements. Then, too, Huffman could have included background research to context the quotations, and thus, by the way, educate his interview subjects in addition to his readers.

But that's just me.

Rent-to-Own? Maybe So, Maybe No

June 2007

By Thomas B. Hudson

Lately I have seen a slew of proposals sent to dealers by companies offering vehicle rent-to-own programs. So far, all the dealers have done is to ask for my general take on these programs. No one has yet asked for a full-blown legal opinion on one of them.

My initial take on the programs is that the literature describing them poses more questions than it answers. Why so, you say?

Well, a couple of arenas come to mind...

Federal Law

True rent-to-own (RTO) transactions, for federal law purposes, are not subject to either the federal Truth in Lending Act and its accompanying Reg. Z or to the federal Consumer Leasing Act and Reg. M. The operative word in the preceding sentence is "true." In order to meet the exclusions from TILA and the CLA, the RTO transactions must be structured so that they do not meet the critical definitions in those laws that determine the laws' scope. In other words, if the transaction is one that is defined as a credit sale in TILA, re-labeling it as an RTO transaction isn't going to matter. It will be a credit sale, and all the required disclosures for credit sales must be made.

State Law

Similar issues arise under state law. Most states have laws that regulate credit sales. Some states have enacted laws that expressly regulate RTO transactions. Again, whether an RTO transaction falls within a state's credit sale laws or within the state's RTO laws will depend on how the program is structured and whether that particular structure falls within the operative definitions.

Even if an RTO program escapes the definitions that would make it a credit sale for federal and state purposes, that doesn't mean the RTO transactions under the program will be totally unregulated. A number of state laws may well apply to these transactions.

State laws to worry about include those relating to licensing, advertising, unfair, and deceptive acts and practices, requirements for simple language or "Plain English" contracts, and foreign language requirements. These are samples; there may well be more in a particular state.

Dealer Licensing Laws

You should also check the dealer licensing laws in your state. It is possible that your state limits or prohibits the practice of operating any business other than a car sales business from your dealership's location.

Financing

Also keep in mind that RTO isn't just another type of financing. With RTO, your dealership will own the vehicle. That has important insurance ramifications that will come to light when your renter (loaded with who-knows-what) plows that Dodge Charger into a school bus loaded with children.

So, when the RTO man comes calling, ask him for all of the documents that he proposes that you use in the program, including all the documents that the customer will see; and then ask him for all of those exhaustive legal opinions that he has had prepared so that you can turn the whole mess over to your lawyer for a thorough review.

And don't forget to add your arbitration agreement to whatever forms you elect to use with your RTO program.

So, that's my general take on these programs. These programs can vary, in terms of risk level, from state to state. And it's not hard to fall within state legislative schemes that sometimes were not intended to apply to this business. So, go slow, and let your lawyer be your guide.

You Might Want to Put the Rent-to-Own Man on Hold

June 2007

By Emily Marlow Beck

Many dealers, especially buy here, pay here dealers, are getting visits from salespeople representing companies pushing "rent-to-own" programs as the next great thing. One of the touted benefits of RTO is the comparative lack of federal and state law regulating RTO transactions.

Reminds me of the Wild West before Wyatt Earp arrived. How come?

Because that touted advantage—comparative lack of regulation—may be about to vanish with the introduction of a new bill in Congress that aims to rein in the RTO industry. In fact, dealers who have been given this pitch might want to hold off making a decision for a bit until we see which way the political winds are blowing in Washington.

Senator Charles Schumer (D., NY) has introduced a bill, S. 1530, titled the "Rent-To-Own Protection Act of 2007." The RTOPA, if enacted, would add a new Title X to the federal Truth in Lending Act.

The RTOPA has three stated purposes:

- To provide consumers in rent-to-own transactions the range of protections provided under state and federal laws to individuals who acquire goods in other consumer credit sales;
- To require rent-to-own contracts and tags affixed to items available for acquisition in rent-to-own transactions to disclose material terms of those transactions; and
- To prohibit rent-to-own dealers and collection agents hired by those dealers from engaging in abusive collection practices.

The RTOPA establishes a cap for "interest, fees or finance charges" by providing that state law finance charge caps applicable to other credit sales will apply to RTO transactions, and takes the same approach for the types and maximum amount of fees that can be charged. In addition to the fees and charges permitted by the RTOPA, a rent-to-own merchant is permitted by the RTOPA to charge a "termination fee," not exceeding 5% of the cash price under the contract, provided that the termination fee is disclosed in the contract. The termination fee may be paid at the time the contract is entered into or over the life of the contract, and must be used in the calculation of the finance charge. The merchant may also charge a "recovery fee" when goods subject to the contract are not returned as agreed.

Rent-to-own transactions escape the scope of several federal laws that protect consumers in other credit transactions. The RTOPA closes those loopholes by expressly providing that the Truth in Lending Act, the Equal Credit Opportunity Act, the Fair Debt Collection Practices Act, and the Fair Credit Reporting Act will apply to RTO transactions.

Applying the Truth in Lending Act to RTO transactions requires some fancy footwork. Before a finance charge can be computed, for example, you need a cash price. The RTOPA provides one, defining "cash price" as "the fair market price at which retail sellers not in the business of renting or leasing such goods, are selling and retail buyers are buying the same or similar property for cash in the same trade area in which the lessor's place of business in located." Work on that one for a minute. Can an RTO dealer set his cash price for his goods at the price charged by Neiman Marcus, or is he limited to the Kmart price? TILA disclosures, with some additional RTO-specific disclosures thrown in, will be required.

The bill then turns to collection abuses. In addition to making the FDCPA applicable to RTO transactions, the RTOPA prohibits a laundry list of bad behavior in connection with the collection of RTO obligations. One RTO company ad we saw recently told dealers that they could report the car as stolen as soon as a payment was late in an RTO transaction. That is the kind of practice the RTO bill will attempt to nip in the bud.

The RTOPA provides for civil liability (Schumer is a Democrat, recall) for disclosure and other violations, requires the Federal Reserve Board to issue regulations no later than 12 months after its enactment and names the Federal Trade Commission as the enforcer of the Act.

All in all, if the RTOPA is enacted, the RTO industry will face very much the same regulatory thicket that lenders and credit sellers face.

Looks like the sheriff might be coming to town.

When Close is Good Enough

June 2007

By Thomas B. Hudson

The old saying, "Close only counts in horseshoes (and hand grenades)," usually applies in the compliance world. Unless a law or regulation specifically gives you some wiggle room, you'd better slavishly do exactly as it says because some plaintiffs' lawyer will seize upon any variation from the letter of the law as a violation, and off to the courtroom you'll go.

You'd think that a court would take a common sense approach to compliance every now and then and give a break to a creditor that has tried to do what's required, but hasn't quite crossed every "T" and dotted every "I." That doesn't happen very often, and when it does, it's really a refreshing change. Let's look at a recent case in which the court had a rare attack of common sense.

Jordan Eger leased a car from VW Credit, Inc. Eger breached the lease agreement, and VW Credit repossessed and sold Eger's leased car. Eger sued VW Credit, alleging that the post-repossession notice VW Credit provided to him failed to set forth verbatim the text as required by California's Vehicle Leasing Act. The VLA requires that a person who receives a repossession notice be advised of their legal rights including the right to obtain a professional appraisal to establish the value of the vehicle for the purpose of determining the amount owed on the lease.

Eger argued that because the notice was not a literal recitation of the language required by the VLA, the notice was inadequate and, thus, he was not liable to VW Credit for losses suffered by VW Credit due to the repossession. In other words, close wasn't good enough. VW Credit moved for a judgment on the pleadings, arguing that the "substantial compliance doctrine" applied and that its notice substantially complied with the VLA.

The federal trial court granted VW Credit's motion, finding that the omission of the statutory phrase "to establish the value of the vehicle for the purpose of figuring how much you owe on the lease" did not interfere with the essential purpose of the statute, i.e., consumer protection. The court found that the "doctrine of substantial compliance" excuses literal noncompliance only when there has been actual compliance with the essential objective of the statute. Because the omitted phrase was a mere technical deviation, the court ruled that the statutory objective of consumer protection was not violated by the omission of the phrase at issue.

So, do you throw away the law books and forget about trying to follow the laws and rules precisely, relying on the doctrine that close is good enough? Hardly.

VW Credit hadn't missed much in this case, and what they had provided to the customer was pretty close to the required notice. Because the court felt that the statute's purpose had been achieved by the non-verbatim text, it gave VW Credit a pass. You don't want to be in the position of needing a sensible, practical judge in order to avoid a bad result, however. They aren't that plentiful.

It's far better to get every detail right, even if it means copying the text of a regulation or statute. When we draft documents for our clients, and the language in a regulation or statute can be used verbatim, we use it that way.

You'll be glad you track that statutory or regulatory language when that hand grenade lands in your foxhole.

Usury and Other Mysteries

July 2007

By Thomas B. Hudson

I have a new friend. His name is Adam Goldfein, and he has the sort of resume that makes you wonder, "What did I do with my life?" He hosts "Autoscoop, the Inside to Car Buying," a nationally syndicated radio show dealing with consumers and the retail car business, but he isn't your ordinary journalist/entertainer. The guy went to law school, and then he managed a bunch of car dealerships. He really knows what he's talking about.

When I heard him on the radio awhile back, I was so impressed with him that I prevailed on Jack Tracey, who is the Executive Director of the National Automotive Finance

Association, to invite him to be the keynote speaker at the recent NAF Conference in St. Louis. I was expecting to hear Adam tell on-the-air war stories. Instead, he surprised me by talking about how the banks and sales finance companies who buy retail installment contracts from dealers can close the gap with consumers, educating them, and marketing to them in innovative ways.

Adam and I were at dinner the night after his presentation, and, in the course of our conversation, he asked if I happened to have a chart of state usury rates applicable to vehicle credit sales transactions. He expressed frustration that he had tried to assemble that information and had not had much luck.

It turns out that Adam did what any sensible researcher would do, using "usury" as a search term. He wondered out loud why that hadn't worked to find the information he was looking for.

I responded to Adam by telling him that he had hit upon one of my major hot buttons and launched into my diatribe about the difference between "loans" and "retail installment contracts" or "RICs."

The reason you can't locate the maximum rates that dealers can charge on the RICs that they enter into with their credit buyers by looking at the usury laws is that usury laws, in most states, apply to the lending of money. Look up "usury" in your handy-dandy *Webster's*, and you'll find that it means "the act or practice of lending money at an exorbitant or illegal rate of interest."

That's not what dealers do. Despite the fact that at every conference you attend and in most articles you read there are continuous references to "loans" and "lenders," when retail installment contracts and those who buy them are being described, dealers do not make loans. Neither do GMAC,

Chase, the credit unions, and all of the others who buy RICs from dealers. They are buying contracts, not making loans.

Now, it's true that some state usury laws are written broadly enough to pick up credit sales transactions, but, in many states, the general usury law is inapplicable to RICs. That can be because the law is worded in such a way that it applies only to the lending of money and not to credit sales, or because the courts have adopted the "time sale price doctrine," which carves out of the usury statute credit sales by merchants. In most states, however, the legislature has long since enacted a law, usually called something like a "retail installment sales act," that expressly deals with the maximum rate that can be charged on sales that are subject to the law.

The laws constitute a hodgepodge of varying approaches and can be pretty confusing if you don't deal with them all the time. Some contain a maximum rate that works a bit like the APR concept works at the federal level, but others use arcane "add-on" language (such as, "the finance charge cannot exceed $X per $100 per year") that must be converted to an interest rate equivalent. Some states provide that the interest rate may be "as agreed by the parties," in effect, no cap. And to make things even more interesting, the state may define the various fees and charges in such a way that a charge that is included in the APR for federal disclosure purposes is not interest for state law purposes, and vice versa.

In short, Adam had wandered into one of the thornier legal brambles in auto finance. As I knew he would, Adam immediately grasped the distinctions I described to him. I sent him the chart he sought, and I'm sure that he will be putting it to good use on his program.

Now if I could only get the rest of my friends to see the difference between loans and credit sales.

Familiar Word May Have New Meaning in FTC Holder Rule

August 2007

By Michael Goodman

Did you know that the word "all" might not mean what you were taught it meant way back before you could tie your shoes? What? you say? When might the word "all" not mean every last little bit?

Answer? When judges and federal regulators try to define it. I'm referring to the FTC's Holder Rule. In 1975, the FTC issued the Holder Rule so that creditors that buy sales finance contracts from sellers could be held responsible for the misconduct of those sellers in the course of arranging the financing. Before the FTC issued the Rule, consumers' relationships with sellers and with creditors were not related. Misconduct in one relationship didn't affect the parties' obligations in the other relationship.

The FTC was concerned that, as a result, creditors could (and did) insist that consumers continue to make payments for a product that was defective or that the seller never delivered. In other words, creditors could rightly claim that they were not responsible for a seller's misrepresentations, breaches, or fraud when they bought a sales finance contract from the seller. The Holder Rule tightened the connection between creditors and sellers, tying the two parties more closely together.

The Rule itself is relatively simple. It requires consumer credit contracts to include a conspicuous disclosure explaining that any holder of the contract is subject to *all* claims and defenses the debtor could assert against the seller. Except for some definitions and exemptions, that's all there is to it. The FTC even wrote the text of this disclosure and put it in the Rule.

So, what's the problem? When the FTC issued the Rule, it also issued its official interpretation of what the Rule meant. And, in that official interpretation, the FTC opined that the word "all" as used in the disclosure required by the Rule didn't mean what your dictionary says it means.

Instead, the FTC explained that consumers could use the Holder Rule to maintain an affirmative action against a creditor for a seller's misconduct only if the consumer received little or nothing of value from the seller. According to the FTC, "all" doesn't mean "all"; it means, "Only if the seller did something really, really bad." Over the years, courts applying the Holder Rule have had trouble deciding whom to listen to—their dictionaries or their government.

The courts still haven't settled on one consistent answer; instead, they've settled on two. One set of courts agrees with the FTC's official interpretation and limits the ability of a consumer to use the Holder Rule to make a claim against a creditor to situations of substantial seller misconduct. This appears to be the majority view. A second set of courts has determined that the text of the Holder Rule is clear: "All" means "all," and these courts have elected to ignore the FTC's interpretation to the contrary. This appears to be the minority view. The right answer, of course, is whatever the judge says in the court where the creditor is sued. Both interpretations have substantial support.

The majority view is unconvinced that the phrase "all claims" in the Holder Rule covers all claims that a consumer might make against a creditor. These courts rely on the FTC's official interpretation for clarification. They reason that the FTC wrote the Rule, so its interpretation of what the Rule means deserves deference. They also make an argument on policy grounds. They reason that it can be unfair to hold a creditor responsible for the conduct of an unrelated third party. They state that the FTC did not intend to make creditor liability universal and absolute, so the proper balance is to reserve that liability for the most extreme cases.

The minority view is more protective of consumers. These courts are seemingly less troubled by the prospect of holding creditors broadly responsible for a seller's misconduct. These courts draw support from the text of the disclosure within the Rule. This disclosure states that consumers may bring all claims against a creditor that they could have brought against the seller. These courts explain that elementary principles of regulatory construction say that you don't need to look to a regulator's interpretation (and, indeed, you *shouldn't*) unless the text of the regulation is unclear. And they say that this text is perfectly clear.

For good measure, courts following the minority view also point to statements in the FTC's official interpretation that they say support their view. They point to the FTC's explanation that the goal of the Rule is to stop the unfair practice of requiring a consumer to make payments to a creditor if the seller did not provide what the consumer thought he purchased. If the purpose of the Rule is to protect consumers, these courts reason, then why should that protection be limited to only certain kinds of misconduct by sellers? These courts also point out that the FTC expected the Rule to shift the cost of seller misconduct from consumers to creditors. The FTC explained that creditors were better able to factor in the likelihood of seller misconduct, because, unlike consumers, creditors do repeat business with sellers. Again, these courts ask why this cost-shifting relief for consumers should be limited to extreme cases of seller misconduct.

What does all this mean for dealers? The Holder Rule doesn't address dealer liability directly. This Rule is about creditor liability for dealer misconduct in a credit transaction.

However, the debate between the majority view and the minority view affects a dealer's litigation risk. Courts adopting the majority view cut off a consumer's ability to sue a creditor for some seller misconduct. Consumers in those jurisdictions will have to go after the dealer for relief. Courts adopting the minority view keep alive a consumer's ability to hold a creditor liable for a seller's misconduct. Consumers in those jurisdictions have more options, as to whom to sue, which make it less likely that a dealer will be the target, or at least the only target, of a consumer's lawsuit.

In the end, dealers striving to understand the meaning of the Holder Rule must do more than just consult their dictionary to determine what "all" means. They must also determine if their court has taken a position on the Holder Rule dispute. As with so much in the law, the answer to the question of what "all" means is, "It depends."

Chapter 2

Dealer Compliance Programs

In this chapter, we discuss the all-important issue of compliance. We begin with "Advice to a Brand New Compliance Officer," and then we handle a number of basic concepts that dealer compliance officers need to know. Additional topics include videotaping the F&I process, selecting a lawyer, and constructing a compliance program for your dealership.

What's that? You say your dealership doesn't have a compliance officer?

Well, it's high time it did. If your dealership doesn't have a compliance officer and a compliance program, chances are good that it doesn't have a culture of compliance either. If your dealership doesn't have a compliance-training budget that involves some real dollars, it is announcing that it doesn't think compliance matters. If this describes your dealership, you've got an uphill climb—first you have to convince management that compliance matters, then you have to put together a program.

Don't just sit there—get to work!

Advice to a Brand New Compliance Officer

June 2006

By Thomas B. Hudson

We get letters (OK, and some e-mails). Some make me laugh. Others make me cry. Here's one that really made me shed some tears. As they used to say on "Dragnet," the names have been changed to protect the innocent, and I have given it a light edit.

Dear Mr. Hudson,

My name is Joe Doaks and I work for AnyTown Motors Inc. I have been named the Compliance Officer for the dealership. My problem is that I don't know what I am doing. I have worked in a car dealership for the last ten years as a title clerk. The dealership that I worked with was a new car dealership, and I did not do compliance. My duties are to get a corporate compliance manual per se together for AnyTown Motors, and I don't know where to start and how to do this. I do not know any of the laws when it comes to auto dealerships, and I am lost. The things that my boss wants in the manual are as follows:

1. *F&I policies*
2. *Used car rules*
3. *Forms*
4. *OFAC*
5. *Advertising*
6. *ECOA/FCRA/ADA*
7. *UDAP*
8. *Financing repairs*
9. *Arbitration*

Could you please tell me how to start this process and where I can find all the information I need. I don't even know where to begin.

Thank You,
Joe

Doesn't your heart bleed for this guy? He's obviously sincere; he wants to do a good job, and he's sharp enough to "know what he doesn't know." At our firm, that last quality is one that I always look for in new hires. The problem is that there's no really good place to send him for a solution to his problem. Here was my response, again, lightly edited:

Dear Joe,

Congratulations on your promotion. I admire your frank acknowledgement that you aren't yet equipped to do the job. Maybe we can help.

First, get in touch with the Association of Finance and Insurance Professionals and take their certification course. It's $600 or so, and you can do it online.

Next, what state are you in? Your state auto dealer association or independent auto dealers association may have helpful training materials that you can get for free.

Contact the National Auto Dealers Association and see what they have—start with "Understanding Vehicle Finance" and their Management Guide on the FTC's Privacy Safeguarding Rule ($25 for members, $50 for nonmembers). Don't forget the National Independent Auto Dealers Association, which has some good offerings.

Go to the Federal Trade Commission's Web site. They have materials there on the federal Used Car Rule and federal advertising guidelines. Note that the state will also regulate advertising.

Go to the Web sites of your state's motor vehicle administration, consumer protection agency, and Attorney General (your state may have different names for these organizations), and check them out for freebie stuff.

Go to industry conferences, particularly those put on by the National Auto Finance Association, the World of Special Finance, Leedom and Associates and the National Affiliation of Buy Here, Pay Here Dealers. They all have legal education programs.

There are professional trainers who make money teaching

compliance stuff to dealers. Some are very good, some aren't so good. Do your homework. Get references.

If the dealer will spring for it, subscribe to our publications: ***Spot Delivery®*** *($249/year),* ***CARLAW® Counselor*** *($995/year for one state), and* ***CARLAW®****, the monthly subscription service, not the book by the same name referenced below ($995/year for one state). These are all available at www.counselorlibrary.com. If your boss won't provide you with the tools to do your job correctly, look for another job. Tell him I said so.*

But before you do any of the above, buy ***CARLAW®****, the book ($49.95, plus shipping and handling), also available at www.counselorlibrary.com, and read it. Tell your boss you are suddenly ill, and take off two or three days and a weekend. The table of contents reads like your topic list. When you've finished it, you'll have a good working knowledge of the issues you'll be facing.*

So, what did I miss? If there are suggestions you would have given this fellow, or sources that you'd vouch for, write them in the margin of a $20 bill and send them to me, and I'll forward them along.

You Don't Need a Compliance Program

September 2005

By Thomas B. Hudson

Every once in a while, I hear a description of a dealership that makes me shake my head in wonder just like my four-footed pal Spot does when (one more time), he's outrun by a squirrel to a tree. Now, generally the description of the dealer operation is couched in language like, "Well, I dunno if its true, but I know my uncle married to my ex-cousin said it," or "Old Henry told me, and he's crooked enough hisself to know...." I listen. I commiserate. I wag my head. But inside my head my brain is boiling with just what I'd like to say upfront and personal to such a dealer. In fact, I think I'll just go ahead and say it in this column. Maybe some "crooked" squirrel of a dealer will recognize "hisself."

Your dealership is lucky that it hasn't turned up on one of those candid camera episodes. Your sales and F&I guys know every trick in the book.

You sell unpopular new cars to unsophisticated buyers for MSRP, just because you can. You tag buyers with premium prices for mediocre used cars. You steal trade-ins. You engage in payment packing. You hard-code "etch" protection on every contract and tell buyers that it's required, just like you tell them that GAP, service contracts and credit life are required "by the lenders."

You "spot" cars when you know you can't sell the resulting retail installment contract to any financing source, counting on getting the customer back in to rework the terms of the deal. You occasionally sell a "clipped" car, a flooded car, or a car with an odometer rewind. You treat your customers like dirt, turning a deaf ear to legitimate complaints.

You engage in "bait and switch" advertising, and your radio ads have some guy talking like he's on helium, machine-gunning the required federal advertising disclosures at a speed that ensures that no one will understand them. Or you just ignore the disclosure requirements altogether.

If this describes your dealership, I've got some great news for you. You don't need a compliance program. You can save a ton of money. You don't have to worry about hiring expensive lawyers, having a compliance audit, or sending your salespeople and F&I people off to the occasional 2- or 3-day compliance classes. You can forget about a lot of expensive training. And you don't need to spend any time at all trying to figure out whether ethics training makes sense for your operation.

And it's a good thing you don't need compliance help, because if this is the way you are going to operate, no compliance program in the world will help you. I can't help you, Keith Whann can't help you, Chris Leedom can't help you, Greg Goebel can't help you, the Cat in the Hat can't help you, and the genie in the lamp can't help you.

You need a compliance program like a gravedigger needs a manicure.

I've said it often in this space and others, but the place that every good dealership compliance program has to start is in decent, ethical treatment of the dealership's customers. And if a dealership lacks that necessary base, all the compliance stuff in the world is just a bunch of eyewash.

To paraphrase Joe Lescota, my dear friend who is the Department Chair for Automotive Marketing at Northwood University, if you wouldn't sell a car to your mother or sister, you shouldn't sell it to one of your customers, and the same thing goes for the terms of the financing and every other aspect of the deal.

Now that's a *real* "friends and family" promotion. And it's a good "spell check" toward ethical behavior that prompts me to nod—not shake—my head.

Start 2006 With a Compliance Self-Test

January/February 2006

By Thomas B. Hudson and Cathy Brennan

It looks as if 2006 is going to be the Year of Compliance. Every conference features programs on the topic; lawyers and others are pushing various kinds of compliance services; and dealer and finance companies are beginning to audit, or have others audit, their compliance efforts.

With these developments in mind, we thought a compliance self-test might be in order. If you pass with flying colors, you might be able to rest easy. If you score badly, maybe it's not too late to consider a second career.

So here we go—let's see how you do.

1. You have named a privacy officer, as required by the Gramm-Leach-Bliley Act and the FTC's Privacy Regulations.

   ❑ Yes (2 points) ❑ No (minus 2 points)

2. You have named a Compliance Officer (not required, but a really good idea).

   ❑ Yes (2 points) ❑ No (minus 2 points)

3. You have a written privacy safeguarding policy that you actually follow and keep up to date, and you have trained your employees about the policy.

   ❑ Yes (2 points) ❑ No (minus 2 points)

4. You check all of your customers against the "Specially Designated Persons" list maintained by the Office of Foreign Assets Control, and you scrub your portfolio against the OFAC list every time the SDP list changes.

   ❑ Yes (2 points) ❑ No (minus 2 points)

5. You have had your financing and security interest documents and your buyer order reviewed by counsel within the last 12 months.

   ❑ Yes (2 points) ❑ No (minus 2 points)

6. You have had your application form reviewed by counsel within the last 12 months.

   ❑ Yes (2 points) ❑ No (minus 2 points)

7. You have had your collection letters and your collection procedures reviewed by counsel within the last 12 months.

   ❑ Yes (2 points) ❑ No (minus 2 points)

8. You have written policies dealing with do-not-phone, do-not-fax and financing closing and collection procedures, and you periodically train your employees on these policies.

   ❑ Yes (2 points) ❑ No (minus 2 points)

9. You have your advertisements reviewed by counsel every time you change the content, and periodically even when you don't.

   ❑ Yes (2 points) ❑ No (minus 2 points)

10. You have implemented a mandatory arbitration program for consumer complaints to protect against class action lawsuits and large punitive damages awards.

 ❑ Yes (2 points) ❑ No (minus 2 points)

So, how did you do?

If you scored 20 points, call up your trade association and offer to teach the next course it offers on compliance. If you scored from 10-16 points, consider yourself in need of a compliance tune-up. From 0-8 points, you need serious repairs, and if you score from 0 to minus 10, consider a complete frame-off restoration. If you hit a perfect minus 20, it's time to close your company and open a bait shop.

Videotaping F&I Activities—Good Idea or Not?

March 2006

By Thomas B. Hudson

Don't ever accuse me of being consistent. I've had so many positions on the question of whether it's a good idea to videotape F&I sessions that you'd need a GPS device to keep track of me.

Ten years ago or so, when I learned that some dealers in Alabama were beginning to audiotape, and then videotape, their F&I sessions with customers, I was intrigued. I knew why the Alabama dealers were trying to create records of their dealings with customers. Alabama had become a hotbed of litigation against dealers, and the dealers were looking for defensive measures to slow down the plaintiffs' lawyers.

Not a bad idea, I thought.

Then I thought some more. And as I did, several concerns came to mind. First, if the F&I process wasn't perfect, the videotape would record the imperfections, and the tape would become Plaintiff's Exhibit 1.

Second, the practices of some dealers as reflected by the court opinions we see each month are not the sort you'd want to have on tape. Dealers would have to jettison things like payment packing and phony menu selling before videotaping began. That's not a bad thing, but at some dealerships, it would mean a sea of change in how business is done, a transformation that some dealerships would not want to make.

Third, even an ethical and honest dealership makes mistakes, and some F&I sessions will not be perfect. In order to avoid those imperfect sessions, dealers would have to train their personnel, and train them well, on the intricacies of the laws governing car sales and finance. Given the general level of knowledge about these topics in many dealerships, and given the typically high turnover at most dealerships, I thought that was a pretty tall order.

Fourth, what if the dealership did not tape all F&I sessions? Judges and juries don't like inconsistent procedures—they immediately think, "Why didn't the dealer tape these sessions?" Finally, the tapes would become subject to federal and state recordkeeping requirements. The burden of keeping several years' tapes appeared significant.

So, given all of these negatives, and seeing few positives, I staked out a position against videotaping. That's where my head was last fall, when I was scheduled to talk on the topic at a seminar in Denver.

A week or two before the seminar, though, I got a call from a lawyer friend who works with a large dealership. He asked if my view of videotaping was negative, and I told him it was. He responded by making a pretty persuasive case for videotaping, and, because he was coming to the seminar, I invited him to join me in leading a discussion on the topic.

At the seminar, this lawyer recounted the experience that his dealership had to date with videotaping. He pointed out the value of videotaping in training employees—it drove away employees prone to do bad stuff. He noted that it also drove off customers engaged in identity theft or fraud in an effort to gain financing for their vehicles (that really caught my attention). He also recounted that it warded off threatened litigation.

I'm not the sharpest tool in the shed, but I always pay attention when people start talking real life experiences instead of gut feelings and theory. After listening to this lawyer recount his dealership's real-world videotaping history, I found myself dragged back over the "neutral" line and into "pro-videotaping" territory.

I still had concerns—dealerships need to do the videotaping right. They should videotape all sessions (except where they document a customer refusal and have a process for monitoring which employee's customers are refusing). They should train and re-train everyone how to do it, and have the dealer's lawyer script the sessions and review samples of the tapes. Finally, dealerships must comply with the recordkeeping requirements applicable to the tapes.

That was where I was before the NADA Conference in Orlando last month. In the NADA Exhibit Hall, though, I saw some impressive videotaping technology that further confirmed my position in the pro-videotaping camp. The software was so far removed from, "The video camera is hanging on the wall and we'll turn it on whenever we remember to," that you wouldn't recognize it as the same concept. I won't recount the technology's many features—suffice it to say the stuff was pretty powerful, offering management the ability to measure F&I activities in ways I had not seen before.

The company offering the technology was Intravision (www.intravisiontech.com), but I try not to make product or company recommendations in columns I write, so I will simply say that if this topic interests you, you should look at their stuff, then look at the offerings of other vendors as well. I haven't seen the offerings of other companies, and equipment that is even more impressive may exist. Shop smart.

So, here I am parked pretty firmly in the videotaping camp again. And, for those of you tracking me via GPS, I still think that the warnings above are good ones. But I now think that videotaping, when done right, makes a lot of sense.

How Should a Dealer Choose a Lawyer?

April 2006

By Thomas B. Hudson

Recently someone asked me, "How does a dealer go about choosing a lawyer?" After a smart-mouthed, "Have them call me," response, I stopped to give the question some serious thought. I didn't get very far addressing the question as a "how to," but started making some headway when I thought about "how not to." I'll share those "how not to" and a few "how to" ideas with you.

The Dealership's Lawyer

Most dealers run pretty large business operations and have a regular relationship with a lawyer who does general business law—stuff like incorporations, corporate governance, tax, and the like. That lawyer might, or might not, be the best choice for a serious environmental matter or a trademark question. However, this lawyer can be a valuable resource and a good place to start your selection process. Chances are, the general business lawyer will know, or will be associated with, lawyers who practice in other subject matter areas and will be able to recommend one or more to you.

Price

Don't choose your lawyer based on the cheapest hourly rate. There are two reasons for this. First, the lawyer's hourly rate is only a part of the calculation that determines the fee. A lawyer who charges $200 an hour, but takes 10 hours to do something is expensive compared to the lawyer who charges $300 an hour, but takes only five hours to finish the same task. Second, there's a reason why a BMW costs more than a Kia. A higher rate is usually an indication of either experience or expertise, or both. In lawyers, these are good qualities.

Family Relationships

Don't pick your brother-in-law or your wife's uncle just because of the relationship. The lawyer-client relationship can get strained at times, and you probably want to stay married (or keep peace in the family).

Generalists

Don't assume, just because an "Esq." follows the lawyer's name, that the lawyer will know how to handle your legal matter. Lawyers aren't fungible (you can't swap one for another). If you have an intellectual property issue, the lawyer you want is probably not the one who handles your showroom "slip and fall" cases. You don't go to a podiatrist for brain surgery, do you? Before I hear from some of the few remaining generalists out there, I'll say that there are exceptions to this advice. Those exceptions, in my experience, are rare. You will likely pay a generalist a lot of money to learn the specialization that you are looking for; it would probably make more sense to pay the specialist's (probably) higher rates. If you have an issue in a particular area of the law, go to a lawyer with experience practicing in that area. Don't be bashful—ask for client references and descriptions of matters he has handled for other clients. Also ask about outcomes and results of those matters.

Experience

Experience is better than inexperience. My wife, the tennis whiz, says "Experience and guile will beat youth and talent every time." If you are going to the mat on a serious legal issue with a lot at stake, you don't want a newbie. On the other hand, if your dealership regularly needs to go to a court of limited jurisdiction (a small claims court where the awards are limited) for things like collecting on bad checks, it might be a good idea to use someone relatively inexperienced and with a relatively low billing rate (see the cautionary note above) for such work, as long as the lawyer is properly supervised.

Here are a few "how to" suggestions:

References

Ask for references, then (gasp!) actually call them. When you talk to the references, ask if they were satisfied with the lawyer's work, the outcome of the legal matter, and the legal fees.

Comparable Experience

Ask if the lawyer has handled matters like yours before and, if so, how often, how recently, and with what results.

Job Application

Ask for a resume setting forth the lawyer's academic background and work history. This will serve as sort of a job application form. You might not care whether your lawyer was the anchorman in his law school class, but if you have an insurance problem, you might be interested in discovering that your lawyer worked in the office of the state insurance commissioner for 10 years.

Agree on Fees

Don't hesitate to talk about fees. Get a fee agreement in writing. You may be able to negotiate a fixed fee or a "not-to-exceed" arrangement. Don't hesitate to ask for a discount from standard rates, but keep in mind that the hourly rates are only half the equation. An unscrupulous lawyer (I have heard that some exist) can pad hours and make up for any discount. And don't forget the extra fees and charges. If you don't like being separately charged for copying, postage, long-distance phone calls, secretarial overtime and other parts of the law firm's overhead, the time to bring it up is *before* you hire the lawyer.

So there you are. Good luck, and tell the lawyer you end up with that I sent you.

Who is Responsible for F&I Compliance?

August 2006

By Thomas B. Hudson

Christine A. Dern, of Profit by Design, trains dealers by teaching, among other things, compliance. In an e-mail I received from her a couple of weeks back, she posed the following question:

> *This week I was asked a question while teaching compliance that I have never been asked and I really felt bad about my response...it was inadequate at best.*
>
> *A student who had been doing the finance job was finding out that he had been violating several laws—some federal—and he was truly upset. The problem was that he had been plopped into the job and told to perform. I was his first training a year later.*
>
> *His question...“Who is responsible for making sure I know the laws?” In other words, he didn’t even KNOW that he was doing things incorrectly—a true case of he didn’t know what he didn’t know—or that he didn’t know. (I am practicing to be an attorney.)*
>
> *So the question—“Whose responsibility is it to make sure I know these things?” is a valid question. Is it the dealership’s, the dealer, the agency supplying the insurance products, or the individual’s, for not knowing?*
>
> *I told him it would ultimately be his responsibility, but his objection was, if you have never done it, you don’t even know that there is more to know or laws that need to be adhered to. His point is very well taken and I run into it all the time. People who have never been trained and a year later are just meeting me to find out that they have made a LOT of mistakes that have put them and their dealerships at risk.*

Christine’s concerns are well placed. Let’s try to answer the question her student posed. Luckily, the answer is a short one:

- It is the dealership's responsibility to make sure that those who have responsibilities that involve legal compliance are fully trained to carry out their responsibilities.
- It is the dealership that will be sued for the violations of its untrained people.
- It is the dealership that will have to pay the bill for its lawyers (and, ultimately, the plaintiffs and their lawyers, too).
- It is the dealership whose image will be sullied by the media when the news of a lawsuit hits. Even if some of the risk for operating with untrained people can be shifted to an insurance company (and many sorts of claims are likely to be excluded from coverage), it's always the case that more claims lead to higher premiums.

Certainly, companies that provide products and services like insurance, GAP, and the like for dealers to sell to car buyers have a vested interest in making certain that the dealer follows the law in the sale process. Many advise dealers on compliant sales procedures, and they provide forms that they say are in compliance with the law. But while such advice can be helpful, the dealership is ultimately responsible for compliant sales procedures and forms. It won't be a defense to say "ABC Insurance Company gave me this stuff, and I assumed it was correct."

The student isn't off the hook, though, at least in my book. If I were told to do a job, and didn't know how to do it, or didn't have the tools to do it right, I'd be standing up on my hind legs demanding the necessary training and tools. And the tools are out there.

We've talked before about the wisdom of dealerships providing F&I certification for their employees. Such certification is offered by the Association of Finance and Insurance Professionals. AFIP's Web site is at www.afip.com/

home.asp. Their training is relatively quick and relatively cheap (full disclosure—our firm represents AFIP and has prepared most of its legal training materials). Others may offer such certification. Certainly others offer training. NADA, Universal Underwriters, state and national dealership trade associations, consulting companies, and private trainers like Christine all have training capabilities.

There are other resources. Our own publications, ***Spot Delivery***® and ***CARLAW***® (the book), are helpful, as are our Internet-based monthly legal update, also called ***CARLAW***®, and our ***CARLAW***® ***Counselor*** database. If you don't like the way we part our hair, many other lawyers have resources available that can assist dealerships with their training and compliance efforts.

The resources are out there, and if the dealership isn't availing its new people (and its experienced people, too) of those resources, shame on it. If you were in the jungle, surrounded by bad guys, would you put your newest, raw recruit on guard duty? And without a gun? I think I'd want someone experienced, with the biggest, baddest firepower available. Well guess what? As Monk would say, "It's a jungle out there!"

Twelve Steps to a Basic F&I Compliance Program

January/February 2007

By Thomas B. Hudson

Let's say that you have decided 2007 is the year you are finally going to take all the compliance noise we have been making seriously. How should you go about it?

Dealers ask me that question a lot, and it's always accompanied by a warning that the compliance program needs to be one that won't break the bank. So, recently, I've given the matter some fresh thought. This article outlines a few first steps you can take toward establishing a serious compliance program, and it makes a stab at estimating the "hard costs" that each one will involve, not including management time, implementation time, and the time your personnel spend studying, training, and researching.

Here goes.

Step 1. Make the decision to become a squeaky-clean operation.

Without this step, none of the rest of the stuff we recommend will work. The decision needs to come from the top of the organization, and, if your organization has had compliance problems, all hands need to understand that it is a real change and not just window dressing. Your people need to be told that anyone who does not treat customers honestly and ethically will be fired. Anyone who doesn't buy into the new compliance culture should be told to hit the road. Cost—$0.

Step 2. Appoint a privacy officer.

While you're at it, make that same person your compliance officer. If your organization is large enough, this person may need help in the form of a small committee. The privacy/compliance officer should report to the highest-ranking person in the organization. Have signs made up for your dealership identifying that person. Cost—$5 for the signs.

Step 3. Give your privacy/compliance officer a real budget so that he or she can actually get something done.

No money budgeted for privacy and compliance will assure that you won't have a privacy/compliance program that's worth a hoot. That could be expensive. Several of the tools that the privacy/compliance officer will need are online. These include copies of the federal Truth in Lending Act and Federal Reserve Board Regulation Z, the federal Consumer Leasing Act and Federal Reserve Board Regulation M, the Equal Credit Opportunity Act and Federal Reserve Board Regulation B, the federal Gramm-Leach-Bliley Act and the Federal Trade Commission's privacy regulation, and the FTC's Used Car Rule. They are free, although your privacy/compliance officer might need some training (generally a minor cost) to access them.

As part of that privacy/compliance budget, allocate enough money to send everyone you can possibly afford to send through the Association of Finance and Insurance Professionals' certification program. It isn't expensive—$670 per person (group pricing is less)—and will pay compliance dividends. Have your privacy/compliance officer obtain and read all the books on F&I compliance that he or she can find. We have two good ones, including one that is used in the AFIP certification course. However, I'm sure that there are others out there if you don't like our stuff. Finally, have the privacy/compliance officer subscribe to online legal compliance services—again, we have those, but there are other good ones in the marketplace, as well. Cost—start with $8,000.

Step 4. Train, train, train.

Dealers tend to have high turnover of sales and finance personnel, and this compliance stuff can be less than riveting. So you need to train your revolving sales and finance force and periodically re-train the ones who stay with you. There are third-party trainers, some of whom are quite good, but if your privacy/compliance officer turns out to be a crackerjack, he or she might well be able to handle the training within your dealership. Cost—$0 in-house, $10,000 for outside training twice a year.

Step 5. Download and print copies of "Understanding Vehicle Finance."

This consumer education pamphlet is free on the National Auto Dealers Association Web site (www.nada.org), and is available in English and Spanish. It provides an overview of how car financing at dealerships works, and bears the seal of approval of the Federal Trade Commission. Everyone in your organization will benefit from reading it. Make copies and display them around your dealership, and put a copy into each customer's packet of papers as you close each deal. Cost—the download is free; plan on $1,000 for printing.

Step 6. Download and print copies of "Keys to Vehicle Leasing."

This is also a consumer education pamphlet. It's from the Federal Reserve Board and is a good overview of closed-end auto leasing. It is also available in English or Spanish, and you should use it just like you use "Understanding Vehicle Finance." Cost—the download is free; plan on $1,000 for printing.

Step 7. Require everyone in the sales and financing process to read your buyers order, your retail installment sale agreements and leases, your privacy policy, your arbitration agreement, and all other documents that you ask the customer to sign or give to the customer.

This should include credit life and accident policies and certificates, GAP addenda, service contracts, "etch" agreements, and anything else the customer sees. Make up a test to determine how much of what they have read each employee understands. Cost—$0.

Step 8. Adopt a true, transparent "menu" process for the sale of additional products through the F&I office.

Dealers who do this say that the transparent sales process loses some sales that they might otherwise make, but that offering every product to every customer every time through a menu results in more sales. Follow up with your employees to make sure that they are actually using the menus you've adopted in the manner they are supposed to be used. Cost—$0.

Step 9. Appoint a person to help customers if they have a complaint.

Sometimes referred to (using a ten-dollar word) as an "ombudsman," such a person helps the customer work through a complaint with the dealership. You don't want customers resolving complaints with the dealer representatives that they originally dealt with—who often caused the complaint and get defensive as a result. You want someone who did not take part in the sales and financing process who can look at the customer's complaint dispassionately. Cost—$0.

Step 10. Have your privacy/compliance officer periodically search the Web.

He or she should check the site for your state's Attorney General, so that you'll know what the AG's current hot buttons are. Another site to check is that of your state's motor vehicle dealer regulatory body. Also check the FTC's Web site, the NADA Web site, your state ADA's or IADA's Web site and any other sites you've discovered that are useful, on a regular basis. Use your Outlook program to set up a weekly or monthly reminder to do these searches (I stole this tip from Gil Van Over). Cost—$0.

Step 11. If your dealership isn't using a mandatory arbitration agreement in its sales, leasing and financing transactions, consider doing so.

Some state association-produced buyers orders contain arbitration language, or you can buy freestanding arbitration agreements off-the-shelf from vendors like Reynolds and Reynolds (but make sure your state permits the use of additional documents and doesn't have a so-called "single document rule"). Regardless of which way you go, have a lawyer who is really knowledgeable about consumer arbitration agreements look over the agreement you intend to use. Cost—$2,000 plus any ongoing printing costs.

Step 12. Have a forms and procedures review and a written compliance program.

All of your sales and F&I forms and procedures should be reviewed by a lawyer who is knowledgeable about compliance law. All procedures should be documented and maintained in a compliance manual. You and your lawyer should periodically review your manual, because laws and regulations change. Use the Outlook feature to schedule a review at least every six months. Cost—$10,000 to $20,000 for the initial review, then $2,000 every 6 months.

Your total comes to something north of $32,000, including outside training, AFIP certification, printing, and $10,000 for first-year legal fees. So there you are. If you implement those 12 steps, you still won't have a first-class compliance program, but you'll be miles ahead of most dealers. Once you get these measures in place, we can start talking about how to bring the program to the next level.

Vendor Training—Take It or Leave It?

January/February 2007

By Thomas B. Hudson

A dealer's training obligation is never done. Dealers have to train the F&I department, the sales department, and the service department. They must also train in environmental and human resources areas. I'm sure there are other areas of training I don't know about. But there is one that I do know something about, and that is the F&I training program. That's what I deal with here.

The Capital One commercials ask, "What's in YOUR wallet?" Good question. Another good question you ought to be asking is, "What's in YOUR F&I training arsenal?"

The reason for this latter question is that all training resources are not created equal. Another reason for the question is that a colleague of mine whose family owns several dealerships says that, in her experience, dealers rely heavily on their vendors to provide training. That comment stopped me cold.

Why? Because there are trainers, and then there are trainers, if you get my drift.

I have seen some vendors who know F&I compliance law as well as, or better than, the lawyers at our firm do, and (not to be bragging) that's no small compliment. I remember being invited to a National Auto Dealers Association training session several years ago at which the trainers were two fellows from Universal Underwriters. UU is a "vendor" of insurance products to 7,000+ franchised dealers. Frankly, when I heard that the UU guys doing the teaching were not compliance lawyers, I wasn't expecting much. To my surprise, they turned out to be great.

Some other vendors are not so impressive. I recall one that claimed that the state did not permit dealers to enter into arbitration agreements with their customers. He was chagrined to find out that the Federal Arbitration Act, as a federal law, trumps state laws that prohibit arbitration.

Another vendor trainer insisted that a dealer's federal Gramm-Leach-Bliley privacy notice was required to obtain an opt-out provision. This provision permits the customer to elect not to have the dealer share the customer's information with certain parties. He was mistaken. Such a provision is not required unless the dealer is sharing protected information in ways that most dealers do not employ.

So, the downside to vendor training is there is not much of a guarantee that the vendor trainer will know his or her subject matter. The reality is, some will, but some won't.

The upside to vendor training is the cost. It is often free. When it costs, it usually doesn't cost much. So, how can you get the upside—modest costs—without the downside—inadequate trainer knowledge? I can think of a few ways.

- If your dealership's lawyer is good at F&I compliance issues, you could have your lawyer sit in on the first training session and make an assessment of how good (or bad) the trainer is.
- Failing that, you could request that the vendor submit to your lawyer a detailed outline of the training session, along with copies of all handouts and other presentation materials the trainer intends to use.
- In addition, you could request that your vendor provide assurances that the material presented will be accurate and complete, and that any materials that deal with legal issues have been reviewed by a lawyer familiar with F&I legal compliance issues.
- Also, in addition to the previous three steps, you can ask the trainer for references, and then actually call those

references to determine how good the trainer was. Note that this last step isn't a substitute for the first three steps.

So, do you cheerfully accept the offer of vendor training or not? My advice is to take it slow, do your homework, and insist that the trainer not only be knowledgeable in the subject matter but also prove that's the case.

Reputable vendor trainers will not be put off by your due diligence, but you might just frighten away the fly-by-night operators.

Spring Cleaning Your Operations

March 2007

By Patricia E. M. Covington

Spring is often associated with cleaning out and organizing. It's also a time to get ready. We do that with our gardens, our "stuff," and ourselves. We eat a little less so that we can fit better into our swimsuits; we ready our little plots of land to grow and harvest vegetables; we seed and fertilize our lawns so that our grass is nice and green for the spring and summer (at least early summer, before the sun scorches it in late summer).

Similarly, spring is a good time to take a hard look at your operations. What's working and what's not? What needs more attention? How can the business improve profitability?

When you're doing this, don't forget about two very important areas—legal and compliance. It's easy to overlook these areas because they don't add to the bottom line. Rather, they are known to do quite the opposite; that is, drain the bottom line. Having said that, you probably know that it takes only one really bad case (or several bad cases when you get copycat plaintiffs' attorneys) to turn this commonly accepted economic perception on its head.

So, let's talk. What should you be thinking about? Where should you begin? First, let's talk about what you should be worrying about. That means inventorying the laws that apply to your operations. Let's begin with basic inventory of the laws you need to understand:

- OFAC: Bad guys list
- FCRA: When you can get a credit report and how you can use it, adverse action notices, prescreened firm offers of credit, credit report accuracy
- ECOA: Nondiscrimination, adverse action, credit applications
- GLB: Privacy notices, safeguarding consumer information
- DPPA: Protection of driver's license information
- FACTA Disposal Rule: How to dispose of credit reports
- FACTA Red Flag Rule: Identity theft prevention programs
- FTC Act: Section 5(a) of the Unfair and Deceptive trade practices, commonly known as the federal UDAP
- FTC's Telemarketing Sales Rule: Do not call
- FCC's Telephone Consumer Protection Act: Do not call
- FTC's Used Car Rule: Buyer's Guide and disclosure on sales contracts
- FTC's Preservation of Consumers Claims and Defenses Rule: Disclosure on retail installment contracts
- CAN-SPAM Act
- Junk Fax Prevention Act
- E-SIGN and UETA: For electronic contracts

- USA PATRIOT Act: Awaiting regulations
- State security breach notification laws
- State security freeze laws
- State Social Security Number limitation laws
- State disposal laws: Similar to the FACTA Disposal Rule, but applies to all consumer information
- State safeguarding of customer information laws: Mini-GLB protections
- Dealer documentary or processing fee limitations
- State mini-UDAPs
- Federal and state record retention requirements
- FTC enforcement actions: DirecTV, ChoicePoint, BJ's Wholesale, DSW, Inc., CardSystem Solutions, Nations Title Agency, etc.

Whoa...These are many of them, but certainly not all. After you've inventoried the laws that govern your operations, you need to distill and understand what they require or prohibit—essentially, what the law says; what conduct it regulates.

To demonstrate, let's talk about OFAC. This is an abbreviation for the Office of Foreign Assets Control, which administers the federal mandate (issued in Executive Order 13224) that prohibits persons from transacting business with any person on the Specially Designated Nationals list (also commonly referred to as the "bad guy list" or SDN list). For a bit more clarity, not transacting business means you can't do business in any way with a person on the bad guy list. You can't sell him a product or service, you can't extend credit to him, you can't hire him as an employee, you can't hire him as a service provider or vendor, nothing, nada. And, oh, by the way, the list is not static. It's updated frequently and on no set schedule. So, you are responsible for continually knowing who is on that updated list, and you may not do business with any person added to it. What's the consequence of doing business with someone on the SDN list? Only up to $1,000,000 (yes, that's one million dollars) in civil penalties, along with a big hit on your reputation. Also, you might incur a cease and desist order. Further, if the bad guy uses the vehicle (the subject of the credit extension) to blow up a building, you've got civil lawsuits to worry about.

After understanding the legal requirements applicable to your dealership, it is time to inventory the business practices affected by the law. Using the OFAC as an example, what practices does it impact? Several: the extension of credit, hiring of employees, and contracting of vendors, to name a few.

Knowing what practices are impacted, you should look to see if you have policies and procedures that address and set parameters around the legal requirements. Back to our OFAC example, if you cannot extend credit to someone *on the list*, it's really important that you verify that each person you are considering for credit is *not on the list*.

Basically, this means you need to include a step of examining the SDN list in your protocol for evaluating a person for credit and selling cars for cash. You need to set up a similar protocol when considering employees and vendors.

So, we have considered evaluating credit, hiring employees, and contracting with vendors, is that it? Not quite. After you've done this once, you need to go back and do it again, and again, and again. Recall, the list is continually updated. That means you need to periodically (and not just once a year) scrub your lists of customers, employees, and vendors against the SDN list.

The policies and procedures should be written. They should

be clear, concise, and easy to understand. They should also be realistic. After developing the policies and procedures, you must distribute them to those who need to know about them. You must also practice what you preach. I recommend a full-blown internal marketing program of the policies and procedures. How do you market to your customers? Consider the same for your employees. Your employees can't follow the policies and procedures if they don't know about them.

Then comes training, and not token training; rather, a dedicated effort to make sure employees are not only aware of, but understand and have the tools necessary to follow, the policies and procedures.

Lastly, you need to make sure folks are doing what you have trained them to do. That means you have to periodically audit. Auditing, together with consistent discipline of all employees violating the policies and procedures, reinforces the message that the policies are the real deal, and you will not tolerate noncompliance.

That's about it. If the exercise I'm suggesting seems a bit overwhelming, don't fret. It doesn't have to happen overnight. Pick the law where you've got the most exposure. Start with it. Name a compliance officer, and task him or her with beginning the process. Slowly but surely you'll get your shop in "compliance order."

Like everything else, it's one step at a time.

You've Plugged It In. Now What?

March 2007

By Emily Marlow Beck

My husband and I recently installed a new water heater in our home. Now, I don't know much about water heaters, but the guy at the store assured me that the unit we bought was the super-duper, top of the line deluxe model. So, needless to say, my husband and I were very disappointed when the plumber installed the thing, and the hot water never came. After multiple visits (and numerous excuses) from the plumber, we learned that our deluxe model water heater wasn't worth a darn, because some lines got crossed during installation. Apparently, even the highest quality water heaters need to be connected to the water line to make the water hot. Go figure.

Oddly enough, my adventure with the new water heater reminded me of my recent trip to the NADA convention and the grand unveiling of all the newest and greatest nifty gadgets peddled to car dealers. This year, I was pleasantly surprised to see how many new products out there are geared toward dealer compliance. And, I was delighted to see how many dealers were taking the compliance initiative and investing in these products.

But, like my scald-o-matic water heater, these products and programs are only as effective as their installation. I'm not talking about the computer folks and the IT crews who plug in the wires and push all the buttons to make things happen. What I am talking about is a commitment from management to encourage the cultural changes that will help the new products and procedures take root. You'd be surprised how often I see dealers who don't ever get the full benefit from a good investment in a compliance-conscious product, because they don't follow through and ensure that the program is properly integrated into dealership operations.

One of my favorite compliance review stories involved a dealer that assured me that it was impossible for his employees to be packing payments, because his dealership had purchased a menu software program. But, when I met with the employees in the finance offices, they told me that they weren't using the menu software the dealer bought. In the words of one employee, "Yeah, I know that we're supposed to be using that stuff, but it's really not my style." In other words, the dealer bought a fantastic menu-selling program, but he had not successfully integrated it into dealership operations. (And yes, for the sake of this article, I'm ignoring the fact that, although menus are a fabulous compliance tool, they're no silver bullet for a dealer's compliance woes or packing claims.)

So, how can you, the dealer, get the most out of a compliance-based product or program?

For starters, follow up and make sure that your employees are actually using the program, and that they are using it properly. Just like the story above, dealers shouldn't assume that employees are using a program just because they've bought it. After all, employees may be hesitant to break old habits that have served them well in the past.

Make sure that your employees understand the changes you are making. If you bring your employees into the "big picture" and let them know that the changes they make today could have long-term payoffs, they will be much more willing to stick with the program.

Don't forget that there is no one-size-fits-all compliance program. No matter how wonderful the program you purchased is, you'll need to constantly reevaluate your situation to see if the program is getting the job done. After all, compliance is ultimately the dealer's responsibility.

Predatory Litigators

July 2007

By Thomas B. Hudson

OK, right up front, I stole the title to this article from Chris Leedom, who used it at our firm's recent workshop. Chris was describing a relatively new kind of lawyer—one who focuses his or her practice on car dealers, actively seeking out the dealer's customers to sue the dealer in lawsuit after lawsuit.

These are lawyers who specialize in suing car dealers—they get up in the morning thinking of new ways to sue. If you have one of these sharks swimming in waters near you, what should you do?

I have two suggestions. The first is to get out of the car biz and open a bait shop. When was the last time you heard of a class action lawsuit being filed against a worm purveyor?

If worms just aren't your thing, then you have to think about other strategies. Here are some tried and tested ways to keep predatory litigators at bay:

Sign Arbitration Agreements

If you aren't having your customers sign arbitration agreements when they buy cars from you, start doing so, *now*. Plaintiffs' lawyers hate arbitration agreements. Why? The agreements take away the leverage the lawyers can get from threatening a class action or a jury trial, and, generally, the lawyers are unable to make nearly as much money in an arbitration proceeding as they can make on a lawsuit. Do you recall the joke about the two guys being chased by the grizzly bear? One of the fellows says to the other something like, "I don't have to outrun the bear; I just have to outrun you." If your customers sign arbitration agreements, and those customers of other dealers in your neighborhood don't sign them, the predatory litigator is going to go after those other dealers first.

Review Forms

Have a thorough review of all of your forms. Predatory litigators look for forms violations, because when they find them, they can argue that every deal employing a supposedly defective form violates the law and gives rise to a class action.

Check Your Insurance Policy

Determine whether you are insured against lawsuits that allege violations of consumer laws. Some policies actually cover such claims. If yours doesn't, get a quote from your carrier for such coverage.

Have a Legal Compliance Audit

Lawyers who practice consumer credit compliance law do this best. Many dealers believe that "a lawyer is a lawyer is a lawyer," but it just isn't true. Most lawyers have never been near the Truth in Lending Act, the Equal Credit Opportunity Act, the Fair Credit Reporting Act, and all of the other federal and state laws that devil dealers in their daily operations. If asked to do such an audit, a lawyer unfamiliar with the laws and regulations likely would either have to learn the law on your dime, or would do a lousy job. Get someone who has done the task for other dealers, and get references from those dealers before hiring the lawyer.

Train Your People

They can't be expected to turn square corners when it comes to compliance if they've never seen a road map. Send your folks to the Association of Finance and Insurance Professionals for its F&I compliance certification course. It's relatively inexpensive, and the fact that you have been diligent enough to train your people will help tremendously when the predatory litigator tries to make your dealership look bad before a jury.

Adopt a "Compliance Culture"

From the top of your organization down to the most menial worker in the place, make "doing it right" the mantra of every dealership employee. I've said it before, and I'll say it again—the most effective compliance program you can have is a satisfied, well-treated customer. Train every employee to watch for any signs of customer displeasure—a few dollars to effect a repair can keep your customer out of the predatory litigator's office.

Take Him to the Mat

Last, but not least, if you are dealing with a predatory litigator, take him or her to the mat whenever your lawyer tells you you've got a good case. This advice is 180 degrees different than the advice we give when you are dealing with a lawyer you don't think you will ever see again, or when your case is weak. In both of those instances, settling the case quickly is almost always the way to go. The earlier you can write the settlement check, the fewer zeros it is likely to need.

All this is more trouble than it's worth, you say? I know where you can pick up a bait shop, cheap.

It's Hip to Be Square: Bring a Code of Ethics Into Your Dealership

September 2007

By Emily Marlow Beck

Do you retain all your employees with absolutely no turnover? Do all your employees do the right thing every time? Do you know the intimate details of every deal worked in your dealership? If you answered "yes" to all these questions, please turn the page—this article is not for you. However, if you've answered "no" to any of these questions, please read on.

We spend lots of time talking about all the written policies the federal government requires your dealership to maintain. You've heard us blab about your Safeguard Policy, your Do-Not-Call policy, and the policies that may be required under the soon-to-be-issued Red Flag Rules, to name a few. There is, however, one thing that federal law does not require you to have; that is, a code of ethics. Your dealership may have a code of ethics that it agreed to when it joined the National Auto Dealers Association, or a state ADA or IADA. If you haven't reviewed those documents recently, you should. And it's always a good idea to train all of your employees about the terms of industry association codes.

Note, however, that these codes were designed to apply to the business practices of dealers generally, not to your particular dealership. So, why implement a code of ethics designed for your dealership? After all, you hire only folks who were raised right, and you are convinced they always do what is ethical, right? Right?

Acceptable behavior starts from the top and trickles down. In the same manner that the management must set standards and goals for sales and profits, the management must set the standard for the behavior it expects from its employees. We often read cases discussing the most pinheaded and technical compliance issues that started out with customers who walked away from the dealership feeling like the dealership just didn't treat them right. A code of ethics aims to make sure that employees act with honesty and integrity in every transaction. Treated with honesty and integrity, customers generally walk away satisfied.

Moreover, when something goes wrong (and, sooner or later, it probably will), a code of ethics can mean the difference between the bad acts of a rogue employee versus the accepted practices of a corrupt corporation. When you have to face the jury and explain why your dealership fleeced grandma, you'd be much better off if you could show that grandma was the victim of an employee who acted in blatant disregard of his written instructions, and not by a dealership that neglected to take steps to ensure its employees acted with a mind for doing things right.

OK. Now that we're on the same page, you probably want to know what a code of ethics should contain. Now, I should warn you that I don't know squat about employment law, and I don't know diddly about the sorts of "values" you can require your employees to adhere to. Also, I should warn that the information below is by no means an exhaustive list. But, from a consumer credit compliance standpoint, I believe a dealership's code of ethics should contain some key provisions.

First, I'd recommend that any code of ethics be in writing and be part of the initial training process. Revisit this code often, and incorporate it into everyday routine. Consider posting a code of ethics in your dealership as a reminder of the dealership values. Consider giving a copy to every customer.

Second, I would stress that any policy should require employees to adhere to the letter and the spirit of the law. Of course, this works much better if you actually teach your employees the letter of the law (consider AFIP certification, for example), but actions that may not "technically" violate the law may "actually" be pretty unethical; also, they may attract the attention of plaintiffs' lawyers and the Attorney General. Technical compliance with the law should be the minimum level to which your dealership aspires, and you should tell your people that your standard is higher.

Third, I would suggest that each employee should be independently responsible for doing the right thing in a given situation. This applies even if the employee believes his or her "questionable behavior" would benefit the dealership financially, or if the questionable behavior would have been acceptable in another dealership.

Employees may try to justify packing a payment here and there or bumping the income on a credit application to push a deal through, believing that "bending the rules" is acceptable when it makes money for the dealership. A code of ethics would not only make clear that disregarding the laws and regulations in order to make money for the dealership is unacceptable, it would also make clear that the management's position on this issue is documented in a written policy. And, while some sales tricks spread from dealership to dealership so rampantly I want to call the Centers for Disease Control, a code of ethics could be used to make it very clear that questionable conduct, while perhaps acceptable at the dealership down the street, has no place in your dealership.

To give more than just lip services to you dealership's ethical standards, you should consider giving your policy an enforcement mechanism. After all, implementation is the name of the compliance game. Also, it might be a good idea to require employees to report illegal or unethical behavior to the management, without fear of reprimand.

If you're interested in developing a code of ethics, there are some great resources out there. Many compliance certification programs, such as AFIP, contain an ethics component. Also, as I noted at the beginning, the NADA and many state and local dealer associations contain codes of ethics.

Sometimes, it's hip to be "square." And "being good" gains the prize. Think about this as you chew over developing a code of ethics for your business. And, until then, be good!

Chapter 3

Truth in Lending Act (TILA)

The granddaddy of federal credit protection laws is the Truth in Lending Act (TILA). It has been around so long that it was in place when I started practicing law in 1973. Indeed, most people in the car sales biz cannot remember a time when TILA and the Federal Reserve Board's Regulation Z, which implements it, were not with us.

Both TILA and Reg. Z deal with disclosure of credit terms—not with the regulation of credit terms. You don't look at TILA and Reg. Z to determine the amount of late charge you can charge in a retail credit transaction (that is regulated by state law), but you do look at them to determine the correct way to disclose the late charge. Generally speaking, the feds don't care what you do, but rather focus on how you must disclose what you do.

TILA and Reg. Z have been around long enough to have generated a great deal of litigation; however, over time, the courts have decided enough TILA cases so that most of the mysteries have been solved, and the pace of litigation seems to have slowed. Still, TILA and Reg. Z claims can pack a dangerous punch, since successful plaintiffs can recover actual damages, statutory damages in some cases, attorneys' fees, and court costs. Because TILA and Reg. Z claims frequently deal with a dealer's or creditor's form documents, plaintiffs often seek class relief, upping the ante for defendants even more.

In this chapter, you'll get some "Z" surprises—when the law applies and when it doesn't, when a charge is a finance charge and when it isn't, where in the contract particular disclosures need to go, and what all the talk about "hidden" finance charges involves.

Dealer Credit Insurance Practices Withstand Class Action Challenge

July 2005

By Thomas B. Hudson

Many dealers have formed separate insurance companies to permit them to earn commissions on the sale of credit insurance and other insurance products. Often, these companies are owned by the dealer principals, have no separate staff or offices, and exist only on paper. Attributes like these drive plaintiffs' lawyers nuts, and they look for ways to attack the arrangements. Here's how one such attack came out.

Elise Webb brought a class action against Westborn Chrysler Plymouth Jeep, Inc., on behalf of individuals who bought credit life insurance in connection with car purchases from Westborn. Webb alleged that Westborn violated the federal Truth in Lending Act, the Michigan Credit Reform Act, the Michigan Credit Insurance Act, and the Michigan Motor Vehicle Sales Finance Act. They further claimed that the dealer's Mama wore army boots (just kidding).

The court's opinion recited the following facts: The credit insurance transactions of the class were standard and representative of the way in which credit insurance is bought and sold in Michigan. That is, Westborn's principal owner, Doug Moore, established and owned the "Susan Agency" solely to sell credit insurance to Westborn's customers, because Michigan law requires credit insurance to be sold by a separate entity. The Susan Agency is the only agency a consumer can buy credit insurance from when buying a car from Westborn. The Susan Agency has no employees, does not do commission work, and does not solicit any outside business. It sells credit insurance exclusively to Westborn customers. Westborn's finance managers sell the credit insurance policies on behalf of the Susan Agency, and Westborn retains a 45% commission on the policies issued.

The State of Michigan's insurance commissioner approved the Susan Agency's policy documents and calculation methods. The Susan Agency uses a Reynolds & Reynolds computer program to calculate consumers' insurance rates. It sells only "gross" credit life insurance coverage, which is coverage that includes the total interest accrued through the entire duration of the retail installment contract.

Webb alleged three claims. First, she claimed that Westborn violated the TILA by disclosing commissions paid to a third party as an "amount financed," rather than as a "finance charge." Webb asserted that her TILA disclosure did not identify the Susan Agency on the form, nor did it disclose that Westborn received a commission or the amount of the commission.

Second, Webb claimed that Westborn violated Michigan law by charging premiums, disclosed as an "amount financed," at an unlawful rate and inclusive of excessive commissions. She argued that Westborn's practice of selling gross coverage instead of "net balance decreasing term coverage" violated the Michigan Credit Insurance Act, because gross coverage involves a method of calculating the premium on a total amount that exceeds the amount of unpaid indebtedness on the date of death. Webb argued that, by using the gross coverage method, Westborn charged a premium for amounts that were scheduled and would become due and payable in the future, and, thus, were "not yet earned by the creditor." According to Webb, because the gross coverage method violates the CIA, it also violates the TILA, the MVSFA, and the CRA, because, in effect, it allowed Westborn to impose unearned finance charges at the commencement of the contract.

Third, Webb claimed the Susan Agency was an illegal sham corporation and that Westborn and its personnel were using it to benefit from indirect commissions in violation of Section 492.131(c) of the MVSFA. Webb argued that because the commissions are unlawful under Michigan law, Westborn violated the TILA by improperly disclosing unlawful commissions as part of the "amount financed."

Westborn moved for summary judgment, arguing that its practices complied with both federal and state statutes. Webb also moved for summary judgment. The U.S. District Court for the Eastern District of Michigan ruled in favor of Westborn.

As to Webb's first TILA claim, the court found that Westborn satisfied the exceptions in 12 C.F.R. § 226.4(d)(1), (Regulation Z), which allowed Westborn to exclude from the finance charge premiums paid for voluntary credit insurance. Moore admitted the Susan Agency was the only agency from which Westborn customers could purchase credit insurance. However, based on language in the retail installment contracts, the court concluded that Westborn did not require Webb or any of its customers to buy credit insurance from the Susan Agency as a "condition to the extension of credit."

As to Webb's second TILA claim, the court found that Westborn's sale of gross coverage credit life insurance was permitted under Michigan law, and, therefore, Westborn did not violate federal law. The court based its decision in large part on the fact that the sale of gross coverage insurance has been the prevailing practice in Michigan for decades; there are a great number of such policies outstanding; and the fact that the Office of Financial and Insurance Services (the agency charged with enforcing the statutes at issue) condones the practice. With regard to the prevailing industry practice in Michigan, the court deferred to the *amicus* briefs filed by the Detroit Auto Dealers Association and the Michigan Automobile Dealers Association in support of Westborn's position.

As to Webb's third TILA claim, the court determined that there was no prohibition barring Moore from owning both Westborn and the Susan Agency or barring Westborn from receiving commissions. The court based its decision on a Michigan Financial Institutions Bureau December 1996 declaratory ruling that endorsed the operation of dealer-related insurance agencies for the purpose of selling credit life insurance in Michigan. Since the commissions paid to Westborn were not unlawful, Westborn did not violate the TILA by disclosing them in the "amount financed."

So, at least Michigan dealers can take a deep breath, but how about dealers in other states with similar arrangements? We suggest that they show this article to their lawyers and ask how their insurance arrangements would withstand an attack like this. We also couldn't help but wonder, as we read this account, whether this lawsuit would ever have been filed if the dealership required its customers to sign arbitration agreements.

Webb v. Westborn Chrysler Plymouth Jeep, Inc., Civil Action No. 03-CV-71077-DT (E.D. Mich. May 11, 2005).

What Does Your Insurance Policy Cover?

November 2005

By Thomas B. Hudson

"Hey Boss, welcome back from vacation."

"Thanks. Anything happen while I was away?"

"Well, not much, except we got sued!"

"What does the plaintiff say we did?"

"She claims we violated some provision of the Texas Retail Installment Sales Act. And it's a class action."

"What's the problem? That's why we've got insurance. Just

send the complaint papers to the insurance company, and let me know when they get rid of it."

"I did that boss, but the insurance company refused to cover us. They said we had Truth in Lending coverage, but no coverage for violation of that particular state statute."

"We'll just see about that. Call our lawyers—if we have to sue to make that insurance company cover us, we will!"

The conversation above is imaginary, but something like it might have occurred to create the following dispute.

J.C. Wink, Inc., operated an auto dealership. Wink obtained a commercial general liability insurance policy from Service Lloyd's Insurance Company. The policy provided errors and omissions coverage. Under the policy, Service Lloyd's agreed to defend Wink in any lawsuit alleging violations of any federal, state, or local truth in lending law.

A class of car buyers sued Wink for violation of the Texas Motor Vehicle Installment Sales Act. Believing that claims under the MVISA alleged state truth in lending violations, Wink requested that Service Lloyd's provide a defense for the action. Service Lloyd's refused to defend the lawsuit, claiming the class action did not allege truth in lending violations. Wink sued Service Lloyd's, seeking a declaratory judgment. Both parties moved for partial summary judgment, and the court granted Wink's motion. The trial court ruled that Wink was entitled to a defense by the insurance company.

Service Lloyd's appealed the decision. The Court of Appeals of Texas considered whether the alleged violation of the MVISA constituted a truth in lending violation requiring Service Lloyd's to defend the matter.

Because the MVISA serves the same objectives as the federal Truth in Lending Act, namely to provide meaningful disclosure to consumers and prevent abuse and deceptive practices, and because the MVISA contains provisions establishing substantive disclosure requirements similar to TILA, the appellate court found that the MVISA's disclosure provisions constituted state truth in lending laws. The lawsuit alleged violations of the MVISA's disclosure provisions, which triggered Service Lloyd's duty to defend.

The decision went the dealer's way, but the time to determine whether you have coverage is before trouble arises, not afterward. Have your friendly local shyster take a look at your policy, and if he or she uncovers any ambiguity in the language describing your coverage, get it fixed before you get served with those suit papers.

Service Lloyd's Insurance Company v. J.C. Wink, Inc., 2005 WL 2438350 (Tex. App. October 5, 2005).

Hidden Finance Charge Claims—'They're Baaaaaack'

May 2006

By Thomas B. Hudson

If you don't establish the price you're going to charge for a car until you see the prospective buyer's credit report, the case discussed here is a dangerous one for you. The opinion deals with a number of other issues, but we're going to ignore them for the purpose of this article. Instead, we'll focus on the Truth in Lending Act claim.

Eddie Diaz sued Paragon Motors of Woodside, Inc., and Americredit Financial Services, Inc., claiming that Paragon violated the Truth in Lending Act, the Equal Credit Opportunity Act, New York's Used Car Lemon Law, the federal Magnuson-Moss Warranty Act (breach of express and implied warranties), and New York's deceptive trade practices law.

Diaz alleged that Americredit was liable for damages on all claims against Paragon, pursuant to the Federal Trade Commission's "Holder Rule" (allows the plaintiff to pursue any claims he has against the dealer, against the assignee of the retail installment contract). Diaz moved for partial summary judgment against Paragon with respect to the issue of liability. Paragon and Americredit filed cross-motions for summary judgment on all claims.

The U.S. District Court for the Eastern District of New York granted summary judgment for Diaz as to Paragon's liability under the TILA and state law claims and denied summary judgment with respect to the ECOA claim. Instead, the trial court ruled in favor of Paragon on the ECOA claim. The court also granted summary judgment in favor of Americredit with respect to most of the claims Diaz asserted against it.

What are the facts behind this flurry of motions and cross motions? Let's take a look.

On May 9, 2003, Diaz visited Paragon and told a salesman that he was interested in buying a 2002 Chrysler advertised in the newspaper for $13,495. Diaz made a $500 deposit on the car and signed a document listing "$4,000 Cash Down" in the space provided for price, under which was written, "Subject to Bank Approval," but with no total vehicle price or other fees listed. The document included a description of the vehicle and a notation of the $500 deposit. A form intended to disclose prior use of the vehicle was left blank.

The parties agreed that Paragon would assist Diaz in financing the car, and Paragon submitted Diaz's application to Dealer Track to determine whether he was eligible for financing with a sub-prime creditor, and, if so, at what amount.

Consumer Portfolio Services, Inc., a sub-prime creditor, approved credit to Diaz subject to certain conditions, including an acquisition fee of $199, later charged to Diaz. The pre-approval provided for a maximum monthly payment of $350, at an annual interest rate of 19.95%. Based on these terms, Paragon set a selling price of $16,130 with CPS to provide financing. Additional charges were $1,500 for an extended warranty, $1,454 in taxes and $140 in license, title, state inspection, and processing fees. The total selling price listed on the proposed May 10 bill of sale, was $19,224. The down payment was listed as $6,000. CPS declined to buy the contract for unexplained reasons, and it was eventually assigned to Americredit.

On May 10, Diaz again offered to buy the car for the advertised price of $13,495, gave an additional deposit of $1,000, and again asked Paragon to obtain financing. According to Diaz, there were no further negotiations on the purchase price of the car on May 10. On May 11, Paragon told Diaz that, to obtain financing, he would have to put $6,000 down, instead of $4,000 as provided for in the May 9 agreement.

Diaz claimed that on May 12, 2003, he returned to Paragon to pay the additional $4,500 down payment, but did not sign any documents until May 13. On May 13, he returned to Paragon and signed a retail installment contract dated May 12, which disclosed the final details of the sale and reflected an increase in the car's purchase price.

According to Diaz, the Paragon finance manager told him that the original advertised price of $13,495 was not available because a "primary lender" would not finance the car, because a "secondary lender" had to be used, and because the extended warranty was necessary to obtain financing. *(Note to the GM: Schedule some compliance training.)*

Because he was putting down $6,000, the balance of $14,047 was to be financed by Americredit with 60 monthly payments of $367 and change, totaling $22,072. The total finance charge listed in the contract was $8,025. The "total sale price" for the car including the $16,590 purchase price, $1,517 sales tax, $8,025 finance charge, $1,800 extended warranty, and other license, title, state inspection and processing fees was stated in the contract as $28,072.

On a bill of sale dated May 12, 2003, but not signed until May 13, according to Diaz, the purchase price was listed as $16,590 plus $1,800 for "other equipment" apparently representing the new price for the extended warranty, $1,517 for sales tax, and $140 for license, title, state inspection and processing fees, for a total cash price of $20,047. The bill of sale included a statement, signed by Diaz, that the "principal pride [sic: prior?] use of th[e] vehicle was as a rental vehicle." Diaz stated the bill of sale was the last document he signed before taking possession of the car.

A few days after Diaz took possession of the car, he complained of problems with it. As is so often the case, it was probably the frustration with the mechanical problems that led Diaz to file a lawsuit.

Diaz contended that three charges imposed by Paragon were hidden finance charges. These were the price charged in excess of the advertised price based on the need to obtain sub-prime financing; the bank fee for assigning the credit agreement to Americredit, passed on to Diaz; and the cost of the extended warranty as a condition to obtaining financing. He claimed that these hidden finance charges resulted in a TILA violation. The court agreed with his argument that the increased purchase price for the car was a finance charge for TILA purposes and declined to address the other two arguments.

Diaz alleged that Paragon violated the ECOA by failing to give him notice that it obtained credit in a different amount and at different terms than he requested. Paragon argued that because Diaz accepted its counteroffer to provide financing through a sub-prime lender, the decision did not constitute "adverse action" as defined by Regulation B and, accordingly, did not require notification. The court agreed that notice of adverse action was not required and that notice of Paragon's counteroffer was not required to be in writing.

Diaz claimed that Paragon's violations of TILA constituted a deceptive or unfair practice under New York's UDAP law. Under that law, a plaintiff must prove that the challenged act or practice was consumer-oriented; that the act was misleading in a material way; and that the plaintiff suffered injury as a result of the deceptive act. The court ruled against Paragon on this claim and granted summary judgment for Diaz.

The court's lengthy opinion deals with the concept of "hidden finance charges" under the federal Truth in Lending Act. A number of similar cases were filed several years ago, but we haven't seen these claims recently. The cases a few years back, involving allegations that a car's price included a "hidden finance charge," were tough for plaintiffs to prove, in large part because prices for used cars vary widely. The facts recited in this opinion indicate that the dealer's representatives told Diaz that he would have to pay more for the car, because his credit limited the dealer to sub-prime financing sources. Those statements provided the plaintiff with the "smoking gun" necessary to prove his case.

The lesson here? If your dealership engages in this practice—pricing cars based on the customer's credit situation and conceding this information to the customer—then it's time to schedule another visit to your friendly neighborhood compliance lawyer. Hey, it's better than having a root canal, and the visit may save you money down the road.

Diaz v. Paragon Motors of Woodside, Inc., 2006 WL 802289 (E.D.N.Y. March 29, 2006).

When the Fastball Isn't Working, It's Time for the Curveball

September 2006

By Wingrove S. Lynton and Thomas B. Hudson

One common plaintiff's lawyer ploy is to argue that a fee or charge appearing in a dealer-financed transaction as part of the amount financed is really a finance charge. If a judge buys this argument, it will almost certainly result in a Truth in Lending disclosure violation, because the amount will have to be added to the finance charge that appears in the "federal box" and will have to be included in the calculation of the APR, also disclosed in the federal box.

There are a couple of pretty effective ways of arguing that a charge isn't a finance charge. One is to argue that the charge is one that is imposed in a "comparable cash transaction." Another is to argue that the charge is voluntary, and that the creditor would have extended credit regardless of whether the amount was charged. A recent case illustrates both arguments.

Thomas Colunga bought a car from Sonic Automotive and financed the purchase by entering into a retail installment sale contract. In addition to the cost of the car and other products, Colunga bought a 36-month membership in the Road America auto club. One of the benefits of the auto club membership was an involuntary unemployment benefit.

Colunga sued Sonic, alleging that Sonic violated the Truth in Lending Act by incorrectly including the entire fee for the auto club membership, which included the involuntary unemployment benefit, in the amount financed. Colunga said the fee should have been included as a finance charge. Colunga also alleged that Sonic violated various provisions of the Texas Finance Code.

In its motion to dismiss or, alternatively, for a more definite statement, Sonic argued that an auto club membership is excluded from the definition of a finance charge, if it is offered to, or required of, both cash and credit customers at the same price. Sonic claimed that Colunga failed to plead that the auto club membership was not offered to cash buyers. Although the U.S. District Court for the Southern District of Texas agreed that Colunga had failed to plead that the auto club membership was not offered to cash buyers, the court explained that Colunga's original complaint alleged that the involuntary unemployment coverage portion of the auto club membership was only valuable to a consumer if he or she was buying an automobile on credit.

The court noted that the involuntary unemployment coverage would only benefit credit customers, because the benefit itself is a payment, subject to certain terms and conditions, of the retail installment sale contract. The court could not understand why a cash customer would buy an auto club membership when the involuntary unemployment benefit, one of the membership's major benefits, would not apply to the cash customer. As a result, the court concluded that, when viewed in the most favorable light, the complaint raised an inference that the auto club membership would not be offered to, or bought by, a customer paying cash. Sonic's fastball wasn't working.

Sonic next tried its curveball, arguing that the auto club membership did not qualify as a finance charge under TILA, because Colunga failed to properly allege facts that established that the auto club membership was imposed directly or indirectly by the creditor as an incident to the extension of credit. Although Colunga, in his original complaint, alleged that the charge "was imposed directly or indirectly by Defendant as an incident to the extension of credit," Sonic attached to its motion the Road America membership application, signed by Colunga, which stated that the program was optional and Colunga was not required to buy it.

Colunga replied that the auto club membership could qualify as a finance charge under TILA even if it were not required by Sonic for the purchase of the car. The court concluded that the important question in determining whether the purchase of the auto club membership was an incident to the extension of credit was this: whether Sonic refused to extend credit unless Colunga agreed to the charge. The court found that Colunga's allegation (that the auto club membership was imposed directly or indirectly by Sonic as an incident to the extension of credit) refuted the contention that the Road America membership application established that the program was optional.

The court believed that at this stage of the litigation, it was compelled to accept all factual allegations in Colunga's complaint as true. As a result, the court found that Colunga had alleged enough facts to create a legally cognizable claim that the involuntary unemployment benefit portion of the auto club membership was a finance charge. Therefore, the court denied Sonic's motion to dismiss.

Sonic will win this case if it can prove—as it almost certainly will—that the auto club membership was optional. Looks like the old curveball is still breaking.

Colunga v. Sonic Automotive—3401 Main, TX, L.P., 2006 WL 1967034 (S.D. Tex. July 11, 2006).

What Belongs in Line One?

April 2007

By Thomas B. Hudson

We've heard a lot of noise lately about how dealers should disclose the cost of third-party products, such as paintless dent repair, window etching, service contracts, and the like, when the dealer retains, or receives, some part of the amount the buyer pays for the product.

Do those amounts go into the un-itemized "cash price" of the vehicle, that is, in "Line 1" of a typical retail installment sale contract? Or do the amounts belong in the part of the "Itemization of Amount Financed" where "Amounts Paid to Others" are typically shown? Dealers are getting conflicting instructions from several quarters—notably the sales finance companies that buy retail installment sale contracts from them, the lawyers who represent them (the dealers), state auto dealer associations, and anyone else with an opinion.

Do we have an opinion? Of course!

Here's what we think federal law requires. Note that we said *federal law*. State laws in some few jurisdictions may affect how these disclosures need to be made. As you already know, the federal law that deals with disclosures in motor vehicle retail installment sale contracts is the Truth in Lending Act. The Federal Reserve Board's Regulation Z implements TILA.

Reg. Z requires the disclosure in the Itemization of Amount Financed of the "cash price" of the vehicle. Reg. Z defines "cash price" broadly:

> Cash price means the price at which a creditor, in the ordinary course of business, offers to sell for cash the property or service that is the subject of the transaction. At

> the creditor's option, the term may include the price of accessories, services related to the sale, service contracts and taxes and fees for license, title, and registration. The term does not include any finance charge.

That definition leaves room for a dealer to include lots of things in the "cash price" number. So, a dealer can simply dump any fee or charge in the cash price (as long as state law allows it), and he's home free, right?

Maybe not. Read on.

Another part of Reg. Z requires a creditor (in a motor vehicle retail installment sale agreement, that means the dealer) to disclose "amounts paid to others." The Federal Reserve Board staff, in the Official Staff Commentary (which is a document that sets forth the staff's view of Reg. Z's requirements) says that when the dealer keeps part of those amounts that are paid to others, the creditor (dealer) must indicate that it will retain or receive a part of the charge:

> A sum is sometimes added to the amount of a fee charged to a consumer for a service provided by a third party (such as for an extended warranty or a service contract) that is payable in the same amount in comparable cash and credit transactions. In the credit transaction, the creditor retains the amount. Given the flexibility permitted in meeting the requirements of the amount financed itemization (see the Commentary to §226.18(c)), the creditor in such cases may reflect that the creditor has retained a portion of the amount paid to others. For example, the creditor could add to the category "amount paid to others" language such as, "We may be retaining a portion of this amount."

A typical retail installment sale contract will contain, within the "Itemization of Amount Financed," a category called something like "other charges." The following extract is from the LAW 553-OH Retail Installment Sales Contract with Subsection 4G completed to show a sale of "Road Hazard Protection" from ABC Tire & Wheel when the dealer is retaining part of the fee. It begins with item #4:

4. Other Charges Including Amounts Paid to Others on Your Behalf *(Seller may keep part of these amounts)*:

   A. Cost of Optional Credit Insurance Paid to the Insurance Company or Companies

      Life $______

      Disability $______ $ ______

   B. Other Insurance Paid to the Insurance Company $______

   C. Official Fees Paid to Government Agencies $______

   D. Taxes Not Included in Cash Price $______

   E. Government License and/or Registration Fees (Identify)______________ $______

   F. Government Certificate of Title Fees $______

   G. Other Charges *(Seller must identify who is paid and describe purpose)*:

      to______________ for Prior Credit or Lease Balance $______

      to ***ABC Tire & Wheel for Road Hazard Protection*** $XXX

      to______________ for ______ $______

   Total Other Charges and Amounts Paid to Others on Your Behalf $______

In our humble opinion, a dealer cannot accomplish this disclosure without itemizing the amounts paid to others. That can't be done when these charges are lumped into the cash price, and that means the charges need to be itemized as part of the "amounts paid to others," with an identification of the party receiving the payment, and accompanied by the required disclosure that some of the amounts will wind up in the dealer's pocket. Note that the amount the dealer keeps need not be disclosed—just the fact that he receives some of the charge.

So, before you dump a fee or charge into the "Line 1" cash price number, think about this itemization and disclosure requirement. And don't forget to check your conclusion with your lawyer.

Coming Soon! Debt Suspension Agreements Excluded From TILA Finance Charge

July 2007

By Catherine Brennan

The Federal Reserve Board, the agency that makes the rules that implement the Truth in Lending Act, recently proposed a raft of changes to Regulation Z, most of which impact credit card disclosures. However, hidden within the 214-page proposed amendments to Reg. Z is a little nugget of great interest to auto dealers and sales finance companies. The Board has revived the call to add debt suspension agreements to the list of charges that a creditor can exclude from the TILA finance charge disclosure, under certain circumstances.

Debt suspension agreements, unlike debt cancellation coverage, merely defer a consumer's obligation to make the minimum payment for some time after the occurrence of a specified event, such as an accident or loss of income. During the suspension period, interest may continue to accrue. The Board has proposed allowing creditors to exclude a charge for debt suspension agreements from the disclosed finance charge under circumstances almost identical to those permitted for debt cancellation products.

Since 1996, Reg. Z has allowed creditors to exclude the charge for a debt cancellation product from the finance charge calculation, if the creditor discloses the cost of the product, its term, and the fact that the consumer need not obtain the coverage in order to obtain credit. The consumer also must sign, or initial, an affirmative written request for the product. The proposed rule would amend the current debt cancellation coverage rule to allow a creditor to exclude debt suspension agreements from the finance charge calculation, so long as the creditor satisfied the requirements imposed on debt cancellation coverage. Additionally, the creditor would also have to disclose, for debt suspension agreements only, that the coverage suspends, but does not cancel, the debt.

In addition to adding debt suspension agreements to the list of charges a creditor can potentially exclude from the finance charge calculation, the Federal Reserve Board also proposes to relax the ability to exclude such charges from the finance charge disclosure when a creditor offers a product that does not squarely fit within the definition of either a debt suspension product or a debt cancellation product.

Currently, a creditor can exclude a debt cancellation product from the finance charge calculation only if the coverage is triggered by accident or loss of life, health, or income. The Board proposes, however, to add a comment to Reg. Z to clarify that if a debt cancellation or debt suspension product for two or more specified events is sold at a single charge, the creditor may exclude the *entire* charge from the finance charge, if at least one of the events is accident or loss of life, health, or income. This should offer some relief to creditors that offer hybrid products that go beyond coverage for accident or loss of life, health, or income, such as debt cancellation products that offer protection upon the happening of a divorce or separation.

Interested parties have until October 12, 2007, to submit comments on these proposed rules.

GAP...Do it Right!

September 2007

By Patricia E. M. Covington

The Truth in Lending Act is all about doing it right. That is, a creditor has to prepare accurate disclosures and provide them to consumers exactly as required by TILA and its implementing rule, Regulation Z. This is incredibly important to avoid regulatory rebuke, but, more importantly, to avoid losing a lawsuit.

What's this have to do with GAP and doing it right?

As regular readers of our newsletter, ***Spot Delivery***®, or those of you who own a copy of ***CARLAW***® are aware, GAP, or Guaranteed Auto Protection, is defined as insurance or an insurance-like product that—in the event of a total loss of a vehicle—pays the difference between the consumer's insurance proceeds and the amount owed on the car.

If you sell GAP, you ought to read these words carefully. GAP products are subject to specific TILA disclosure requirements, and those requirements are critical for the GAP charge to be excluded from the finance charge. You might be thinking, "Oh yeah, I know about these requirements—this is old news." Yeah, it's not new, but lots of folks are still getting it wrong. In addition, there are many other issues regarding GAP that must be considered.

Slip-ups that occur in the arena of GAP can be expensive, because they can easily result in class action claims. When you sell GAP, after a while you find that there tend to be a fair number of these deals on the books. GAP is a product that is generally sold and administered pretty much the same way every time. Consistent sales and administrative procedures invite class actions.

Most creditors (a term that includes dealers and sales finance companies) know that GAP is a debt cancellation product. There are two types of GAP products: two-party and three-party.

Two-party GAP is an agreement between the creditor and buyer where the creditor agrees not to pursue the buyer for monies owed when the transaction vehicle is totaled (after, of course, the creditor receives the insurance check). In other words, the creditor waives collection of any deficiency after it receives the insurance check. Most of the time, the insurance check isn't large enough to pay off the entire balance owed on the installment contract. GAP provides the difference.

Three-party GAP works much the same as two-party GAP. Rather than being an agreement between the creditor and buyer, however, guaranteed auto protection is provided by a third party—hence the designation three-party GAP. The creditor would still sell the product, but it would belong to a third party, much like an extended warranty or insurance product.

Though creditors may consider the TILA implications of GAP, many forget other issues such as insurance. GAP is considered insurance in many states. This is usually the case with three-party GAP and sometimes with two-party GAP as well. When a state doesn't consider two-party GAP to be insurance, it's because the state understands that it is simply an agreement between the seller and buyer to waive monies owed.

If GAP is considered insurance in a state, there are several implications: Among others, these include (1) special disclosures to be provided; (2) proper licenses to sell it; and (3) limitations on charges for it. So, it's pretty important to know what type of GAP is being sold, and whether it is insurance or not.

Another largely disregarded detail about GAP is the situation that occurs when the buyer pays off his or her installment contract early. It's not always, "Hooray, we got paid, and since the debt has been paid, our risk of providing coverage is gone." While an understandable reaction, the correct response is to ask the question, "Do I have any responsibility regarding the GAP, because the installment contract has been prepaid?" Boring though it may be; nevertheless, it is correct. Why?

Well, remember the discussion above about insurance? Here's yet another implication. If GAP is insurance, there is a very good likelihood that state insurance law will require a creditor to "rebate"—that is refund—any unearned amounts. Unearned amounts? you say. What is that? Think precomputed installment sales; the concept is similar.

The GAP product provides value over the whole term of the installment contract (never mind that the benefit payable would decrease over time as the contract is paid down). If the installment contract is paid off early—let's say two years into a four-year term—there is some value that is left on the table (the remaining two years). Some laws and regulators take the position that, like finance charges, the charge for the GAP product is earned over the life of the installment contract; that is, slowly but surely, as time passes. So, if the contract is paid off early, then the charge for the GAP is only partially earned resulting in unearned amounts.

Prepayment may not mean gravy on the deal. Rather, it may mean refunding unearned amounts. But who refunds? Well, it depends. State law will dictate who has to pay out of pocket. It could be the dealer, the sales finance company, or the insurance company, depending on the type of GAP. While it's not usually the dealer, the dealer and/or sales finance company may still have other obligations. A creditor may be required to notify the consumer that he or she may be entitled to a refund. Bottom line, this issue deserves some attention because many states have requirements along these lines. Be alert to the fact that just because GAP isn't insurance doesn't mean a creditor is off the hook. Some states may require rebating of a non-insurance GAP product.

What else could there be?

Well, a state may not allow a creditor to sell, charge for, or finance GAP. The answers to these questions depend upon state law and the type of GAP product involved. For example, a state may allow the GAP charge to be financed, but it would have to be a finance charge. That's not fun. That means it has to be included when calculating the APR. Most creditors won't like that!

The case of *In re Matthews (Matthews v. Johnson)* provides a perspective on what TILA and Reg. Z require. The dealer in this case successfully defeated the plaintiff's challenge that the GAP was not disclosed properly.

Holly Matthews bought a 2005 Chevrolet from Johnny Johnson, a motor vehicle dealer. Matthews entered into a retail installment contract and security agreement with Johnson. Johnson assigned the contract to Centrix Funds, LLC. Matthews sued Johnson and Centrix, claiming violations of the Truth in Lending Act. Matthews alleged that a $399 processing fee and a $330 premium for GAP insurance were not properly disclosed because they were not included in the finance charge.

Matthews also alleged that the proper party did not make the GAP insurance disclosures. Finally, Matthews alleged that because the $399 processing fee and the $330 GAP insurance premium were excluded from the finance charge, the disclosed APR was misstated by more than the tolerance allowed under TILA. Matthews dismissed Centrix from the lawsuit after Centrix filed for bankruptcy, and Johnson was left as the only defendant. Johnson then moved for summary judgment.

The U.S. Bankruptcy Court for Middle District of Alabama found that the processing fee was not a charge incident to the extension of credit, because it was charged on all sales—cash or credit. Therefore, the court ruled that Johnson did not violate TILA by failing to group the fee with the finance charges.

The court went on to find that Johnson advised Matthews in writing that debt cancellation coverage was not required *(the first disclosure requirement, which must be done in writing)*. The court also found that Johnson had advised Matthews of the cost of the premium *(the second requirement, and if the term of the coverage is less than the term of the contract, the term of the coverage must be disclosed)*.

The court determined that Matthews had signed a request for coverage after she was advised that coverage was not required and after she was advised of the cost of coverage *(the final requirement is that the consumer sign or initial an affirmative written request after receiving the prior two disclosures)*. Consequently, the court concluded that the GAP insurance premium was properly excluded from the finance charge. Because the court determined that both the $399 processing fee and the $330 GAP premium were properly excluded from the finance charge, the court rejected Matthews' claim that Johnson misstated the APR. Accordingly, the court granted Johnson's motion for summary judgment.

GAP—it's a good thing when it's disclosed properly and a creditor knows all its responsibilities relating to it. It can be a source of future headaches and the loss of big dollars if it's not done right. Consequently, if you "do" GAP, you must do it right!

In re Matthews (Matthews v. Johnson), 2007 WL 1589553 (Bankr. M.D. Ala. June 1, 2007).

How to Keep Insurance and Other Charges Out of the Finance Charge

September 2007

By Thomas B. Hudson

Long ago and far away, in a very odd place called Washington, D.C., some pointy-headed bureaucrats at the Federal Reserve Board were sitting around a conference table concocting yet another federal regulation. This one was to be Regulation Z, and it was supposed to implement the federal Truth in Lending Act.

As usual, arguments broke out among the participants regarding what the regulation should say. One of the arguments dealt with what fees and charges in a credit transaction the Feds should require creditors to include in the finance charge.

One group insisted that premiums for credit insurance be part of the finance charge. Others argued that unless the creditor required the credit insurance, it wasn't appropriate to include the premiums in the finance charge. If a consumer could get credit without incurring the premium charge, they reasoned, it wasn't logical to call the premium a cost of credit, which is what the finance charge is supposed to represent.

As usual, since this meeting took place in Washington, the participants reached a compromise of sorts. Creditors could exclude premiums for credit life, health, and loss-of-income insurance from the finance charge, but only if certain conditions were met.

First, the creditor could not require the coverage, and that fact had to be disclosed in writing. The premium for the initial term of the insurance had to be disclosed. If the term of the insurance was to be shorter than the term of the credit transaction, the insurance term had to be disclosed. Finally, the consumer had to sign an affirmative written request for the insurance after receiving the required disclosures. There were somewhat similar requirements for keeping the charge for debt cancellation coverage (sometimes called "GAP") out of the finance charge.

Another part of Reg. Z says that any charge a creditor imposes in a "comparable cash transaction" is not a finance charge. That permits dealers to charge for doc fees, service contracts, and services, like "etch," and not include the charges for these items in the finance charge, as long as they impose them in comparable cash transactions. Now, dealers make money on credit insurance, doc fees, GAP, service contracts and etch, so there is always a temptation to tell the customer, suggest to the customer, or hint to the customer that some or more of these fees and charges are required in order for the customer to obtain financing. Usually, the dealer places the blame on the finance company—"We cannot get you financed, Mr. Customer, unless you sign up for [fill in the blank]."

Oops. A dealer who utters these words has probably just stuffed the charge for whatever product appears in the blank back into the finance charge. That means the charge must be added to the "regular" finance charge and included in the calculation of the APR. Since the dealer almost certainly isn't going to take those steps, we have a TILA/Reg. Z violation. And if the dealer fabricated the bit about the bank or finance company "requiring" the customer to buy the product or service, the dealer has also committed a state law unfair or deceptive trade practice. If the dealer regularly does these things, he is exposed to class action liability, as well.

It is for these and other reasons that many compliance folks urge dealers to use a true, transparent "menu" sales approach, in which every customer is offered the opportunity to buy or decline everything the dealer sells in connection with the car sale, and that fact is documented in writing.

Such a process (assuming that the dealership representatives aren't using winks and nods to get around it) will go a long way toward keeping the dealership out of the courthouse.

Chapter 4

Equal Credit Opportunity Act (ECOA) and Fair Credit Reporting Act (FCRA)

After passing the Truth in Lending Act, Congress was so tickled with itself for creating disclosure requirements for creditors that it decided to address two other areas:

- Discrimination—with the Equal Credit Opportunity Act; and
- The regulation of credit reports—with the Fair Credit Reporting Act.

Both of these laws impose upon dealers a requirement that, under certain circumstances, creditors provide an "adverse action" notice to credit applicants; otherwise, the laws are pretty much unrelated.

Dealers have been swept up in class action litigation, alleging that their practices of "marking up" the "buy rates" of banks, finance companies, and other creditors violates the ECOA, because the markups are higher for protected classes (so far, that's usually African-Americans and Hispanics) than for others. Some dealers have even been the targets of federal and state investigations for alleged discrimination in credit pricing.

The ECOA doesn't require any sort of intent to discriminate. For example, a dealership that does not actually set out to discriminate, and who would fire employees found to be intentionally discriminating, can find itself faced with the charge if its seemingly innocent business practices permit discrimination to occur. Dealerships should pay heed to their vehicle and credit pricing strategies to assure that discrimination—intentional or not—isn't rearing its ugly head.

The Fair Credit Reporting Act regulates how dealers, as users of credit reports, must behave. Dealers need to take care that they actually are entitled to pull credit reports before they do, and that they tend to their duties regarding adverse action notices. But the FCRA holds some surprises, too, in unexpected areas. Dealers who buy advertising mailer programs from vendors—compiled from credit bureaus and other sources—need to be mindful of duties the FCRA imposes on people who "prescreen."

Seems like there are nasty surprises everywhere.

Guidance on Credit Report Fraud Alerts

April 2006

By Emily Marlow Beck

Your dealership lands a customer in a car, gets a signed credit application, and pulls credit. Everything checks out on his credit report, and you, the salesperson, are about to sell the customer the whole ball of wax. Then, you take a second look at his credit report and notice something: It contains a fraud alert.

What do you do? Pretend you didn't notice? (After all, this deal is too sweet to pass up.) Send him packing? (If there's a slight chance fraud is involved, you don't want to touch this deal with a 10-foot pole.) Or do you panic and call your lawyer?

Fortunately, the Federal Deposit Insurance Commission has provided us with some guidance on how to handle this issue. On March 9, 2006, the FDIC issued Financial Institution Letter 22-2006, and even though the letter was directed at FDIC-supervised financial institutions (not including car dealers), the guidance in the letter should help all creditors (including car dealers) comply with the Equal Credit Opportunity Act (ECOA) and the Fair Credit Reporting Act (FCRA) (i.e., car dealers).

ECOA's Regulation B makes it unlawful to discriminate against an applicant for credit simply because the applicant has, in good faith, exercised a right given to her under the FCRA. Among those rights provided by the FCRA is a special protection for active duty military personnel and consumers that believe they are, or may be, the victim of identity theft. This right allows active duty military personnel and consumers who believe they have been targeted by identity thieves to put an alert on their credit reports. The goal of these alerts is to help protect consumers' information from identity theft, and to help prevent new extensions of credit using stolen identities.

A consumer establishing an alert has the option of providing information, such as a phone number, to potential users of his or her credit report. When a user of a credit report, such as a dealer, pulls a credit report containing an alert, the FCRA requires the user to take steps to verify the identity of the credit applicant. In such a situation, the user of a credit report must contact the consumer using the phone number provided in the alert, or, if no number is provided, the user must take reasonable steps to verify the consumer's identity and confirm that the application is not the result of identity theft.

Unless the user of the report takes reasonable steps to verify the customer's identity and is able to form a reasonable belief that he knows the identity of the applicant, the user is restricted from extending credit to that customer. However, if, after taking reasonable steps, the creditor cannot verify the customer's identity, the creditor may deny credit to the applicant on the basis that he could not verify the customer's identity.

The FDIC wrote its letter after learning that some creditors were denying credit applications without attempting to verify the applicant's identity when they saw fraud or active duty alerts on the applicant's credit report. The FDIC emphasized that, when a creditor denies credit or takes other adverse action based on the presence of an alert, such action constitutes unlawful discrimination based on the exercise of a right granted by the FCRA and is therefore prohibited.

So, why should dealers care about a letter written by the FDIC? In a nutshell, the FDIC reminds all creditors (that includes car dealers) that it is unlawful to deny a credit application simply because the credit report contains an active duty or fraud alert. Smart dealers will have the right procedures in place to make sure their sales and finance employees know what to do when they see an active duty or fraud alert.

Is Offering Less Than Best Financing Rate 'Adverse Action' Requiring Notice to Customer?

April 2006

By Jean Noonan

Several courts have held that insurers who have charged customers more for their insurance than the best rate available were required to send adverse action notices to the customers. The cases have created a lot of buzz among car dealers and sales finance companies; they are wondering how these cases apply to car credit. If you are one of the ones doing the wondering, then you and the United States Congress are thinking along the same lines.

As part of the Fair and Accurate Credit Transactions Act, and amendments to the Fair Credit Reporting Act, Congress directed the Federal Trade Commission and the Federal Reserve Board to come up with a rule that would address risk-based pricing. There are two approaches to such a rule under consideration: (1) a notice, similar to an adverse action notice, that tells a consumer after the offer is made that he or she didn't get the best terms, due to his or her credit history; or (2) a generic notice, probably at the time of application, that says an applicant's credit history may affect the terms he or she receives. These are two very different approaches.

The agencies have been unable to agree on which approach to follow, even for the purpose of a proposed rule. Until there is a final rule, we find no legal requirement to give a notice based on risk-based pricing in a credit transaction.

The situation is different for insurance transactions. Several courts have found that a higher insurance premium, based on the applicant's credit report, triggers an adverse action notice under the FCRA. We think that the answer is different for creditors for two reasons.

Reason #1

First, under the Equal Credit Opportunity Act, it is not adverse action to offer the consumer less than the best financing terms *unless* (1) the consumer requested certain terms; (2) the creditor offered different, less-favorable, terms; *and* (3) the consumer rejected this counteroffer. The first criterion is the tricky one. Most dealers and auto finance companies try to set things up so the consumer doesn't request specific terms—the dealer or finance company just makes an offer. But this is a very fact-based situation, and sometimes consumers do request specific financing terms. If the consumer tells the dealer, "I can pay only $1,000 down," or, "I want financing for six years," and the dealer or finance company offers a deal that requires a larger down payment or a shorter repayment period, a court might conclude that the dealer or finance company made a counteroffer. That gives rise to the requirement to give an adverse action notice, if the consumer doesn't accept the offer.

In situations where the consumer doesn't request specific terms (or in which the dealer or finance company meets those terms), but the rate is not the lowest available, there is no adverse action.

Reason #2

The second reason the answer differs for insurance companies and creditors is that the FCRA has separate, specific definitions of adverse action for insurance and credit.

- For credit, the FCRA adopts the ECOA/Regulation B definition. So, if a situation is not "adverse action" for the ECOA (as described above), it is not adverse action under the FCRA.
- For insurance, the FCRA adverse action definition specifically mentions an increase in cost due to credit history. It is this language the courts have relied on in holding that FCRA adverse action notices are required when the premium is higher due to credit history.

Notice that, even when a rule is promulgated under the FCRA risk-based pricing amendment, it will not be an "adverse action" notice within the meaning of either the FCRA or ECOA. I don't feel that dealers must give adverse action notices to all borrowers who get a less-than-best rate due to credit history. However, I would encourage you to do two things:

- Keep an eye on the regulatory agencies' actions on the risk-based pricing notice rule. (***Spot Delivery***® and other auto finance publications will cover this issue and provide updates.)
- Take a look at your counteroffer procedures to be sure you are in good shape regarding your adverse action notices.

Once again, this is a tricky area, so be sure, and discuss your procedures with your lawyer.

CHAPTER 4

Bankruptcy Discharge Lists—Good Business or Litigation Nightmare?

October 2006

By Jean Noonan

You have a dealership lot full of good used cars that you are eager to move out. You also have good sources for deep subprime financing, including a list of people recently discharged in bankruptcy. Do the names of recent "bankrupts" promise deals made in heaven or litigation nightmares?

The answer is, "It depends."

Folks on lists such as these can be good prospects for your business. Many of the customers turned in a car they were financing as part of their bankruptcy; now, they need affordable transportation. Because they have recently had their credit card and other unsecured debts wiped out, they could be good credit risks, especially if they have steady incomes. Targeting them with a letter offering financing despite their credit problems can be an effective sales technique. So what's the problem?

The problem is the bankruptcy discharge list itself. That is, specifically whether it is regulated by the Fair Credit Reporting Act. In some cases, the list will legally be considered a consumer report on each listed person. If so, you'll have strict compliance obligations under the FCRA. In other cases, the list might be outside the FCRA, and you have much greater flexibility in how you use it. Here's the rub—it can be hard to tell whether the list is covered by the FCRA or not.

Potentially, each listed contact is a consumer report (and covered by the FCRA), even if the list only gives the consumer's name and address. Why? Because you know that each person appearing on the list—by definition—has recently been discharged in bankruptcy. Hence, this fact conveys information about that person's creditworthiness.

The FCRA governs the use of the list if it meets any of three criteria:

- Why were the names collected?
- How will they be used?
- Was the information collected, used, or expected to be used to determine the consumer's eligibility for credit, insurance, or employment? The last question is the most critical.

For starters, you need to know exactly where this list came from. For example, if the list provider got the information from a credit bureau, the list is definitely covered by the FCRA, because credit bureaus collect information to help businesses determine a consumer's eligibility for credit. If the list provider got the names directly from courthouse records, you may be OK on the "collected" issue. The courthouse collects these names as part of judicial records—not to help creditors determine credit eligibility. But *why* is the list provider collecting the names, and *how* will other business customers use the list? You need to know the answer to these two questions.

A good list provider will have an enforceable provision in its contract to prohibit any user of the bankruptcy discharge list from using the information to determine a consumer's eligibility for credit, insurance, or employment. The list provider's marketing materials and oral statements can't contradict the prohibition. Also, the list provider's contract should promise you that the list information was not collected for a purpose protected by the FCRA.

These contract provisions are especially important if the list provider obtained the names from another information broker, rather than directly from courthouse records. If the names have been collected, used, or are expected to be used for an FCRA-covered purpose anywhere along the line, they are "tainted."

If the List is Covered by FCRA

If the list is covered by the FCRA, you can obtain it only if you are prepared to make a "firm offer of credit" to everyone listed. Why? Because you can get consumer reports on potential customers only if you have a "permissible purpose" under the FCRA. When a consumer has not applied to you for credit—and, in fact, hasn't yet initiated any business deal with you—the only way to legally get a "consumer report" is to comply with the FCRA's prescreening rules. These rules include the duty to make everyone on the list a firm offer of credit, and you might not be able to make that promise to everyone.

Why not?

Well, first, you can't be sure that all listed persons will meet the credit criteria of your financing source. The FCRA permits you to condition your firm offer on some additional criteria, such as proof of income. But this is a tricky legal area, and you definitely need the help of your legal compliance counsel.

Second, courts have been imposing requirements on creditors who make prescreened offers. Some courts require that all terms of the offer appear in the solicitation letter. This is a tough requirement for auto dealers, because, without more information from the potential customer, the dealer won't know the exact terms for which the customer might qualify. Furthermore, if a court decides that you used a list covered by the FCRA, but your mailer was not a "firm offer of credit," the law provides for statutory penalties of $100 to $1,000 *per mailing*. That's enough to ruin your day.

Don't Invite Trouble

If the FCRA does not cover your bankruptcy discharge list, you do not need to make a firm offer of credit—or any offer of credit. Your mailer should focus on selling cars. You may mention that you might be able to get financing, even for people with credit problems, including recent bankruptcies. However, avoid any suggestion that you have prescreened customers for credit eligibility. Doing so could submit the list to coverage by the FCRA.

What other precautions should you take?

- Make sure the mailer language is true.
- Avoid stretching the truth. Don't say, "This is a limited time offer," if it's not. Don't promise the lowest prices or best financing terms in the metro area, unless you can back the claim with facts.

If the list provider offers to do the mailing for you, examine the solicitation—and the envelope—carefully. Don't rely on a contract provision that says the list provider is responsible for the content of the solicitation. If there is a problem with it, consumers and the government will come after you.

Be sure the statements in the mailer are true and not misleading to a reasonable consumer. Avoid trickery: Does the envelope imply that the mailer is from the bankruptcy court? Does the mailer look like a real check? Such tricks invite trouble.

Conclusion

There are currently more than 180 cases pending in federal court against businesses accused of making prescreened offers that don't meet the FCRA's "firm offer of credit" requirements. Many of these companies are facing the possibility of penalties that will put them out of business. So here's one final suggestion: If you are confident that your bankruptcy discharge list is not covered by the FCRA, consider putting a little notice in your mailer that says: "We did not consult your credit report in selecting you for this offer." Maybe that will help the plaintiff's attorney decide to pick on someone else.

Helping a consumer who has been through bankruptcy to purchase an affordable car can be a great service for the consumer; it also can be good for your business. But for unsuspecting auto dealers, using bankruptcy discharge lists from list providers can be a legal minefield. Unless you can make a firm offer of credit to everyone on the list, make the list provider satisfy you that his list is not covered by the FCRA.

A Scam for All Seasons: 'Seasoned Trade Line' Score Enhancement

April 2007

By Jean Noonan

Auto finance creditors are beginning to experience unexpected defaults from customers with good credit scores. On close examination, they are finding that many of these customers have credit scores that have been artificially inflated by a new fraud technique known as, "credit score enhancement," from seasoned trade lines.

Credit score enhancement occurs when a person with less-than-good credit pays to have seasoned trade lines—belonging to other people—added to his or her credit file. Using various online services, the deceptive person (let's call him Mr. DP) pays a fee ranging from hundreds of dollars to several thousand dollars to become an "authorized user" on a credit card account belonging to a stranger with good credit history. Mr. DP can't actually use the stranger's credit account. (Any card issued is typically held by the operators of the Web site.) But he or she does get the credit history because creditors typically report the credit history on an account in the names of all account holders, including authorized users. By adding one or more of these good accounts to his credit records, Mr. DP can see a major increase in his credit scores—an increase that does not reflect his true repayment history.

The fraud investigators of one of our clients have identified more than 40 Web sites that offer these services. For a typical example, look at www.tradelines.biz or www.seasonedtrades.com.

Are these services legal? Maybe yes, maybe no.

To the extent that they say they can improve a consumer's credit rating (and they typically do), the services are covered by the federal Credit Repair Organizations Act. The CROA imposes three main requirements on a covered credit repair organization: (1) It can't lie about its services; (2) It can't collect payment for services until they are rendered; and (3) It must make an affirmative disclosure to customers, including a three-day right to cancel.

Obviously, the biggest stumbling block for credit enhancement services is (2), no payment before services are complete. This requirement is intended to make it impossible for these services to operate legally as a credit repair organization, and it accomplishes that pretty well. Even if the services are successful in raising their customers' credit scores (and thus are not deceiving them), they still cannot collect their fees until the consumer's credit rating has been successfully raised (or perhaps until the consumer has been successfully added as an authorized user, depending on the promise originally made to the customer). It is doubtful that any of these services would be willing to wait on payment—a particular irony since they are providing a mechanism to deceive auto finance companies and other creditors into taking a bet on these customers' repayment habits.

What is the future for such practices? I see two directions looming:

- The FTC will bring enforcement actions, shut them down, and scare others out of the business; or
- Creditors, especially card issuers, will become more skittish about reporting an account's credit history in the names of authorized users. This is a risky option for creditors, however. The Equal Credit Opportunity Act requires a creditor to report the credit history on a spouse who is an authorized user. This requirement was intended to let a married woman share in her husband's credit history. As a result, creditors routinely report credit history on *all* authorized users, because they often cannot be sure whether or not the authorized user is a spouse. A creditor, who decides to furnish credit history only on an authorized user married to the primary cardholder, runs the risk of violating the ECOA, if the creditor fails to accurately identify an authorized user who is a spouse.

Hudson Cook has shared information with the Federal Trade Commission about this scheme, but it is not yet clear whether the agency will take action. In the meantime, auto finance creditors should take the following steps to prevent being victimized:

- Do not rely on the credit score alone. Look carefully at the repayment history on the trade lines.
- Be suspicious of credit files that contain a positive history on an open-end account on which the customer is an authorized user. Ask yourself, "Is this history consistent with the rest of the applicant's repayment history?"

- Ask for a copy of the credit card for any authorized user accounts you question. If the customer has acquired the credit history through one of these schemes, he or she probably won't be able to produce the card, and the auto finance company should consider disregarding the positive credit history.

As long as schemes like these exist, auto finance companies will lose money, both from consumers who default, and from those who pay a lower interest rate than their true risk profile warrants. Careful underwriting is necessary to avoid falling victim to this one.

No Actual Damages Equals No ECOA Recovery

June 2007

By Thomas B. Hudson

In a spot delivery gone bad, James and Tricia Bertin sued Grant Automotive, Inc., claiming that Grant Automotive violated the Equal Credit Opportunity Act, the Illinois Consumer Fraud and Deceptive Business Practices Act, and the Illinois Uniform Commercial Code. The couple also claimed that Grant Automotive had committed the common law tort of trespass to chattels or conversion. Both parties moved for summary judgment, which is lawyer talk for asking the judge to decide the case based on the pleadings, motions, and perhaps some additional evidence, but without a trial. Here is the blow-by-blow case description...

Tricia completed a credit application at Grant Automotive on January 2, 2004. She indicated on the application that she was employed as a waitress. Grant Automotive's salesperson, Michael Cherry, advised Tricia that he would try to secure financing approval for her and her husband, and that he would contact her with the status of the application.

Nuvell Financial Services conditionally approved the application, provided that the Bertins submitted additional proof of their monthly income. The Bertins returned to Grant Automotive the next day with the required paperwork and decided to buy a car. The parties signed a Retail Installment Contract, a Bill of Sale, a Bail and Hold Harmless Agreement, and a document titled, "I Understand Form."

The Bill of Sale provided that the dealer was not obligated to sell the car until a bank or finance company was willing to buy the retail installment contract from the dealership. The Bail and Hold Harmless Agreement stated that, in the event the terms were unacceptable to the financing institution, the purchaser was required to return the car to the dealer or pay the purchase price in full. If the purchaser failed to return the car, or pay, the dealer had the right to take possession of the car.

The "I Understand Form" required the Bertins to remain employed for the next 30 days in order to complete the financing agreement. The dealership did not provide a copy of this form to the Bertins.

The Bertins signed all the documents, paid a $400 down payment, bought temporary insurance for $145, traded in their vehicle, and left the dealership with the new car.

On January 8, 2004, Cherry contacted Tricia and told her that Nuvell Financial had declined to buy her retail installment contract, because Tricia had been terminated from her job. Cherry asked the Bertins to return the car. Tricia wanted to keep the car, and Cherry said they might be able to get financing if she could find another job. Neither Grant Automotive nor Nuvell Financial gave the Bertins written notice of the denial of their loan application. On January 12, 2004, Tricia returned to

Grant Automotive with the new car and stated that she wanted to proceed with the deal, but she was unable to find another job. Cherry again asked Tricia to return the car and offered to return her trade-in vehicle. She refused and drove away in the new car. Grant Automotive later repossessed the car and returned the trade-in to the Bertins.

In their suit, the Bertins claimed that Grant Automotive violated the Equal Credit Opportunity Act by not providing a written adverse action notice. Grant Automotive admitted that it should have sent such a notice.

The court determined that the Bertins failed to show that they sustained any damages as a result of Grant Automotive's not sending a written notice. The $400 down payment had not been debited from their account, and the $145 for insurance was not connected to Grant Automotive's failure to provide written notice of adverse action. The court refused to award punitive damages, because the Bertins were unable to show that Grant Automotive's failure to provide written notice was wanton or malicious or in reckless disregard of the ECOA notice provision.

The Bertins claimed Grant Automotive violated the Illinois Consumer Fraud and Deceptive Business Practices Act, because their down payment and trade-in vehicle were not returned. The court concluded that the trade-in was returned and would have been returned sooner, had Tricia not refused to accept it. Again, the court found that the down payment checks, though not returned, had never been cashed, and the checks had been marked "Void." Because the Bertins were unable to show actual damages, the court denied their motion for summary judgment on this issue.

The court denied the Bertins' claim that Grant Automotive violated the Uniform Commercial Code by not providing notice of disposition. The court held that Grant Automotive had a legal right to take possession of the car, because it owned the car. The court reasoned that the sale transaction was subject to finance company approval, the approval never came, and therefore Grant Automotive never stopped owning the car. The court denied the trespass to chattels claim for the same reason—Grant Automotive owned the car, and the Bertins did not have an absolute and unconditional right to it.

The court denied the Bertins' motion for summary judgment and entered summary judgment for Grant Automotive on all counts.

This case started as a typical, "throw everything against the wall, and see what sticks," attack on a plain vanilla spot delivery transaction. It ended up as a clean-sweep win for the dealership. That's always good news.

The court's determination—absent proof of actual damages—that the consumer could not recover under the ECOA will be very useful to dealers charged by plaintiffs' lawyers with failing to provide adverse action notices. In our experience, plaintiffs often have difficulty showing actual damages for notice and disclosure violations.

Dealers engaging in spot deliveries should find especially interesting the court's discussion of the Uniform Commercial Code claim. We think the court got this one right. The court concluded that the dealership's interest was an ownership interest and not a security interest that would be governed by the UCC. We've seen courts get that analysis wrong in other cases, perhaps because the lawyers representing the dealers didn't think to make the argument and assumed that the UCC applied to the dealer's actions.

File this one away somewhere. It might come in handy.

Bertin v. Grant Automotive, Inc., 2007 WL 1257183 (C.D. Ill. April 30, 2007).

Joint Users—Probably Not What You're Thinking

August 2007

By Jean Noonan

Ah, the law of unintended consequences! So often when Congress writes a new law to "fix" a problem, it creates new ones. As a result, lawyers and compliance officials scramble to figure out if the law applies to situations beyond those Congress originally had in mind. Recently, one alert lawyer had just such a question. This is his story...

A few years ago, Congress amended the Fair Credit Reporting Act to limit the ability of a consumer-reporting agency to report medical information in credit transactions, unless the medical information was relevant to the transaction, and the consumer provided specific written consent.

Reading the amendment, the alert lawyer wondered: What about the situation, when a consumer lists income from social security disability payments as a source of income on an application for auto financing?

He reasoned thusly: The disability payments probably qualify as "medical information" under the new—broader—definition in the FCRA. And, in some cases, credit applications qualify as "consumer reports." Does this mean, he wondered, that the dealer must get the consumer's specific, written consent before sharing the credit application with a bank or finance company that might buy the retail installment sale contract?

Good question, but no, Congress did not anticipate this particular mess when it added the FCRA provisions about medical information. However, the alert lawyer's question creates an opportunity to review how dealers and financing sources avoid becoming consumer-reporting agencies themselves, when they share information about a consumer's creditworthiness.

Every day, dealers share application information about consumers with banks and other financial institutions. A credit application is potentially a consumer report (and covered by the FCRA), because it bears on creditworthiness, and it is collected for the purpose of determining eligibility for credit. So, if the dealer furnishes a credit application to a third party (for a fee or on a cooperative nonprofit basis), and the application meets all the requirements for being a consumer report, then the dealer becomes a consumer-reporting agency. This analysis leads some dealer counsel to worry that the dealer should not pass along an application containing medical information (the consumer's receipt of disability income) without first obtaining the consumer's specific written consent.

Fortunately, the Federal Trade Commission staff recognized this problem a long time ago. The problem goes beyond getting consent to share medical information—a relatively new concern. If dealers were to become consumer-reporting agencies when they share credit applications with potential assignees, they could not do business. Why? Because if you think there is a lot of government regulation of auto dealers, just try being a consumer-reporting agency! The FTC staff appreciated that the world of indirect credit could not exist if auto dealers and other retail finance sellers had to comply with the same FCRA requirements that apply to consumer-reporting agencies. So, the FTC made up a legal doctrine, called the "joint user" doctrine, for just this situation.

Under the joint user doctrine, the dealer is not a consumer-reporting agency furnishing a consumer report to the potential financing source. Rather, the dealer and financing source are joint users of the credit application, and no consumer-reporting agency is involved in the transmittal of the application.

The FTC codified this interpretation in the FTC

Commentary, and courts have generally respected it, although the Commentary doesn't have the force of law. The joint user doctrine lets dealers share credit applications with other companies jointly involved in credit decisions, as well as those with a permissible purpose under the FCRA to obtain consumer report information. When it shares this information with a joint user, the dealer does not become a consumer-reporting agency, the FTC says. Once we conclude that the dealer is not a consumer-reporting agency, the FCRA provision requiring written consent to furnish medical information does not apply.

Whew! One problem off our list. But wait; there's another one. What about the financial institution's communication back to the dealer on whether it will approve the consumer's deal? Isn't that a communication of information bearing on creditworthiness, and, thereby, a consumer report under the FCRA? And doesn't that make the financial institution a consumer-reporting agency?

Congress actually spotted this potential problem when it wrote the FCRA more than 35 years ago. Happily, it supplied a solution designed for indirect credit in the form of an exclusion from the definition of consumer report.

The FCRA specified that the financial institution's communication to the dealer about the consumer's creditworthiness is *not* a consumer report, provided that the dealer does one simple thing: Tell the consumer the name and address of every creditor the dealer has asked to consider the consumer's application. In other words, a dealer should tell the consumer the name and address of each creditor to which it sends the consumer's application for credit.

Oddly enough, if the dealer does not give creditor information to the consumer, it is the financial institution, not the dealer, that has a compliance problem. The financial institution becomes a consumer-reporting agency. That status, I can tell you, makes the financial institution as unhappy as it would make the dealer.

Apparently, some financial institutions are paying more attention to this legal problem. Several dealers have contacted us recently, saying, "One of my financing sources has made me promise that I will always give customers their name and address when I refer a credit application to them. What's going on?" If you have received one of these instructions from a financing source, now, you know why. The creditor has realized it cannot legally tell you its application decision unless, first, you have informed the consumer of the creditor's name and address.

So, with a bit of effort, dealers and their financing sources can escape the problem of being a consumer-reporting agency under the FCRA. Dealers can thank the FTC staff for getting them off the hook with its joint user doctrine, and financing sources are off the hook if the dealer tells customers the names and addresses of creditors that receive the consumer's credit application.

Are You Making 'Firm Offers'?

September 2007

By Thomas B. Hudson

In 2001, an Illinois car dealer sent out a mailer to potential customers whose names had been obtained from a credit bureau. The Illinois dealership had come up with the bright idea of obtaining such a list and then making a "firm offer of credit" in the amount of $300. Now, $300 isn't much credit when you're talking about buying a car. But, the dealer noted, the FCRA didn't specify a minimum amount—it just required that the offer be "firm."

What the dealer had not counted on was this: The practice of getting lists of potential customers is one that is pretty heavily regulated.

Under the federal Fair Credit Reporting Act, you cannot get such a list to use in any manner you please, but you can get a list of people who meet certain criteria (for instance, a credit score of 550-650 who live in a particular geographic area) if you are willing to make them a "firm offer of credit." That gives you a "permissible purpose" in FCRA-speak.

Let's consider an example of why it is important to understand FCRA-speak.

Oneta Cole received one of the Illinois dealership's mailings. She sued the dealer, objecting that her credit report had been accessed by the dealership without a permissible purpose, and claiming that the offer of $300 in credit for the purchase of a car was a sham. She further asserted that the real reason the dealer had accessed her credit file was to sell her a car. Because of that, she argued, the sham offer didn't qualify as a firm offer, and the dealership had no right to access her credit report. Cole's case was filed as a class action.

"Whoa, Nellie!" says the dealer. "There's no minimum credit amount in the FCRA—we're permitted to access the credit report provided that we are willing to shell out whatever we say we're willing to shell out, which in this case is $300."

The U.S. District Court (the federal trial court, as opposed to an appellate court) agreed with the dealership, finding that it had a permissible purpose to access Cole's credit report. Dissatisfied with this result, Cole appealed to the U.S. Court of Appeals for the Seventh Circuit (the only higher federal court is the U.S. Supreme Court).

The appellate court bought the argument that the trial court had rejected, finding that the $300 offer was a sham and was made in order to access Cole's credit report for marketing purposes. Most lawyers knowledgeable of the law in this area claimed that the appellate court had invented law where there was none, since the FCRA required no minimum amount of credit to qualify as a "firm offer."

The appellate court reversed the trial court's decision, and, as we in the legal profession say, the compost hit the cooling system. In very short order, copycat lawsuits were filed all over the country.

Car dealerships, mortgage companies, and credit card issuers were all hit with "firm offer" cases, and, at one point, there were more than 250 class action firm offer cases pending around the country. You might say, a regular cottage industry for plaintiffs' lawyers had been created.

As things go, those cases are slowly producing decisions of their own. Some of the trial judges followed the decision in the *Cole* case (indeed, those in the Seventh Circuit pretty much had no choice but to do so), but other trial courts, and, later, other appellate courts disagreed with the *Cole* analysis. The result, at the moment, is a mishmash of cases that come down both ways. So, what should a dealer do when the marketing company shows up with a "firm offer" marketing program? Do you throw the salesman out the door, or do you sign up?

Your call, Bunkie. But if you are tempted to sign up, this is one time you really, really need to listen to us when we say your lawyer needs to review the program. After *Cole*, these firm offer programs can still be used, but the legal requirements are dicey, and they can change from jurisdiction to jurisdiction. So, fork over the money for the mouthpiece, Bunkie. The lawyer needs a new boat anyway.

Chapter 5

OFAC/ USA PATRIOT Act/ Cash Reporting/ Identity Theft

All of our lives changed after 9/11. Why shouldn't the lives of car dealers change, as well?

The short answer is, they did. The long answer is, in a variety of ways, the changes were, and remain, significant...

Change #1

First, the industry rediscovered a provision that had been in place for years—the federal prohibition against any American citizen "doing business" with any person or entity named on the Treasury Department's "bad guy" list, maintained by the Office of Foreign Assets Control. The penalties for doing such prohibited business are draconian. Hence, the only way that dealers and others could avoid the possibility of incurring the penalties was to run the names of everyone they did business with against the list before they engaged in any transactions. Our experience is that the majority of dealers don't check the list, and the dealers who do, seldom check it for everyone, including employees and vendors. This is a mistake.

Change #2

Shortly after September 11, in 2001, the same year of the World Trade Center and Pentagon attacks, Congress came along with the USA PATRIOT Act, which was supposed to impose on dealers and others, a sort of "know your customer" regimen. Congress directed that the federal agencies come up with regulations to implement the law, and they all did—except for the regulators charged with drafting regulations for car dealers. The law's requirements depended on the issuance of the regulations: so, car dealers are still in limbo.

Change #3

Meanwhile, agencies continued to work on another statutory requirement that imposed similar burdens on dealers and others. The FACT Act amended the Fair Credit Reporting Act and required creditors to come up with ways to prevent identity theft. Again, Congress left it up to the agencies to provide the detail the regulations would require, and the result was a proposed "Red Flag" Rule. As we go to press on ***CARLAW®*** *Street Legal*, we are waiting for the Red Flag Rule to become final.

Change #4

Finally, you'd think that being given a wad of cash for a cash automobile sale would be a good thing. It is, except when that cash transaction triggers the fed's cash reporting requirement rules. Dealers need to step carefully through what can only be described as a minefield of detailed instructions that apply when enough cash is involved.

Your tax dollars at work.

Can We Have Your Cave Address?

March 2006

By Thomas B. Hudson and Emily Marlow Beck

We hang out with all sorts of car people. Last week, we were in the company of some fellows who work for an insurance company that insures car dealers. Since the insurance company has a vested interest in keeping its insured dealers out of trouble, it tries hard to educate dealers about their responsibilities under various state and federal laws and regulations.

According to one of these fellows, at a recent meeting of

dealers he attended, the topic was the Office of Foreign Assets Control, and the OFAC "Specially Designated Persons" or "Bad Guy" list. After a discussion among several of the dealers about how stupid the law is (and they are right), one dealer raised his hand and said, "I haven't heard of this requirement. How are we supposed to keep up with developments like this?"

It's rather hard to surprise us, but we have to tell you, our jaws dropped. We can understand dealers who are not yet in strict compliance with the OFAC rules. We can even understand dealers who know about the OFAC requirements, but who have not yet started to bring their dealerships into complete compliance.

But not to have heard of the requirement? Our reaction was: *Do you live in a cave?* With all of the ink spilled over the last few years on this topic, how could anyone not have heard of the requirement?

This article is not about OFAC. It's about keeping up with new developments. How does your dealership make sure that a new law or regulation doesn't sneak up on you and put your business at risk if you aren't in compliance? I'll say it again: *How do you get out of your cave?*

Let's look at some ways dealers address the problem and the steps they take to emerge from dingy caves of ignorance into the sunshine of enlightenment. To challenge you a bit, I'll do this Socratically; that is, by asking questions before giving answers.

1. Do you have a compliance officer?

If not, appoint one. *(Hint: This could be the same person you appointed as your privacy officer.)* Tell him or her that the job is to identify new laws and regulations that affect your business. The compliance officer should report to the top of your organization—this would send the message that compliance is an important part of your company's management.

2. Do you insist on regular written reports, perhaps quarterly, in which the compliance officer identifies new laws and regulations?

You should. And he or she should either identify new laws and regulations, or he or she should affirm that none have arisen since his last report.

3. Are you giving the compliance officer the tools to do the job?

For instance, he or she will need to subscribe to a few publications, to join a few organizations, and to acquire Internet access and skills to find new developments. Also, you should find a lawyer who knows the compliance areas you want to track. You may need more than one, for topics like employment law, environmental law, and consumer protection law. Make sure the compliance officer has access to whatever legal help he or she needs for each area.

4. Have you joined your state auto dealers association or independent auto dealers association?

Not all of these associations do a good job of keeping on top of new developments; but most do, and some are superb. Join NADA or the NIADA. Attend the meetings with your compliance officer, and actually go to the meetings—not just to the golf sessions and the cocktail parties.

5. Does your compliance officer regularly crawl all over the Web?

Your state Attorney General, motor vehicle administration, and consumer protection bureau all have Web sites on which they post recent developments. The Federal Reserve Board, the Federal Trade Commission, and other federal agencies also have useful Web sites. Your compliance officer should find these sites, learn to navigate them, and create a tickler file as a reminder to check the sites frequently. (We check them daily, but you can probably get by with less frequency than that.)

6. Have you recently checked with your insurance company?

Several insurers offer compliance training. They may be willing to assist without charge.

7. Is your compliance officer F&I certified by the Association of Finance and Insurance Professionals?

He or she should be; he or she also should be recertified periodically. It costs, but it's worth it.

8. Are you reading?

Many publications have helpful stuff. You are reading one of them right now. Check out *The World of Special Finance*, *Ward's Dealer Business*, *Automotive News*, and ***Spot Delivery*®** (in the interest of full disclosure, that one is ours). You can bet that the plaintiffs' lawyers read sources like these. You should, too.

9. Final question: What's the alternative to doing a good job of tracking new developments?

Turn around and head back to your cave of ignorance and wait for (1) your customer's attorney to point out which laws you violated in a formal complaint; (2) your friendly state Attorney General to come knocking on your door; or (3) the legal compliance fairy to appear.

Security Breaches Prompt New Laws

October 2005

By Patricia E.M. Covington

*[**Editor's note:** This is one in a series of articles emanating from NHEMA's Business Technology Committee, which hosted the annual Business Technology Roundtable in Costa Mesa, CA, during February 2005. Topics centered on the use of technology in organizations. Web site: www.nhema.org.]*

New laws seeking to protect consumers from losses in the theft of personal data have stretched across 22 states, and more are expected as Congress contemplates federal regulations.

Senate Bill, S. 1408, approved by the Senate Commerce, Science and Transportation Committee in 2005, requires companies to give notice to consumers when their personal information is compromised and there is a "reasonable risk of identity theft." S. 1408 also requires businesses to safeguard sensitive consumer information, gives consumers the right to freeze credit reports, and limits the use and disclosure of Social Security Numbers. This federal action bolsters state rules governing a growing concern: identity theft.

By October 2005, the Identity Theft Resource Center had reported 110 security breaches affecting 56.3 million individuals in the United States. The number was made more startling by the familiar corporate names impacted, like Choicepoint, Bank of America, PNC Bank of Pittsburgh, and CardSystems.

As a result, elected state officials enacted laws at a rapid pace. At the start of 2005, only one state had a security breach notification law; by the end of 2005, the number of states had risen to 22. In addition, new requirements imposed on businesses and government agencies govern the use, retention, and disposal of consumers' personal information.

In 2002, California was the first state to break ground in security breach procedure by enacting a law (effective on July 1, 2003) that requires companies and governmental agencies to give consumers notice when an unauthorized acquisition of unencrypted computerized data occurs, which compromises the security, confidentiality, or integrity of consumer personal information.

Personal information is defined as first name or initial and last name, when paired with one of the following:

- Social Security Number
- Driver's license or California ID number
- Account, credit card or debit card number in combination with the security code, access code or password to gain access to the account

It does not include public information made lawfully available in governmental records. The notice to affected persons must occur expediently, without unreasonable delay. However, if law enforcement determines that the notification will impede the criminal investigation, a delay is permitted.

Similarities and Differences

With the passage of the California security breach notice law, other states followed suit with their own security breach notice laws. These states include: Arkansas, Connecticut, Delaware, Florida, Georgia, Illinois, Indiana, Louisiana, Maine, Minnesota, Montana, Nevada, New Jersey, New York, North Carolina, North Dakota, Ohio, Rhode Island, Tennessee, Texas and Washington.

Many of these laws, in effect by 2005 and 2006, are modeled after California; however, some differ.

For example, certain laws apply to all businesses, and governmental agencies—as in California and Connecticut.

Others apply only to governmental agencies—such as Indiana. In Georgia and Maine, the laws apply only to data brokers. At least one state, Minnesota, exempts financial institutions as defined under the Gramm-Leach-Bliley Act (GLB), as well as entities subject to the Health Insurance Portability and Accountability Act.

Scope

The scope of the laws may also vary. For instance, the definition of "personal information" has been refined in some states. North Carolina excludes from the definition an individual's electronic identification numbers, mail names or addresses, Internet account numbers and identification names, a parent's legal surname prior to marriage, and passwords, unless such "information would permit access to a person's financial account or resources."

The exclusion definition has been broadened by other states. Medical information is included in Arkansas and Delaware definitions of excluded material. Georgia includes a password alone, if it can access data identifying a consumer by name. North Dakota's exclusion definition includes a consumer's date of birth, mother's maiden name, employer ID, e-signature, and birth, death, or marriage certificate.

Also, note that some states have expanded the format or medium of the personal information covered by the notice requirements. North Carolina elected to apply the notice requirements to all data, no matter what form, written or electronic; while California, Montana, and North Dakota laws apply only to computerized data.

Safe Harbors

Many of the new laws contain safe harbors. North Dakota, Nevada, and North Carolina provide a safe harbor, or exclusion, for financial institutions, as defined under GLB, if such institutions are in compliance with its applicable laws and regulations.

Risk Threshold

Some of the new laws contain a harm or risk threshold, triggering the requirement to give notice. States that have opted to limit notices in this manner are Arkansas, Connecticut, Florida, Louisiana, Montana, Nevada, North Carolina, and Washington.

For instance, Arkansas does not require a consumer notice, if the covered entity's investigation finds "no reasonable likelihood of harm to customers." Similarly, Connecticut's law requires no notice if, after investigation and consultation with the relevant law enforcement agencies, it is determined "that the breach will not likely result in harm to individuals whose personal information has been acquired and accessed."

Finally, at least one state, Illinois, does not provide for a delay upon the request of law enforcement. It does contain instructions as to how the notices should be delivered, depending upon the number of affected persons.

Consumer Information

When it came to data privacy and security, breaches were not the only thing on legislators' minds. Many of the security breach notice bills also contained measures to protect consumer information and prevent identity theft. Common provisions include safeguarding requirements similar to those under GLB, limitations on the use and disclosure of Social Security Numbers, the right of consumers to freeze their credit reports, and the imposition of requirements in connection with the disposal of consumer information. When not included in the security breach bills, many of these provisions were passed separately in other bills.

All in all, the threats of identity theft and security breaches caused a flurry of new bills in 2005. You should expect to see more state measures unless the federal government steps in with a measure that trumps state laws.

*[**Editor's note:** As we go to press with this book, there has been no preemptive legislation, and other states have joined those described in this article in enacting security breach legislation.]*

King Cash—Touching-Up Your Cash Reporting Requirements

May 2006

By Emily Marlow Beck

So, what's it like to wrestle with the IRS about compliance with the Form 8300 cash reporting requirements? Ask the Virginia dealer who just fought its way back from a $100,000 civil penalty due to what the IRS claimed were "intentional violations" of the federal reporting requirements. In a case that was a real close shave for the dealer, a federal district court awarded the dealer a refund of the $100,000 penalty, plus interest. The judge took more than a year to decide the case, which appears to be the first decision involving failure of a business to comply with IRS cash-reporting requirements as a result of error.

What did the dealer do to get himself into this mess? Let's take a look...

When conducting a review of Tysinger Motor Company, the IRS determined that the dealership failed to comply with federal law, which requires any business accepting $10,000 or more in cash to file a Form 8300 to report the details of the transaction to the IRS. Specifically, the IRS determined that the dealership failed to report four out of eight reportable transactions during the 1999 and 2000 tax years. The agency assessed a $100,000 penalty against the dealership for noncompliance (that's $25,000 per non-filed form, for those finger-counters out there). The IRS claimed the hefty penalty was justified due to the dealership's "intentional disregard" of the federal requirements. Tysinger paid the fine but filed a claim in federal court seeking a refund of the $100,000. Tysinger claimed the dealership's failure to comply with federal law was a mere error, and that the dealership did not "intentionally disregard" the law.

Fortunately for the dealer, the U.S. District Court for the Eastern District of Virginia agreed and ordered the IRS to give back the $100,000, plus interest. The court concluded that the dealership carried its burden of proving that it did not "intentionally disregard" its obligation to file Form 8300s in the four transactions. The court found no proof that anyone at the dealership consciously decided not to report the transactions. Instead, the court agreed that the failures were simply mistakes. The court's decision to refund the dealer's money was based, in no small part, on the dealer's demonstrated efforts to comply with the cash reporting requirements. These efforts included developing internal systems designed to identify transactions that would be subject to the cash reporting requirements, and conducting training sessions for employees.

This was a close call for the dealer. A different day, a different situation, could have earned a different result. But one thing is for certain—the dealer could have avoided the whole mess by not making mistakes.

Tysinger Motor Company, Inc. v. United States of America, 2006 WL 940320 (E.D.Va. April 6, 2006).

What steps have you taken at your dealership to make sure that you're complying with the cash-reporting requirement? Do you know where to start?

A recently released Internal Revenue Service Motor Vehicle Technical Advisory may be able to help. This document, "Cash Reporting and Your Dealership," provides informal guidance in the form of 31 "frequently asked questions" and answers involving dealers' compliance obligations under the IRS Cash Reporting Rule. The MVTA issued the document following a request for compliance guidance on several cash reporting scenarios not directly addressed by the Treasury Regulations or IRS publications.

The document contains too much information to include here. But, below is a sampling of those questions. Some (should be) easy. Some are a little trickier.

What does "cash" mean for the purposes of Form 8300?

Cash is money—currency and coins of the United States and any other country. Cash also includes certain monetary instruments, such as a cashier's check, bank draft, traveler's check, or a money order, if it has a face amount of $10,000 or less and the business receives it in (1) a designated reporting transaction; or (2) any transaction in which the recipient knows the payer is trying to avoid the cash reporting requirements.

Is a personal check considered cash for purposes of the reporting requirements?

Nope. Personal checks aren't considered cash.

What is a "related transaction"?

Transactions between a buyer and a seller that occur within a 24-hour period are related transactions. Transactions more than 24 hours apart are related if the recipient of the cash knows, or has reason to know, that each transaction is one of a series of connected transactions.

A customer purchases a vehicle for $9,000 cash. That same year, the customer pays the dealership additional cash of $1,500 for a repair to the vehicle's transmission, accessories, etc. Is a Form 8300 required?

No, unless the dealer knew or had reason to know the sale of the vehicle and the subsequent transactions were a series of connected transactions, e.g., if the dealer and the customer agreed, as a condition of the sale of the vehicle, that the customer would be obligated to pay the additional $1,500.

A customer purchases five cars, each separately, through the year, totaling $15,000. Is a Form 8300 required?

No. These are separate transactions.

If a buy here, pay here dealer receives weekly payments in cash and the total of these payments is more than $10,000 in a 12-month period, is a Form 8300 required?

Yes. The weekly credit payments constitute payments on the same transaction. As such, the dealership is required to file a Form 8300 when the total amount exceeds $10,000.

A customer wires $7,000 from his bank account to the dealership's bank account and also presents a $4,000 cashier check. Is a Form 8300 required?

No. A wire transfer does not constitute cash for the purpose of Form 8300 reporting.

So, how did you do? If the IRS showed up at your dealership for one of its "reviews," how would your dealership hold up? Think of it this way: You already pay Uncle Sam gobs of money. Don't add to it with unnecessary penalties and fines.

'Red Flag' Guidelines Tricky for Dealers

August 2006

By Patricia E.M. Covington

Remember that law that brought you the "Disposal Law" (the one that requires that you properly dispose of consumer reports)? Well, it's back! I'm talking about the Fair and Accurate Credit Transactions Act of 2003 (FACTA).

We warned you in our June 2006, issue of ***Spot Delivery®*** that the federal banking agencies and the Federal Trade Commission (the FTC, your regulator) were up to their old tricks again. You may recall that in May they made public their proposed rules for the "Red Flag" guidelines and address reconciliation procedures. Sections 114 and 315 of FACTA required the agencies and the FTC to make these rules. The draft made public in May was officially published on July 18.

If you were ambitious enough to read the May draft, you're in luck—the published rules are unchanged. Now, I use the word, "luck," loosely. I don't think anyone is really lucky when it comes to having to comply with these rules.

Within the proposed rules for dealers, there are two parts: the first deals with the "red flags" creditors have to look out for to prevent identity theft. The second contains the rules for spotting an address discrepancy between a credit report and a credit application.

In this article, we'll talk about "red flags."

The proposed red flag guidelines require dealers to put into place an "Identity Theft Prevention Program."

What's that? It's a program with "reasonable policies and procedures" to address risks of identity theft *and* risks to the safety and soundness of the dealer's business. Safety and soundness—that's a new one. Banks have had to worry about it for decades, but not dealers—not until now.

The obvious purpose of the program is to detect, prevent, and mitigate possible risks of identity theft. What's not so obvious is that we're talking about *possible* risks of identity theft. That sounds like fun, huh?

The proposed rules insist that a dealer's program *cannot* be static. It's not one of these, "I've put it into place and now I can forget about it," type of deals. The proposed guidelines make painfully clear that the dealer has to *constantly* keep up-to-date with the changing risks of identity theft. That means the dealer needs to be constantly aware of the following factors:

- Changes in its own experiences with identity theft;
- Changes in the methods of identity theft (how identity theft is done);
- Changes in the methods of detecting identity theft (new ways to spot identity theft);
- Changes in the methods of preventing identity theft (new ways to prevent identity theft);
- Changes in the methods of mitigating identity theft (new ways that one can lessen the damage from identity theft happening); and
- Changes in the dealer's business.

And we're not through. Once a dealer becomes aware of a change, it has to consider whether its program needs to be updated to address it. If the dealer decides that an update is necessary, it has to implement it promptly. Not an easy task, and certainly not one the FTC wants you to forget.

Another really important thing that a dealer needs to understand is that if you get a vendor or some other third party to help you comply, you'd better make sure that the solution (or performance) is sufficient. That's because dealers will remain responsible and liable for any and all third parties hired whose performance impacts the program. So, if you buy some software to get into compliance, or hire a firm to provide some service to help prevent identity theft, you need to make sure that what they provide, or how they perform, complies with your program *and* the guidelines. You see, you can't just turn over this matter to a third party, because the proposed guidelines require that you have a program to oversee and manage the vendor's performance. (Having third parties do things on your behalf just got a little harder.)

Now, let's get to the nitty-gritty. What specific things need to be in a program? There must be processes and procedures for the following:

- To identify red flags that will help in detecting a possible risk of identity theft (you have to have a way you're going to pick the red flags to include in your program);
- To verify the identity of persons opening an account (for dealers, that means confirming the identity of *every* customer who is buying a car on credit or setting up an account for service work);
- To actually detect the red flags;
- To assess whether any red flag detected evidences a risk of identity theft (determine whether the facts show that there is a possible risk of identity theft);

- To mitigate the risk of identity theft (lessen any ill effects of identity theft or of identity theft happening);
- To train staff about identity theft and the dealer's program;
- To oversee its vendors; and
- To receive board of director approval, oversight, management and reporting.

One of the first things a dealer is going to have to do to develop this program is to conduct a risk evaluation. (Sound familiar? Think GLB, Safeguards Rule.) The program must be in writing. And, it has to be appropriate to the size, complexity, and nature of the dealer's business and the scope of its activities.

Now, how is a dealer to know what red flags to include in its program? Recall that risk evaluation I just mentioned—that's how. Based on the findings of the risk evaluation, the dealer has to pick out what red flags are relevant to its operations. Then it has to make sure it's going to actually detect those red flags. The concept is that you don't have to just identify the red flags; you need to detect them as well. For example, in your home, you identify fire as something you want to protect against; accordingly, you install smoke detectors to actually detect the fires.

What happens after you detect a red flag? You have to assess whether the red flag detected reveals a possible risk of identity theft. If you determine that it doesn't, then you have to have a "reasonable basis" for making this conclusion. That means take out your pen and paper—you ought to either document your "reasonable basis" or have a policy of what constitutes a "reasonable basis."

Now, let's say you've assessed the red flag and determined that it is a possible risk of identity theft. Then what? Well, you've got to do something to mitigate any ill effects from it. Most of the time, that'll mean not selling the car to the customer or not taking his credit card.

The banking agencies and FTC were kind enough to give us a list of some things that could be red flags. Only one small problem—it's a scary list. One of the red flags they suggest is examining the customer's credit report to see if it indicates a pattern of activity that is "inconsistent with the history and usual pattern of activity of an applicant or customer." That's a mouthful! What does that mean? Is the dealer supposed to be an expert analyzer of credit reports to spot "inconsistent" or "unusual patterns of activities?" Well, I don't know about you, but I don't feel fit to perform that type of analysis. Don't fret too much; not all of them are hard. There are some easy ones. For instance, one is a fraud alert on the person's credit report; another is an alteration on the customer's driver's or other identifying document. Take a long hard look at the list the regulators suggest. Your program should include some of what they list.

A couple of other points you ought to know:

- First, the guidelines call for training your employees. You have to train them regarding how to detect red flags and how to mitigate identity theft.
- Second, the dealer's board of directors has to approve and be right on top of what's happening with the program. The proposed guidelines not only require that the program be presented to and blessed by the board, but the board has to get an annual report on how well it's performing, and if it's in compliance with the guidelines. The FTC and banking agencies mean business—everyone from the top down must be involved and is responsible.

If you haven't read the draft since it was first made public, I'd strongly suggest you do so now, *and* talk to your lawyer. The period for offering comments to the regulators has expired, so you will be stuck with whatever final version of the rule the regulators adopt. It could be drastically changed, or it could track the draft closely.

One thing I'm pretty sure about—we're going to have to live with some rendition of these rules. So, you ought to see what they require sooner rather than later—you'll need all the lead-time you can get to comply.

We Get Letters...

September 2006

By Thomas B. Hudson

Once again, Spot fell asleep and failed to bite the mailman, and a couple of letters actually got through. A lawyer friend of ours wrote as follows:

> *I came across something in the Supplementary Information to the proposed interagency "Red Flags" Rule that I thought you might have a field day with in one of your columns. The FTC estimates the burden on motor vehicle dealers to create and implement the newly required Identity Theft Prevention Program to be a mere 5 hours (with an annual recurring burden of 1 hour). 71 Fed. Reg. 40786. This is in addition to 2 hours to train the staff (1 hour in subsequent years) and 4 hours to prepare the written report (1 hour in subsequent years). The FTC's estimate assumes dealers will borrow heavily from the programs of financial institutions to which they assign their credit sales and leases.*
>
> *One has to wonder how long the FTC thinks it will take the average dealer employee who is responsible for this program to read through and become acquainted with these new*

requirements, let alone conduct a risk assessment, determine which red flags are applicable to its business, develop procedures to protect against the risks it identifies, analyze its service provider arrangements and develop an institution-specific written program (among other things). And all this by entities that never have had to develop and implement Customer Identification Programs (under section 326 of the USA PATRIOT Act) upon which they could build their programs. One would think with the Safeguards Rule a mere three years old that the Commission still remembers the huge challenges dealers had to overcome to rearrange their business operations to conform with that rule's separate anti-identity theft measures.

What our friend is referring to are the proposed "Red Flag" Rules. Several federal agencies (including the FTC, which regulates car dealers) have jointly issued these proposed regulations for comment. If enacted in their proposed form, these Red Flag Rules will impose a serious additional burden on dealers. See "Proposed 'Red Flag' Guidelines Tricky for Dealers" in the August 2006 issue of ***Spot Delivery®***.

Our friend's points are, as lawyers like to say, well made. Based on our experience, we think that the percentage of dealers who have actually implemented a Safeguards Policy is probably not very high.

Many dealers simply are not aware that they are "financial institutions" under the Gramm-Leach-Bliley Act and, as such, are required to create and maintain a privacy Safeguards Policy. We know this because we've had dealers screaming at us that the Safeguards requirements only apply to "lenders" and not to dealers. (The erroneous reference to "lenders" is, as Mama would say, "a whole 'nother problem.") Screaming or not, dealers must have a Safeguarding Policy—those who don't face potential enforcement activities.

But we digress. Back to the Red Flag Rules. Dealers WILL have to face more federal requirements when these proposed rules become final. Those requirements will be burdensome, and any dealer who believes the FTC's estimates of hours necessary to comply with them probably also believes in the Tooth Fairy.

So, You Think You Know Privacy? Let's Talk...

October 2006

By Patricia E.M. Covington

If you thought that privacy law was limited to Gramm-Leach-Bliley, you're about to get a reality check. GLB is the veritable tip of the iceberg. Just ignore the fact that icebergs are shrinking every year, because—quite to the contrary—privacy-related laws are increasing with every year that passes. When you think about the subject of consumer information privacy, it's best to step back and take a "panoramic" look at the landscape.

Understanding the complete picture is not only necessary for compliance, it's critical for not overspending when complying. It also promotes a more robust and efficient program that is more likely to achieve the laws' intended goals.

I'll start with a description of the lay of the land. Privacy-related laws can be broken down into three types: (1) Don't share my information and protect what you've got (confidentiality and security related); (2) Respect my privacy and don't contact me when I've said that I don't want to be bothered (marketing related); and (3) Don't steal from me (identity theft protection related).

The granddaddy of all privacy laws is the Fair Credit Reporting Act. How is it a privacy law, you ask? Well, for one, it says that companies that collect data about a person's credit (i.e., credit reporting agencies) can't willy-nilly share that data (i.e., consumer reports) with others. This information may be shared only with persons who have a valid need under the law (i.e., permissible purpose). Also, persons who do obtain these credit reports can't indiscriminately share the information. If they do so, they might find themselves deemed a consumer-reporting agency. And, if you have an affiliate, you can only share credit report information if you provide the consumer with an opportunity to opt out of that sharing. Finally, it contains the rules on making prescreened offers. Consumers have the right to have their names removed from the prescreening lists.

In a nutshell, the FCRA contains two types of privacy-related laws: "Don't share my information," and "Respect my privacy by not contacting me." There is a third variety, but we will discuss it later.

The most well-known privacy law is GLB. There are two components, the Privacy Rule and the Safeguards Rule. The Privacy Rule requires companies to tell consumers what information they collect, how they share it, and with whom they share it. The Safeguards Rule requires that companies actually do what they say they're doing in privacy policies. Companies must protect consumer information against unauthorized access and anticipated security and integrity threats.

Now back to FCRA. The Fair and Accurate Credit Transactions Act amended FCRA. FACTA added quite a few privacy-related laws, including the truncation of all but the last four digits of the Social Security Number on receipts, the prohibition of selling debts that are the result of identity theft, the right of identity theft victims to obtain copies of transaction documents used in connection with identity theft, fraud alerts (initial, extended and active duty), the Disposal Rule, the Red Flags Rule and the Address Discrepancy Rule. The requirements to truncate Social Security Numbers, to not sell debts that are the result of identity theft, and to give identity theft victims copies of transaction documents used in connection with identity theft are pretty self-evident. These all are, "Don't steal from me," type of laws.

The Disposal Rule requires that companies properly dispose of credit reports (or any compilation of credit reports). This, of course, is to prevent the unauthorized access and use of them. Fraud alerts give consumers the right to put an alert on their credit files. If an alert is on a file, a creditor is required to verify the consumer's identity. Initial alerts are placed when someone thinks she may become the victim of identity theft (e.g., I lost my wallet). Extended alerts are placed when an identity thief already has victimized the consumer. Active duty alerts are for individuals in the armed services and on the road. The goal of alerts is to give the creditor notice that identity theft is a real risk and it better make sure it's dealing with the *real* person and not a thief.

The Red Flag and Address Discrepancy Rules are the newest kids on the block. The Red Flag Rule requires that companies put in place an "Identity Theft Protection Program." This program must include reasonable policies and procedures to address the risks of identity theft and the safety and soundness of the dealer's business. The Address Discrepancy Rule requires that creditors confirm the identity of consumers when the address provided by the consumer is different than what is listed in the credit file. Again, all of these requirements are the, "Don't steal from me," kind.

FACTA does have a "Don't contact me," component—it's the amendment to the Prescreening and Affiliate Sharing Rules.

In addition to other requirements, the Prescreening Rule requires that the right to opt out from prescreening lists be clearly and conspicuously disclosed. The Affiliate Sharing Rule limits how information shared with affiliates actually can be used when it comes to marketing.

Other "Don't contact me" laws are the federal "Do Not Call laws" (FTC's Telemarketing Rule and FCC's Telephone Consumer Protection Act), CAN SPAM, and Do Not Fax laws. These laws contain specific requirements regarding how and when you may contact consumers via phone, e-mail and fax.

The states then have their own privacy-related laws. Some are mini-versions of the federal ones, and some are completely new, such as security breach notice laws. These require that consumers be notified of security breaches involving their sensitive information. The company who owns the information breached must provide the notice. In almost every case (except North Carolina and Hawaii), the security breach applies to computerized data. North Carolina and Hawaii apply it to all data, no matter the format. As of October 2006, the number of states having this type of law has grown to 34.

The states also have Social Security Number limitation laws. These laws limit how Social Security Numbers can be used, published, and transmitted. Some states prohibit Social Security Numbers from being printed on any materials that are mailed. There are some exceptions, such as applications. At least 13 states have this type of law.

Then there are disposal type laws. These laws are very similar to the FACTA Disposal Rule, except they apply to all records and documents that contain sensitive consumer information. They generally require that a company have reasonable policies and procedures to dispose of sensitive customer information (to prevent unauthorized acquisition and use). There are at least 16 states with this type of law.

Many states have their own safeguarding laws. These laws are similar to GLB in that companies must implement a safeguarding program to protect the confidentiality, security, and integrity of consumer information. Approximately nine states have this law.

Lastly (at least as we go to press), there are credit or security freeze laws. These laws don't require dealers to *do* anything, but instead give consumers the right to lock down their credit reports. If a security freeze is in place, creditors are "frozen out" of the credit report and cannot gain access. There are usually exceptions for current creditors and law enforcement. To gain access, the consumer has to request that the credit file be "thawed." This is of interest to dealers because it inhibits the credit process and the ability to get the customer in a car and off the market.

Why is it important to know about all these laws and how they are interrelated? Well, first, it enables you to build a cohesive program—one that will comply with all the requirements and actually function better. For example, the effort you invest to comply with the FACTA Disposal Rule will certainly help you with the state's disposal law. That effort also helps you comply with the GLB Safeguards Policy, but only if you take the time to document it in writing and add it to your plan.

Many of your compliance efforts can do double duty. But, first, you need a clear picture of what you're required to do and where you're going. This will enable you to use your resources more efficiently. You won't duplicate efforts, and you'll build on existing programs when creating new ones (e.g., Red Flag Rule). In the end, you'll wind up with a stronger overall program. To top it off, you may actually prevent identity theft and fraud, which saves you even more money.

Common Sense: The Best Tool in Your Dealership's Identity Theft Arsenal

December 2006

By Emily Marlow Beck

Those of you who have been reading our lawyer babble for a while know that Uncle Sam has recruited car dealers into his war on terrorists, drug dealers, identity thieves, and other unsavory characters. Many of you have kicked your efforts into high gear, stepping up your compliance efforts to meet new federal and state requirements head-on.

You've bought a fancy-schmancy software system that scrubs every potential customer against the OFAC or "bad guy" list. You've tightened up your cash reporting requirements, and you've been tracking your state's legislation for enactment of any new data breach laws. You keep a copy of the US PATRIOT Act at your bedside for emergencies (yeah, right!), and you're waiting with bated breath to see the new federal Red Flag Rules so that you can start revising your dealership polices immediately. It's enough to make a compliance lawyer tear up with pride.

So, it came as a bit of a surprise to me to read a news report in which a dealer in Texas is feeling heat from the district attorney's office over a car the dealer sold to an identity thief. Based on a recently issued news report, a Houston-area dealer may be held responsible for not preventing identity theft that occurred in its dealership.

According to the report, prosecutors got all fired up when a 19-year-old black, cross-dressing man bought a car at a Dodge dealership using a 48-year-old white woman's identity. The district attorney claimed that red flags at the dealership should have gone up immediately, but the finance manager who handled the deal said it was not apparent that the customer was a man, because he was dressed as a woman. The report quotes the credit manager as saying that the customer misled him with make-up and cornrows. Anyone else would have made the same mistake, right?

Well, not quite. Especially when you consider that the victim's credit report already had a fraud alert on it. According to the dealership employee, "The credit warning said, 'Verify ID,' and we had ID." Apparently, the dealership didn't notice (or didn't care) that the customer provided the ID of a person of a different race, gender, and age—the ID showed a person nearly 30 years older than the customer presenting the ID.

Either way, the dealership's actions surely did catch the attention of the county district attorney's office. The report quotes the district attorney's office as saying, "When [dealers] sit and watch a piece of their property walk out the door, we have to go find it...[and] the taxpayers have to pay for it." As a consequence, the district attorney's office is planning to ask a judge to forfeit the car to the county to help pay the expenses for locating cars bought by identity thieves. The report also notes that the district attorney has informed the Texas Auto Dealer's Association that he plans to do the same in similar cases.

We don't know whether such a move by the DA would succeed, but no dealership wants to have to go to court to defend something like this.

As for the identity thief, his luck ran out and he got snagged when he tried to use the stolen identity to purchase a vehicle at another dealership, which actually did its job and acted on the red flags.

What to do When the Exterminator Comes Knocking (and Other Things to Train Your Employees)

January/February 2007

By Emily Marlow Beck

I've got a confession to make. I love watching those TV exposé shows. You know, the ones with secret cameras that impose a form of vigilante justice by blasting businesses' mishaps all over the Channel 8 News?

I saw one lately that really blew me away. Fortunately, the piece wasn't about car dealers (phew!), but it just as easily could have been.

In this little ditty, a crack team of bandits for hire was tasked with robbing a bank. These crooks weren't hired to snatch gold or money. Instead, the thieves were told to steal as much personal information as possible without getting caught. They pulled it off without breaking a sweat.

These crooks didn't use any fancy-schmancy, code-cracking computers or any James Bond-like tricks. Instead, dressed like exterminators, they told the employees at the door that they were responding to a call about critters in the building. The bank employees promptly escorted the "exterminators" to the file room, where they were left unattended with as much personal account information as you could imagine. And, if that wasn't enough, they pulled the same trick in multiple banks in town.

Most of the bank managers responded to the news outfit by talking about the top of the line, technologically advanced security features they employed at their branches, and their strong commitment to customer privacy. I have no doubt that these banks took strong measures to take a stand against identity theft and spent gobs of money to protect customer information. What I'm not so sure about is whether they trained their employees.

How do I know? This is the type of thing I have seen many times when I show up at a dealership to do a dealer audit. You'd be surprised how many times dealership employees don't ask any questions or bring me to the attention of their manager and just let me go about digging through personal information. If, after I have rummaged through the deal files, I ask the employee why he or she didn't stop me from digging, the employee usually says something like, "Well, I wasn't sure exactly who you were and what you were doing, and I didn't want to ask," or "You were wearing a suit and looked like you knew what you were doing, so I didn't say anything." (Apparently, people dressed like exterminators and lawyers can go anywhere and do anything they want—and please, no jokes about exterminating lawyers.)

Here's the deal. You may have your dealership's safeguarding policy tattooed to your forehead. You may be able to sing your state-specific data breach law to the tune of Yankee Doodle. And, you may have the tentative federal Red Flag Rules at your bedside for your nighttime reading enjoyment. But, all of these things don't mean squat if you don't train your employees on how to carry out the policies and rules' requirements.

Your employees will be on the front lines and making the day-to-day decisions that will determine exactly how safe your customers' non-public personal information is in your dealership. You should equip them with the training and tools to help them do their job.

For example, consider training your employees to ask for credentials and to check with a designated person before permitting any vendors or service providers to roam through sensitive areas of the dealership. Inform employees of the types of things to look for, and instruct employees to alert the safeguards coordinator (or similar person) if something seems out of place.

Don't limit this sort of training to vendor access to customer files. Consider helping your sales and finance employees stay up on the latest and greatest identify theft and fraud schemes floating around out there so that they know how to avoid being duped when making day-to-day decisions. Also, consider conducting periodic self-tests to see how well your internal policies and procedures are holding up, and make adjustments as necessary.

After all, you'd feel awful silly if you had to tell those TV reporters about how much money you spent developing privacy policies and procedures, but that you forgot to train your employees on what to do.

Chapter 6

Unfair and Deceptive Acts and Practices (UDAP) and Fraud

Dog may be man's best friend, but a plaintiff's lawyer's best friend is a special kind of law, found in most states, which does two things:

- It *prohibits* "unfair and deceptive acts and practices" by retailers and others.
- It *permits* consumers—and sometimes even consumers who have suffered no injury—to sue for these so-called "UDAP" violations.

Plaintiffs' lawyers love UDAP laws for several reasons. First, they impose fuzzy and subjective standards of deceptiveness and unfairness that usually will permit very broad allegations by a plaintiff to withstand a defendant's motions to dismiss. Also, the UDAP laws usually permit the recovery of attorneys' fees for the plaintiff. Because the attorneys' fees in these cases often dwarf the actual damages recovered by the consumer, and because there is no required relationship in most of these laws between the amount of the consumer's damages and the attorneys' fees award, the attorneys' fees awards alone can be staggering. Finally, most UDAP laws permit a successful plaintiff to recover a multiple of two or three times his or her actual damages.

Then, too, UDAP laws are adaptable. For instance, a Florida lawyer sued a dealer on behalf of his client, alleging that the dealer violated the FTC's Used Car Rule. That's really interesting, because there is no so-called "private cause of action" under that rule or the law it implements; in other words, a private plaintiff cannot sue for a violation of the Rule. Only the FTC may do so.

No problem, says this plaintiffs' lawyer. "You, Mr. Dealer, had an obligation to comply with a federal law, and you failed to do so. Your failure to comply with your *federal* law obligations constitutes an unfair or deceptive practice under our *state* UDAP law."

This plaintiffs' lawyer bootstrapped his way into a state claim based on a federal law violation. Look for more claims like this one.

Court Upholds $500,000 Award for Dealer 'Reprehensible Conduct'

January/February 2006

By Teresa Rohwedder and Emily Marlow Beck

Frank and Shelly Krysa visited Payne's Car Company, a used car dealership owned and operated by Emmet and Terri Payne, to buy a dependable truck that had room for their family and could tow at least 8,000 pounds. After a couple of visits to the dealership, the Krysas noticed a 1991 Ford F-350 extended cab truck, its engine running, at the back of the dealership lot. When asked why the engine was running, the salesman said the battery was recharging. The salesman told the Krysas that the truck was in perfect shape and that it would have no problem pulling an 8,000-pound load.

Upon opening the hood, the Krysas noticed that it was a different color than the rest of the truck. The salesman said the hood color was different, because the truck had recently been painted, and when the Krysas inquired as to the history of the vehicle, the salesman said the truck had been a "one-owner trade-in." The Krysas bought the vehicle, but, at the time, the dealership did not provide them with a title.

The Krysas quickly discovered many problems with the truck, such as inoperable power windows, poor towing capacity, a smashed radiator, a missing thermostat, and broken glass on the floor beneath the seats. At one point, it took the vehicle three hours to start. The Krysas obtained a *CARFAX* report for the truck and learned that the vehicle had 13 prior owners. Armed with the *CARFAX* report, the Krysas returned to the dealership, where Emmet Payne acknowledged the problems but offered only to provide the Krysas a credit toward the purchase of a different vehicle on the lot.

The Krysas hired an automotive expert who quickly discovered that the truck was actually two vehicles that had been welded together. Upon the advice of the expert, the Krysas ceased driving the vehicle because of safety concerns. The Krysas sued the Paynes, asserting various claims of fraud and misrepresentation. Evidence at trial suggested that the dealership owners were aware of the prior damage to the truck and took active steps to mislead the Krysas as to its true condition. The jury awarded the Krysas $18,449 in compensatory damages and $500,000 in punitive damages. The trial court entered judgment in that amount, and the Paynes appealed.

The Paynes challenged the punitive damages as being constitutionally excessive, contending that the verdict was so grossly excessive as to violate their substantive right to due process. The Missouri Court of Appeals rejected this argument and affirmed the damages awarded by the trial court.

In considering the reasonableness of the punitive damage award, the appellate court considered the reprehensibility of the dealer's conduct (the most important factor), the disparity between the harm, or potential harm, suffered by the plaintiffs, the punitive damages award, and the difference between the punitive damages awarded by the jury and the civil penalties authorized or imposed in comparable cases. The appellate court observed that the dealer's conduct in this case could constitute grounds for discipline and result in suspension or revocation of its license, which could potentially be costlier than the jury's punitive damage award. Thus, the appellate court concluded the award was not out of line with potential civil sanctions. The ratio of punitive to actual damages in this case was approximately 27:1.

After carefully considering the factors above, the appellate court said it was "simply not left with the impression that the jury's award was grossly excessive," given the relatively small amount of actual damages awarded, the egregious nature of the defendants' acts, an established pattern of similar behavior by the defendants, their open refusal to alter their behavior, and the magnitude of the potential harm that could have resulted.

Krysa v. Payne, 2005 WL 3038853 (Mo. App. November 15, 2005).

Keep Your Eyes on the Prize

April 2006

By Maya Hill

Back when my dad had his Buick and Chevy stores, a prime focus was getting people in the door. One of the first lessons I learned in the business was that car dealers would do almost anything for an "up," that is, a customer who simply shows up. My dad, like most dealers, was always looking for ways to attract customers, and his favorite lure was the old-fashioned contest, or sweepstakes. With these events, the theory is, of course, you entice customers to come into your store for a chance to win this or that—this discount, or that gift. If you are lucky, they may drive up in their beat-up station wagon, but they'll drive away in their brand new Buick Lacrosse.

My favorite contest was the one where the dealership mails out 10,000 keys, each with a note explaining to the potential "up" that the key he has received might unlock the door of a brand new Pontiac Solstice parked in the showroom of the dealership. All the customer has to do is to come in and see if the key worked. Presto! People poured into the showroom, trying their keys, seeing shiny cars they liked on the way in, wondering if it was time to trade up, asking about financing, taking test drives—you get the idea.

Of course, there are a million other contests that dealers can, and have, utilized to get people in the door: hole-in-one, odometer match, guess how many in the jar, dice roll, Frisbee toss, even weather promotions, such as, "Buy a car during the promotional period in November, and if it snows on Christmas Day, receive a $5,000 rebate." Many dealers also used promotions or contests that take place outside of their dealership—running lotteries in shopping malls, or sponsoring basketball shootouts at the nearby courts for a chance to win a new car.

While a contest is a fun and innovative way to increase sales traffic, it is also a potential legal hazard if the promotion is run in violation of your state's unfair and deceptive acts and practices (UDAP) statute. State UDAP statutes come in one form or another in nearly every state; these statutes are modeled after Section (5)(a) of the Federal Trade Commission Act, which prohibits unfair or deceptive acts or practices. Do you know how these statutes may apply to the contests your dealership is running? Or are you running the risk of losing the compliance contest?

Generally speaking, an "unfairness" challenge will likely be raised by a regulatory agency, if the act or practice in question (1) causes or is likely to cause substantial injury to consumers; (2) cannot be reasonably avoided by consumers; and (3) is not outweighed by countervailing benefits to consumers or competition. A "deceptive" act or practice is a representation, omission, or practice that is likely to mislead consumers who are acting reasonably in the circumstances presented. To be unlawful, the representation, omission, or practice must be material; that is, it must be likely to affect a consumer's choice to buy or use the product. Usually, information about costs, benefits, or restrictions on the use or availability of a product or service is material.

The FTC defines a representation as deceptive if (1) it is not true; (2) it might imply something that's not true; or (3) it might be a statement that's unsubstantiated, such as performance claims for products. Keep in mind that UDAP statutes vary from state to state. You should check with local counsel to determine what acts and practices are covered, and which are excluded.

OK, fine. Let's say you have determined that your contests are legitimate. You are a good natured, honest dealer who wants to put nice people into nice cars, and you use contests to help you achieve that goal. Spot, our mascot, who seeks out bad guys, delinquent payers, and suspicious practitioners, likes that attitude. We consulted him; he likes games; he suggested we have one. A contest? we asked. Spot answered in his usual (unless napping), enthusiastic way. So, we agreed that Spot will describe a contest/promotion variety that dealers typically run, and you get to guess a UDAP violation that is likely attached to it. Spot will send everyone who answers correctly a new Chevrolet Malibu Maxx.[1] Here goes...

Contest/Promotion

The 10,000 keys described above.

[1] Disclosure: There is no such thing as a Chevrolet Malibu Maxx; contest expires March 31, 2006; there are no right answers; there are no winners; no implied warranties; contest rules and regulations subject to change without notice.

Possible Violation

You'd better be certain that one of those keys you mailed out actually does unlock a car door; otherwise, you may be in violation of a UDAP prohibition against using sham contests to gain sales leads. Such contests fail to offer the prizes and awards advertised. Another promotion variation occurs when a dealer is sponsoring a citywide treasure hunt, such as, "Stop in any number of times per week and get a clue," and the person who puts all the clues together wins a car. Be sure that your clues actually add up to win the hunt. Sending customers on a wild goose chase can wind up sending you to court.

Contest/Promotion

Putt a hole-in-one on the showroom floor, and qualify for "special financing," this Saturday only—in honor of the PGA kickoff. We'll even let you putt twice.

Possible Violation

If you don't disclose, for example, that the offer is contingent on the customer's passing a credit check after he makes the hole-in-one, you may be in violation of a UDAP provision prohibiting the offering of goods or services to a consumer without disclosing all conditions and limitations on the offer. Similarly, if your promotion involves winning a brand new GMC Envoy, and you fail to disclose that the customer is responsible for the tax, title, license and doc fees, you may have committed a violation.

Too easy? OK. Try this one. It's not really a contest, but it promotes your vehicle brand, which is, of course, a goal of advertising. You know that some people don't like car dealerships; they don't want to deal with car salespeople. So, no matter what you do in your store, you won't be able to reach them. So, you park a Cadillac Escalade in the parking lot of a popular mall with a sign that says, "For Sale. Call Steve, 410.555.5555." People see the car and start calling Steve. Now, Steve is your GSM, and that number is his home phone number. Steve negotiates the sale of the car over the phone. See anything wrong? Maybe not. After all, the car wasn't even sold in your dealership. Steve sold it out of a mall parking lot after hours, so the above UDAP rules don't apply, right? Wrong.

UDAP laws apply whenever and wherever your dealership is operating, and chances are if you're advertising something outside of the confines of your store, additional rules and regulations apply. In the above scenario, if you don't disclose to the customer that the car is being sold by the dealership, you may have committed a UDAP violation by selling the vehicle under false pretenses (you represented that it was Steve, not a dealership, who was selling the car). It might be seen as concealment of a material fact, deception, or fraud. Such was the situation in *Long v. Enterprise Motors, Inc.*, 2005 WL 2861034 (N.J. Super. November 2, 2005). In this case, the defendants, who owned a used car operation, represented to the plaintiff car buyer that they, as individuals, were selling the car. They never disclosed that the car was, in fact, inventory of a retail establishment. Many states impose additional rules governing off-premises advertising and promotion, and these rules are often found in unsuspecting places, such as state criminal codes and lottery rules and regulations.

Some readers might remember Chris Shields and Toyota of Portsmouth, where the dealer ran $200 coupons in the paper, and Shields collected 207 of them (that's $41,400 in coupons) to purchase a 2002 Toyota Sequoia. When he got to the dealership, Shields was told that there was a limit of one coupon per person. Noting that no such limitation was printed on the coupon, Shields contacted the Maine Attorney General's Office, consumer protection division. The dealer principal at Toyota of Portsmouth commented that there was nothing deceptive or misleading about the coupons, and that no reasonable person could possibly expect to piggyback coupons like that and walk away with a new car.

Thankfully, common sense prevailed on this one, and no action was taken by the Attorney General's office. Reportedly, an Assistant Attorney General in Maine told the dealer that Shields' case had "no legs to it at all." So things worked out for Toyota of Portsmouth, and we hope that in running future promotional coupons, dealers will be careful to print all relevant limitations, however commonsensical they may be, on the coupon.

In summary, before you advertise a contest or promotion ask yourself certain questions:

- Is there a possibility that the offer could mislead someone?
- Are all fees that are likely to be charged clearly disclosed?
- Are any limitations on the offer clearly disclosed?
- Does the offer reference any products or services that might not actually be available?

Of course, this list is not exhaustive, but it is intended to get you thinking about what to be on the lookout for when running contests or promotions. Perhaps, better yet, have your attorney check everything over to make sure you didn't miss anything.

So, go ahead—set up the casino tables, put your F&I manager in the dunk tank, send out those scratch-off discount coupons. But while you're busy counting the "ups," who will be taken in by your contests and promotions, don't forget to keep your eyes on the prize—and in this case, the prize is legal compliance.

'If We Don't Got Jalopies, We Got Nothin' To Sell'

May 2006

By Maya Hill

"We ain't sellin' cars-rolling junk—I got to get jalopies—What cut do you make on a new car? Get jalopies. I can sell 'em as fast as I get 'em—if I could only get a hundred jalopies. I don't care if they run or not."—John Steinbeck, *The Grapes of Wrath*

There's a scene in Steinbeck's *The Grapes of Wrath*, in which a depression-era car dealer is bemoaning the fact that he can't sell new cars and is calling for more junkers, because those are the cars he can sell. Sound familiar?

Steinbeck wasn't a car dealer, but he sure could think like one. We all know that dealers don't turn much of a profit by moving new cars off the lot—the real money is made in the used car shack. But if you're not careful about what you're selling, and how much you're selling it for, you may be setting yourself up for a potential lawsuit that could cost your dealership millions in restitution and even more in public image costs. Don't make the mistake of thinking that once that jalopy rolls off your lot, the deal is done. Just because you don't hold the paper doesn't mean you don't hold the liability.

J.D. Byrider of Louisville, a subsidiary of J.D Byrider Systems Inc., of Carmel, Indiana, recently agreed to pay more than $7 million—the largest settlement ever with an auto dealer in Kentucky history—to settle a lawsuit in which the Kentucky Attorney General accused the dealership of selling shoddy cars and trucks at exorbitant prices. How exorbitant, you ask? Try $7,935 for a 1995 Chevrolet Cavalier bought in 2002 with 80,192 miles, a vehicle, which the customer alleged, broke down within six miles of being driven off the lot. Other vehicles were found to have been sold for more than twice their book values.

The lawsuit accused the dealer of violating the state's Consumer Protection Act by falsely claiming that the vehicles were inspected prior to sale. The suit also alleged that Byrider and its finance company were forcing credit customers to buy life insurance and a $1,095 service warranty, and then illegally including those charges in the amount financed, for which some customers had to pay 24.9% interest.

Under the terms of the settlement, certain customers who bought vehicles between January 1, 2000, and December 31, 2005, were entitled to receive $500 from Byrider. Those who paid off their vehicles received a check for $500. Those who are still paying off their obligations received a $500 credit. Customers did not have to participate; if they felt they were entitled to more money, they could forego the settlement and hire an attorney. The settlement affected more than 14,000 customers.

In addition to restitution, J.D. Byrider Systems was obliged to comply with certain specific provisions regarding all future sales at any Byrider franchise or store in Kentucky. These requirements included: establishing maximum retail prices in writing for each vehicle disclosed upon inquiry by a customer; posting notices informing customers that credit insurance was voluntary and not a condition of extending credit, ensuring that the forms used in transactions complied with Truth in Lending and other state and federal laws, ensuring that implied warranties were not improperly disclaimed through an "As Is" clause, and ensuring that deductibles were not charged for repairs that would be covered under an implied warranty. The local franchise also agreed to inspect a specific list of items (a checklist of sorts) before selling a vehicle to ensure that the sale met the standards of the settlement. The dealer was required to provide the inspection report to the customer upon request.

Both J.D. Byrider Systems and J.D. Byrider of Louisville denied any wrongdoing and stated that the settlement was the most efficient way to resolve the issue and get back to business. J.D. Byrider Systems has since cancelled the local franchise, citing failure to meet a deadline to renew its contract as the reason.

If the list of requirements and restrictions arising from this settlement seems burdensome to you, you likely are not alone. The list is long, and at first glance it may seem as though compliance with this settlement would be difficult. But take a closer look. While no one should minimize the magnitude of this settlement or its far-reaching implications for dealers across the country, note that many of the settlement terms are reinforcing what is already required of dealers by federal and state law.

Let's be clear. We see nothing wrong with a dealer's turning a good profit on a used car—that's what good business people do. We see nothing wrong with a dealer's selling a car that's had work done, that needs work done now, or that will need some work done in the near future. But a dealership that sells cars at outrageous prices without providing the disclosures that dealers are required to make under a state's consumer protection statute or other laws runs the risk of incurring millions in restitution, legal fees, and image costs. In addition, such a practice is likely to create a feeding frenzy for plaintiffs' lawyers.

So go ahead. Get excited when auction day rolls around, or when a customer drives up in a trade-in that you know you can turn around in under three days. Take out your *Kelley* books and calculators and dream about the projected profit margins on those beauties—it's all part of the game. But think before you sell. If, like Steinbeck's car dealer, you don't care if your jalopies run or not, chances are, the people who buy them will.

CHAPTER 6

On the Lookout for Fraud

May 2006

By Emily Marlow Beck

I try my best to stay informed about the goings-on of dealers and dealer mischief. A couple of months ago, I typed in "car dealer fraud," and some similar search terms in "Google E-Mail Alerts." As part of this nifty program, Google e-mails me daily about any new information on the Internet that discusses dealer fraud.

I set this program up thinking that Google would pick up an occasional dealer fraud story here and there. To my dismay, my e-mail box has been flooded with recent news stories about dealer fraud. Fraud against customers, fraud against finance companies, fraud against the state—you name it, I read about it.

Take, for example, the case of a recent enforcement action brought against a car dealer in Vermont. According to an April news article from the *Burlington Free Press*, a dealer in Vermont recently agreed to settle consumer fraud charges brought by the Vermont Attorney General's Office to the tune of $90,000. This amount includes restitution to consumers and payments to the state.

And that was just for starters!

As if a $90,000 penalty didn't have enough sting, as part of the consent order, the dealer agreed to terminate his dealership and not to work in auto sales or financing in Vermont for seven years.

You might ask—what type of behavior would get an Attorney General worked up enough to ban a dealer from working in the car business for seven years?

The facts were a little thin, but the news article reported that the state Attorney General brought an enforcement action against the dealership for activities in violation of the Vermont Consumer Fraud Act. Investigations by the Attorney General's office turned up a bunch of allegedly naughty deeds.

For example, the investigations revealed that the dealership had, in numerous cases, failed to properly submit documents and fees to the Department of Motor Vehicles so that consumers would receive valid title to their vehicles. Also, the Attorney General's office claimed that the dealership provided false information, such as prices and other terms, to banks and finance companies when trying to assign installment contracts.

The dealer admitted that the dealership engaged in conduct that violated the Vermont Consumer Fraud Act. Now, he's stuck with paying a big fine and looking for a new job.

While the Vermont dealer learned that fraudulent behavior could certainly earn a visit from the state's Attorney General, an Oklahoma dealership recently learned that fraudulent deeds could attract a civil lawsuit as well.

According to a recent article from the *CNHI News Service*, a used car dealership in Oklahoma was on the receiving end of a civil lawsuit filed last month by a disgruntled customer and an angry credit union for more than $500,000 in damages. The credit union allegedly discovered that the dealer was "power booking" deals by misrepresenting the value of the purchased collateral to the finance company.

The credit union's lawyer described "power booking" like this: If a customer chooses a plain-Jane car worth $12,000, the dealership would submit a buyers order and description of the vehicle to the credit union that showed a fully-loaded car, worth $18,000. The credit union would then cut a check to the dealership for $18,000, and the dealership would pocket the extra $6,000. The petition alleged that the credit union elected to finance some 400 vehicles purchased at the dealership, basing its credit decisions on representations made by the dealership. The credit union discovered that many of the booking sheets were materially false, and, if the accurate valuation/description had been provided, the credit union would not have financed these transactions According to the news article, the dealer denied any wrongdoing.

Keep in mind that much of what is recited above came from an AG's press release or a plaintiff's as-yet-unproven allegations in a complaint. But if the alleged facts are true, there's a lot more that I would like to know about the two cases above. For example, were these acts performed at the hands of the dealers, or by dealership employees? Did the dealers know this stuff was going on? Were they asleep at the switch? Or, did they turn a blind eye?

I also would like to know what, if any, active steps the dealers took to prevent fraudulent behavior in their shops. Did they develop any written policies to address fraud? Did they require any sort of compliance or ethics training for their employees? Did they periodically audit their own deals to look for signs of fraud? Or, did they ever hire auditors to detect fraud in their dealerships? If they knew about fraud at the hands of their dealership employees, what steps did they take to remedy the problem?

Correct answers to the questions above could have seriously reduced the risk of dealership fraud, and could have put the dealership in a much better position in the event fraud occurred at the hands of a rogue employee.

So, maybe it's time to do a little investigative work and see what's really going on in your dealership. Or you might just be the featured story in the next news article I read on the Internet about fraud.

Car Buyer—No Damages— Hits Dealer for $30,000 Attorney Bill

May 2006

By Thomas B. Hudson

OK, Tom, let me get this straight...A car buyer sues a dealer because the car she bought as "new" turns out to be a demo with 9,800 miles on it. However, at trial, the jury finds that the buyer paid fair market value for the car, so she's unable to show that she suffered a loss. Despite what looks like a win for the dealer, the dealer gets whacked for nearly $30,000 for the buyer's legal fees. Whazzup with that?

Welcome to the world of state consumer fraud acts, sometimes called "Unfair and Deceptive Acts and Practices" or "UDAP" laws. UDAP claims can arise anywhere in the dealership—sales, servicing, or parts. UDAP laws are some of the most powerful weapons that plaintiffs' lawyers can wield, and the following case illustrates that point very well.

Zefkiser Sema bought a 2000 Nissan Altima automobile from Automall 46, Inc. According to the complaint Sema later filed against the dealership, the Automall salesperson told her the car was "new" and had been driven only 10 miles. All of the documents in connection with the sale confirmed the vehicle as being "new" with 10 miles on the odometer. Sema paid $17,600 for the car. In her lawsuit, Sema claimed breach of contract, violation of the New Jersey Consumer Fraud Act, and violation of the federal Odometer Act.

At trial, Automall conceded that the car was used as a demo and had been driven approximately 9,800 miles. The trial court told the jury that the measure of damages was the difference between the price Sema paid for the car and the retail value of the car with the excess mileage. Sema's expert testified that the value of the car with the additional mileage was $14,800. The defense expert testified that the value of the car with the additional mileage was between $17,700 and $18,300.

The jury found against Automall on all three claims. However, the jury concluded that Sema paid fair market value for the car even with the extra mileage. Thus, the court concluded that Sema failed to prove that she suffered an "ascertainable loss." Despite this failure, the trial court awarded Sema attorney's fees under the CFA in the amount of $28,153. The trial court concluded that the adverse jury finding on the ascertainable loss issue did not bar Sema from recovering her attorney's fees.

The trial court denied Automall's post-trial motions, and Automall appealed. The Superior Court of New Jersey, Appellate Division, affirmed the trial court's decision. So long as the plaintiff shows a "*bona fide* claim of ascertainable loss" related to a CFA violation, the appellate court said, then, even if the plaintiff ultimately loses on the damages claim (but the jury finds a CFA violation), the plaintiff will be entitled to an award of attorney's fees. The appellate court rejected Automall's claim that it was entitled to attorney's fees based on its offer of judgment. Sema rejected.

So there you have it. The jury found that the dealer violated the CFA; so, damages or no damages, Sema gets her $30,000 in attorney's fees. Sema gets nothing; the dealer, required to pay its own lawyer and Sema's lawyer, gets a lot less than nothing; and Sema's lawyer gets nearly 30 big ones.

Is this a great country, or what?

Sema v. Automall 46 Inc., 2005 WL 3881264 (N.J. Super. App. Div. March 24, 2006).

'Strange As It Seems...'

June 2006

By Thomas B. Hudson

One of the most startling lines in rock & roll music, in my humble opinion, is from the Cornelius Brothers and Sister Rose. In their 1971 hit, "Treat Her Like a Lady," the lead singer intones the following head scratcher: *"Strange as it seems, you know you can't treat a woman mean."* Every time I heard that one, my reaction was, "Well, duh."

The line came to mind as I was reading an account in the *Carolina News Wheel* (the Carolinas Independent Automobile Dealers Association's newsletter) of a North Carolina dealer who got tagged by a jury for $500,000 in punitive damages. A number that large—big enough to put a lot of smaller dealers out of business—always gets my attention.

What had this hapless dealer done to incur the jury's wrath? Well, according to the *Wheel*, the facts were as follows.

East Coast Imports sold a 1993 Saturn to the unnamed customer for $1,900. The customer was told that the car had 77,000 miles on the clock at the time of the sale. A DMV License and Theft Inspector determined that the mileage was a tad understated. Seems the Saturn actually had 226,000 miles on it (a rounding error, no doubt). To add insult to injury, the Inspector also determined that the car was a 1992 model, rather than a 1993. And to put a cherry on top, the Inspector found that the car had been sold to East Coast Imports by a Maryland auction as a "parts only" car. These are things that those in the detective business call "clues."

Not surprisingly, "the customer" quickly became "the plaintiff," suing for VIN fraud, failure to disclose, and some other stuff. The jury, evidently steamed by the dealership's actions, returned a punitive damages award against the dealership and its owners for $500,000. The *Wheel* reported that the trial judge cut the punitive damages award to $250,000 to comply with North Carolina's statutory cap on punitive damages. That's an improvement for the dealership, but I hear that in most parts of North and South Carolina (and all over Georgia, as Daddy would say), $250,000 is still real money.

Note that in a state without a cap on punitive damages, the dealer's pain here would have been quite a bit worse. Whether such a cap applies in your state might be a handy little thing to know.

It's difficult to believe that the dealership acted innocently here, but I wasn't at the trial and didn't hear the testimony, so I suppose there's some remote possibility that the dealership didn't intentionally do bad. However, for a jury to award $250,000 in punitive damages, it's almost certain that the jury concluded that the dealer was engaging in some pretty reprehensible conduct. That kind of hammer blow isn't usually directed at a dealer who makes some technical disclosure error.

And $250,000 was the reported amount just for punitive damages. Chances are the plaintiff also recovered his actual damages (probably not a lot of money, considering it was a $1,900 car). Depending on the laws under which the suit was brought, it's possible that the plaintiff was also awarded his attorney's fees and costs of suit. And the dealership was on the hook for its own lawyer's bill too.

All of which makes me want to do a remake of that song, changing the words just a little. I can hear it now, *"Strange as it seems, you can't treat a customer mean."*

This is a lesson that some dealers never seem to learn. If you treat a customer in a way that you wouldn't want a jury (or your Mama) to hear about, you're just asking for trouble.

Bad Apples in Your Apple Bin? What's a Dealer to Do?

July 2006

By Thomas B. Hudson

The Associated Press reported on June 24 that a former North Carolina auto dealer and ten of his employees were sentenced for their roles over several years in connection with fraudulent "loans" (we're sure that the AP meant to call these transactions "credit contracts" and not "loans") that cheated "lenders" (again, probably "sales finance companies") and stuck some customers with inflated vehicle payments they couldn't meet.

According to the AP's report, prosecutors claimed that the dealer, who owned and operated three auto malls, used widespread corrupt practices. Specifically, the dealer was accused of using his laptop computer to generate false pay stubs, Social Security benefits letters, tax returns and other documents that could be used to support a buyer's inflated claims about a buyer's income. He also sold fake documents to co-workers preparing "loan" applications, prosecutors said. He charged $25 for a false pay stub and $100 for two year's worth of faked tax returns, according to the indictment. Sometimes the car buyers knew about the fraud, sometimes they didn't. When the buyers wouldn't themselves engage in the fraud, the dealership employees simply forged the buyers' signatures and went on with the sales.

The dealer got three years in the federal pen, while the former General Manager got a two-year stretch. The remaining nine employees' sentences ranged from a year's probation to 366 days in prison. Each of the eleven was ordered to pay restitution of $1.5 million.

The prosecutor did some crowing about the result, stating that it should serve as a warning to the auto industry to clean up its act. That's a cheap shot, in my opinion, unless the prosecutor has evidence that the practices of this dealer and his employees are typical of the practices of dealers as a whole.

I don't believe that is the case. I do believe, though, that the manufacture and use of fake documents does happen at some dealerships. While most people who work at dealerships are professional and ethical, there's a very low "barrier to entry" to people who want to work for car dealers. Educational requirements aren't that high, and sometimes the background checks aren't what they should be. So, some folks of marginal and sub-marginal integrity can end up in positions in which they can engage in bad acts like those described by the AP in this case.

Assuming that top management isn't involved in bad acts, as was the case here, how can a dealership protect itself against bad apples in the F&I room? I can think of four ways:

- First, dealers may want to consider using mystery shoppers to see if dealership employees are urging customers to engage in fraud and to see how dealership employees portray the credit credentials presented by the mystery shoppers to the sales finance companies.
- Auditing will really help, as well; that is, carefully examining credit documents in customers' files, contacting customers after the deal has closed, and finding out how the customer's information provided to the F&I department differed, if at all, from the information provided by the F&I folks to the sales finance company. You can pay someone to do this, but if you are budget-minded, you can do it yourself.
- Videotaping F&I proceedings will make it very difficult for some aspects of these frauds to be carried out.

- Last, but never least, serious training is in order. If everyone in the dealership knows that he or she could go to jail and have to pay restitution to customers and finance companies that might—just might—keep some employees from getting caught up in these activities.

Are you certain that shenanigans like these are not happening at your shop? If not, perhaps it's time to consider what you can do to reduce the possibility that they are.

Scams for Sale: Dealers Watch Out for Rebate Promoters

November 2006

By Emily Marlow Beck

I read lots of juicy stories about the mishaps of car dealers. Some of these stories are about dealers who try to do the right thing, but just get caught in the crossfire. Other stories involve dealers who behave badly. And some stories, like the one below, involve dealers who are asleep at the switch.

Why do I say asleep at the switch? Read on.

An RV dealer in Washington may be in some hot water after hooking up with an organization called "CashBack America" and offering "deferred rebates" of $10,000 to its customers.

How did the rebate deal get the dealer in trouble? After all, rebates have been around for years, right?

For starters, the rebate offered by the dealer was only available to customers 54 months after the sale, and even then only if the customer completed a rigid, multiple-step rebate process. Depending on how and when the customer claimed his or her rebate, the customer, who was expecting a $10,000 rebate, might receive as little as nothing (yes, that's zip, zero, nada).

And as if that wasn't enough, the dealer allegedly made blatant false advertisements and misrepresentations to customers by deducting the rebate from the RV's bottom line price in advertisements. The dealer also allegedly told customers that they would receive a $10,000 rebate, knowing that they might not qualify for the rebate.

So, what does this RV dealer have to look forward to for his alleged dirty deeds? It is quite possible that someone, among all the folks who were promised a full $10,000 rebate, will file a class action lawsuit against the RV dealer. It is also very possible that the dealer may be forced to make good on all rebate offers, not to mention that the dealer may have earned himself or herself a friendly visit from the state Attorney General.

The Rebate Promoter

At this point you may ask, who is "CashBack America," and how does the "CashBack" program work? Based on information on its Web site, CashBack America is a "Sales Promotion Company" that works with various approved merchants and retailers. CashBack's participating vendors are required to provide each and every customer with a CashBack America voucher, which, depending upon the merchant, may be redeemable for hundreds or thousands of dollars. In all situations, the CashBack rebates are only available following the expiration of a 54-month waiting period, and only then if the customer redeems the voucher within a 30-day window.

The explanation CashBack uses as to how it can actually afford to pay these rebates is a term referred to as "slippage." The CashBack Web site describes "slippage" as the proportion of promotional vouchers that are never redeemed for all kinds of reasons. In other words, CashBack is banking on customers' forgetting to submit their vouchers. In fact, the CashBack

America brochure and Web page ask customers to take the "CASHBACK CHALLENGE," and states: "We believe you won't remember the date you made this purchase."

Based on information from the Massachusetts Attorney General's Web site, if roughly 15% of customers redeem CashBack rebate vouchers, CashBack will reduce rebates below the full rebate price. What makes matters worse is that if CashBack believes that the customer was reminded to file the claim for its rebate at any time and in any way, the claim becomes invalid and the customer gets nothing. *(Reminded by whom?)*

Now, you may wonder why I think this is a story of a dealer "asleep at the switch" and not a story of a dealer "behaving badly."

Blame it on my rose-colored glasses, but here are my thoughts. I have no first-hand knowledge on how, or why, this dealer chose to implement this rebate program. But, my guess is that CashBack's rebate program was one of many of the "latest and greatest" ways to "bring traffic and increase sales" that are so often hurled at car dealers. Odds are, when the dealer heard about a great program that could boost traffic in a slow time, the dealer took the bait. The dealer probably bought into the ol' line, "This program has worked for lots of other dealers," and jumped on board without doing any research.

What kind of research? For starters, did the dealer explore whether, under state law, a "rebate" could be offered by anyone other than the manufacturer? Or, did the dealer think about the potential unfair and deceptive trade practice liability (not to mention the public image damage) that could be caused by selling RVs to customers who, based on the representations of the dealer and CashBack, would overextend themselves to purchase vehicles, expecting to receive a $10,000 windfall in five and a half years? Or, did the dealer "Google" the company to learn that enforcement actions had been brought against it in multiple states?

I doubt it. But, one thing is clear—someone at the dealership level should have vetted this program.

Beware Those 'Unfair and Deceptive Acts and Practices' Laws

January/February 2007

By Thomas B. Hudson

The sharpest tool in the plaintiffs' lawyers' toolbox just got a little sharper.

Plaintiffs' lawyers really love state "unfair and deceptive acts and practices," or "UDAP" laws. And what's not to like? Most UDAP laws are pretty subjective in their application; there are lots of practices that can be alleged to be either "deceptive" or "unfair." Those fuzzy standards give the plaintiffs' lawyers a lot of maneuvering room.

But wait, there's more! Most UDAP laws permit a successful plaintiff to recover some multiple of his or her "actual" damages. So, the plaintiff gets to recover two or three times the amount of damages he or she can prove.

But what damages is the plaintiff entitled to recover, and to multiply by two or three? Is the plaintiff limited to "economic" damages, such as lost wages, or can he or she recover "noneconomic" damages such as those for "pain and suffering" and "mental distress?" That was the question in a recent Ohio case.

Craig Whitaker sued M.T. Automotive, Inc., doing business as Montrose Toyota, in connection with his unsuccessful attempt to lease a vehicle from Montrose. Whitaker sued Montrose for violating the Ohio Consumer Sales Practices Act (a UDAP-type law), and also brought several tort claims.

The trial court awarded Whitaker $105,000 in damages for the CSPA violations. The trial court then trebled the CSPA award to $315,000 and awarded attorneys' fees and expenses. (This represents still another reason why plaintiffs' lawyers like UDAP laws—a successful plaintiff can recover his or her attorney's fees and expenses.)

Montrose appealed the CSPA damage award, the treble damages award, and the attorneys' fee award to an intermediate appellate court, which found that Whitaker could not recover noneconomic damages under the CSPA and found insufficient evidence of economic loss. The court also reversed the attorneys' fee award and remanded the case in order for the trial court to determine the basis for that award.

Whitaker appealed to the Ohio Supreme Court, arguing that noneconomic damages should have been included in the damage award. The Supreme Court concluded that, in an Ohio CSPA action, "all forms of compensatory relief, including noneconomic damages, are included within the unrestricted term 'damages'" under the Act. The high court also concluded that any actual damages proven are subject to trebling under the Ohio CSPA. Finally, the high court concluded that Whitaker could recover for mental anguish or emotional distress under the CSPA.

I'm just guessing here, you understand, but my bet is that the dealer will be out-of-pocket to the tune of something pushing a million dollars by the time he pays the UDAP award to Whitaker, Whitaker's legal fees and expenses, and the legal fees and expenses for the dealer's own lawyers. It's no wonder that plaintiffs' lawyers love those UDAP laws.

Whitaker v. M.T. Automotive, Inc., 111 Ohio St.3d 177 (Ohio November 8, 2006).

Don't Misrepresent the Buyer's Income to the Finance Company

March 2007

By Thomas B. Hudson and Catherine C. Worthington

What happens when your dealership's F&I folks misrepresent a customer's credit qualifications to a bank or sales finance company? We've pointed out before that this type of conduct could violate federal and state criminal laws, subjecting those who engage in such conduct to jail time and monetary fines.

That's bad enough, but, as this case illustrates, such conduct can also expose the dealership to a civil lawsuit brought by the buyer. This case involves alleged violations of a Connecticut law. Even though you may live elsewhere, the case is worth reading, because almost every state has a similar law.

Priscilla Farlow went to Barbarino Brothers, Inc., to buy a car and discussed financing options with the manager of the dealership. According to Farlow, she unknowingly signed a credit application that was filled out by the manager. On the application, the manager misrepresented Farlow's annual income as $78,000, when she actually earned an hourly wage of $11.

Based on the information in the credit application, Wells Fargo Financial extended financing to Farlow, but eventually repossessed and sold the car when Farlow missed her monthly payments. Farlow was also responsible for the remaining deficiency after the sale of the car.

Later, Farlow sued Barbarino for violating the Connecticut Unfair Trade Practice Act as a result of its misrepresentation on the credit application and alleged slander of credit. Barbarino moved to strike both counts.

The Connecticut Superior Court first denied the motion to strike the CUTPA claim, finding that Farlow alleged sufficient facts to show that Barbarino's false misrepresentation of her income on her credit application proximately caused harm to her. The court noted that without the misrepresentations, Wells Fargo would not have extended credit to Farlow; therefore, she would not have sustained the financial injury upon repossession. "Since the purpose of the credit application is to determine what amount an applicant can afford to pay and whether the applicant is a viable candidate for an extension of credit of the amount requested, the damages sustained by [Farlow] are a reasonably foreseeable result of a monthly payment that is grossly disproportionate to [her] overall monthly income."

However, the court granted the motion to strike the slander of credit claim. Noting that slander of credit is not recognized as a cause of action in Connecticut, the court looked to other jurisdictions to determine whether Farlow pleaded sufficient facts to maintain such an action and found that she did not. Without recognizing a distinct cause of action for slander of credit, the court found that Farlow did not allege facts to show that Barbarino made a defamatory statement, thereby injuring her reputation to a third party.

If you were looking to illustrate the dangers of misrepresenting your customers' credit information to financing institutions, you'd be pressed to find a better example than this case. The law this dealership allegedly violated is a typical "unfair and deceptive acts and practices" law. Most states have such a law, and the laws are particular favorites of plaintiffs' lawyers. Why? Because they usually provide for a doubling or tripling of the plaintiff's damages and provide for an award of the plaintiff's attorney's fees as well.

These can be serious, big dollar cases...training your folks might be a good alternative to having them face charges like those encountered by this dealer's manager.

Farlow v. Barbarino Brothers, Inc., 2006 WL 3755219 (Conn. Super. December 1, 2006).

Chapter 7

'Doc' Fees

I have to tell you a funny story about document preparation fees, otherwise known as "doc fees." Right after I wrote one of the following articles grousing about dealer doc fees on the basis that they constituted "nickeling and diming" customers, a reader responded by buying our first book. After he'd gone through the process of ordering the book online, he had to e-mail me and rib me for our pricing—the book was $49.95, but there was an additional $5.95 "shipping and handling" charge.

I was busted. The best I could do was to point out—lamely—that those who bought the book at conferences and meetings, where we sold them, could avoid the charge, but I had to concede his point.

But doc fees, in general, aren't very funny. The practice offers a very "target-rich environment" for plaintiffs' lawyers. If dealers are not careful, they will find that their doc fee practices violate a host of laws: federal and state disclosure laws, usury laws, and advertising laws. What's more, they may even constitute the "unauthorized practice of law."

Because doc fees tend to be charged on all transactions, cases challenging those fees tend to be brought as class action suits, making them especially dangerous. All in all, if I were a dealer, I'd have to consider whether I wanted all of the aggravation involved with doc fees, if I could get rid of it by simply charging a little more for the car.

'Doc Prep Fees' Policies and Why You Need Them

September 2005

by Patricia E. M. Covington

A proposed class-action lawsuit settlement in Hawaii reminds us why dealers should consider carefully whether they should be charging doc fees and, if so, in what amounts.

Depending upon the state, and sometimes even among dealerships within a single state, these fees have many names—doc prep fees, document fees, doc fees, processing fees, transfer service fees, dealer administrative fees, and closing fees ("doc prep fees"). Whatever the name, doc fees are attractive targets to plaintiffs' lawyers, as a Honolulu dealership sadly learned.

In the class-action suit, Honolulu Ford, Inc., was sued for unfairly and deceptively charging license and documentation fees. The plaintiffs' lawyer claimed that the license and documentation fees were duplicative and unsubstantiated by the dealer's "processing costs." Honolulu Ford agreed to settle the class action to the tune of $1.6 million. At press time for this article, the court was considering the proposed settlement.

Under most states' law, doc prep fees fall into two categories: (1) those assessed by the dealer in connection with the retail sale (typical dealer doc prep fees); and (2) those assessed as part of, or incident to, the credit transaction. This article will consider typical dealer doc prep fees.

Generalities

In general, my review of the 50 states reveals the following broad-brush approaches to doc prep fees:

- Specific regulation of these fees in dealer laws or administrative rules, with one or more of the following requirements or limitations: a cap on the amount;

required disclosure in the transaction documents; required inclusion in the advertised price of the vehicle; required posting of signs regarding the charging of the fee; reasonableness of the amount assessed and some relation to the services actually provided; the customer's consent to the amount of the fee; and, in at least in one state, required negotiability of the amount of the fee.

- A prohibition on the charging of the fee either by statute, administrative rule, Attorney General, or regulator opinion (formal or informal).
- No specific dealer regulation of the fee, but the relevant credit or installment sales act speaks to the fee. The credit act requires either that the fee be separately disclosed or included in the finance charge.
- No specific dealer regulation of the fee, but the Attorney General or relevant regulator has opined that so long as the doc prep fee is charged by a dealer on both cash and credit transactions, and included in the cash price, it is permissible. The Attorney General or relevant regulator also may impose parameters on the charging of the fee (e.g., reasonableness of amount; relation to actual services provided; required disclosure in transaction documents; required inclusion in advertised price of the vehicle; required posting of signs regarding the charging of the fee; customer's consent to the fee, etc.).
- No specific dealer regulation of the fee nor any guidance from the Attorney General or relevant regulator.

Note that both the dealer act and relevant credit or installment sales act prohibit the charging of such a fee or only allow the charging of fees specifically itemized in these statutes.

Specifics

Given the general descriptions that apply to all states, specific dealers need to know what's happening in their own corner of the U.S. Where to start? First, look at your state's dealer laws and its installment and credit acts. See if these fees are specifically addressed. Next, look to your Attorney General and specific regulator to see if either has taken a position on the issue. For instance,

- In Alabama, the Attorney General has informally stated that anything over $150 is a violation of Alabama's unfair and deceptive practices act.
- In Massachusetts, according to an online resource regarding motor vehicle purchases, the Attorney General states, "There is no specific limit on how much a dealership can charge consumers for these [doc prep] services. The fee just has to be reasonable."
- In Alaska, the Attorney General issued a Business Advisory providing that dealer doc prep fees are "[i]n reality, ... merely additional payments to the dealer for services that are an essential part of the deal." *Business Advisory from the Fair Business Practices Section, Alaska Attorney General's Office, Re: New car price-comparison advertising and other related issues (January 11, 2000).*
- In Georgia, the Georgia Office of Consumer Affairs has taken the informal position that a vehicle's advertised price must represent the actual total purchase price of the vehicle, excluding only tax, tag, title and WRA (Warranty Rights Act) fees. Any additional fees or charges (e.g., doc prep fees, freight charges, transportation charges, destination charges, dealer preparation charges, etc.), and any required options must be included in the advertised

price. Alaska similarly takes the position that failure to include the doc prep fee in the advertised price of the vehicle is deceptive.

Other Laws

Sometimes doc fees can run afoul of other laws.

Beware: If you charge a fee only in credit transactions, it is deemed to be a finance charge under the federal Truth in Lending Act as well as many state laws and must be included in the calculation of the APR. If it's not included, you've committed a TILA violation—a potential claim on which plaintiffs' attorneys can capitalize. By inconsistently charging the fee, you could even end up on the wrong side of a discrimination lawsuit.

Beware: Applicable unfair and deceptive trade practices acts, both federal and state. The unfair and deceptive practices act aspect actually garners more attention from the state in relation to advertising practices; that is, whether or not the advertised sale price of the vehicle includes or discloses the doc prep fee. In those states where the Attorney General or regulator has taken a position that the doc prep fee is pure profit to the dealer, the fee must be included and disclosed in the advertised price of the vehicle. For instance, the Florida Unfair or Deceptive Acts or Practices Act provides, "The advertised price must include all fees or charges that the customer must pay, including freight or destination charge [and], dealer preparation." F.S.A. § 501.976(16).

Crafting Your Dealer Doc Fees

What specific items should you consider when crafting your dealership's position and policy on the charging of fees? To start, does state law allow a doc prep fee? If it does, are there any mandated amounts, caps, or requirement that the fee be substantiated? Does state law require that it be disclosed on purchase contracts or installment sale contracts? And if so, is there specific wording? Must it be included in the cash price or is there a requirement to separately itemize it? Is there any signage requirement or posting of a disclosure of the fee in the dealership? Are there any advertising restrictions? Does a dealer have to include the amount of the fee in the advertised price, or can a general disclaimer be placed at the bottom of the ad that additional fees may apply? Finally and fundamentally, are your doc fees reasonable?

Your policy should also address when the fee is charged and whether it can be waived. Remember, if there is inconsistent assessing of the fee, you can get into truth in lending trouble when the fee is frequently waived for cash transactions, but not for credit transactions.

Note that sometimes the relevant credit or installment sales act prohibits the charging of a doc prep fee in a finance transaction, because only those fees itemized in the relevant statute may be charged. So, if you charge these fees in credit transactions, you'll need to review your state's credit act. If your state law specifically regulates what can be financed, and the doc prep fee is not included in an itemized list of what's allowed, and dealer law or regulator opinion allows for the charging of the fee, then you'll have to include it in the cash price of the vehicle. If dealer law or regulator opinion does not allow for the fee, then it may not be permissible to charge the fee.

With regard to whether the amount is a finance charge and necessary to include in the APR calculation, you'll want to look at the definition of "finance charge" in the TILA and in your state's relevant credit act. Generally, so long as the charge is assessed in both cash and credit transactions, it is not a finance charge. In Massachusetts, the Division of Banks has stated that the doc prep fee is not a finance charge and not subject to its credit act.

Massachusetts Division of Banks, Opinion No. 03-127.

Which reminds me, if your state requires that the fee be substantiated, it's best not to include the preparation and/or services performed to finance the sale. Again, that's because it could be deemed a finance charge under TILA.

Caps and Reasonableness

As noted earlier, another matter to consider is the reasonableness of the fee. If your state regulates the amount of the fee, that could be an easy putt. For instance, caps are placed on the maximum amount of doc prep fees that may be charged in the states of California, Illinois, Maryland, Michigan, Minnesota, Oregon, Rhode Island, South Carolina, Texas, West Virginia, and Wisconsin. Be aware, however, that although a state may permit a fee of "$XX" or "up to $XX," a plaintiff could still argue that the fee is unreasonable given the amount of work involved. If your state doesn't cap the fee, then you'll need to look at whether your Attorney General or regulator has commented on the issue. In Indiana, Iowa, Kansas, Montana, Pennsylvania, Washington and Wisconsin, the Attorney General or regulator has taken a position that the fee must be reasonable and/or reflective of the services performed.

If the amount of the fee needs to be substantiated, then you'll need to consider what services or costs are included in determining the amount of the fee. If your state's law, Attorney General, or regulator requires substantiation of the fee, take a look at Wisconsin and Maryland's doc prep fee statutes and interpretive materials. They both give a laundry list of items that a dealer does in consummating a sale. California's statute can also be helpful.

Then, there are "unfair and deceptive acts and practices" considerations. If a fee is labeled a "doc prep fee" or something similar, it may give an impression to the consumer that the fee is somehow covering the preparation of documents or processing of paperwork, or even worse, that it's a fee paid to state officials. If the fee is pure dealer profit and isn't related to or is not meant to cover any of these items, a consumer could claim that the fee is "deceptive" because its label doesn't accurately describe what it actually represents. What you call the fee implics to the consumer what they are paying for.

Worries

So, what should be on your "worries" list?

To start, statutory or punitive damages under your unfair and deceptive practices act—that's the first thing. Also, attorney's fees are generally recoverable under unfair and deceptive practice act claims. In states that regulate doc prep fees, the law may dictate penalties. Bad press, erosion of consumer confidence, and trust are of constant concern. As a dealer, you know that the business is all about relationships. Finally, you don't want the tax collector coming after you. In some states, the fee may be taxable. If so, you need to determine whether you or the consumer is responsible for paying the tax, collect it, and then you'll have to remit it to the proper state authority.

In addition to consumers, class action lawyers, Attorneys General and regulators, your finance companies may also be concerned with these fees. As discussed, state law may require disclosure of the fee, and your finance company may have a policy on whether the fee can be financed and, if so, how much can be financed. Review your dealer agreement, program materials, and bulletins to see if the fees, or similar ones, are addressed.

Say it Again, Sam

In summary, do your homework on doc fees. Understand your state's position on doc prep fees; examine your dealership's practices (charging of the fee, amount of the fee, disclosing of the fee, waiving of the fee, posting of the fee, advertising of the fee, taxing of the fee, etc.); and develop a standard policy on the matter. Don't overreach. Be fair about the amount you charge consumers. Don't forget to publish that policy, and communicate it to all employees, particularly those who interact with customers. Employees need to understand the fee to accurately describe it to your customers, because, even if you do everything right, it will likely be a "he said, she said" boxing match at your local court if you get sued.

We've said it before; we'll say it again. When in doubt, consult your lawyer or call your local ADA or IADA. They'll likely be informed on the issue. Good luck!

Doc Fees Make Mainstream News

November 2006

By Emily Marlow Beck

You've heard Spot barking over the years about dealership practices and policies surrounding document prep fees. So, it came as no real surprise to us when the *Wall Street Journal* picked up on this topic in early October.

According to the *Journal*, states are increasingly passing laws that permit dealers to up the fees they charge for preparing and processing the paperwork involved in a car deal. Citing estimates provided by automobile club AAA, the *Journal* claims that the average doc fee in 30 or so states is 400 to 700 bucks a deal.

Better yet, the *Journal* article tells us that these fees run as high as $900 (gulp!) in some states.

Many state laws have reflected this trend. The *Journal* reported that a new law in Ohio bumps the permissible fee up from $100 to as much as $250. Also, in recent years, limits on paperwork-processing fees have been raised, or set, in Michigan, Washington, and Maryland.

So, why the rise in these fees? The *Journal* article was quick to point out that in many instances dealers are looking to doc fees as an additional revenue source in light of slipping profit margins in car sales. Citing numbers provided by the NADA, the *Journal* reported that net profit on an average car deal was $60 last year—down from $172 in 2004. According to the article, doc fees are a way for dealers to squeeze an extra dime or two out of a deal.

But, dealers claim that they've had to bump the fee to compensate for the increased costs of compliance with federal and state laws (think Gramm-Leach-Bliley, OFAC, etc.) and to cover the time and manpower needed to process tag and title documents.

Either way, one thing is clear—dealer practices of charging doc fees are, at the moment, under a microscope. If you don't believe me, just look to Arkansas and Florida, where the *Journal* reports that class action lawsuits against dealers for dealer fees are pending.

So, what lessons should dealers take from all this?

First, dealers should make sure they understand their state laws. If laws have changed, dealers may need to make some changes to their forms and procedures to comply. They should pay close attention to any disclosure requirements or limits on what particular costs the fee can represent. They should consider whether state advertising laws require them to disclose any such fees. And, let's not forget to state the obvious: State law may permit dealers to charge a higher fee, and they just may not want to leave that money on the table.

But, dealers shouldn't stop there. Even if a dealership charges a doc fee that is within permissible state law limits, certain dealer practices could implicate federal law issues. For example, does the dealership charge the same fee to all customers? If the answer is no, that's a red flag. It might be worth your doing a little homework on the issue.

Maybe it's time to talk to your state dealer association. Or, consider giving your lawyer a call. After all, if you're the dealer charging $900 in doc fees per deal, odds are you can afford it.

Another Reason to Dislike Doc Fees

March 2007

By Thomas B. Hudson

I hate doc fees for the same reason I hate it when a hotel charges for local calls or when a mechanic tags onto my repair bill another $30 for "shop supplies." I'm sorry. Those items should be overhead—not nickel and dime additional charges—to a customer, who is paying a substantial sum for the room or the repair.

And when I pay $20,000 or $25,000 for a car, I don't want to be dinged for another $99, or $199, or whatever, for a doc fee. My reaction is, if I can't buy the car without paying it, it's part of the price of the car.

That describes my reaction to doc fees as a consumer. As a lawyer, I have a couple of additional observations.

First, dealers in several states are charging doc fees without a clear statutory basis for doing so. A couple of years ago, a client complained that we had answered a doc fee question for his state incorrectly—we had said that there was no authority to charge the fee. The client complained that "everyone was doing it," so it had to be legal. We hear that a lot.

But since (believe it or not) we occasionally make mistakes, I asked one of our lawyers to revisit our answer. When his research confirmed that we could find no basis for charging a doc fee, he started nosing around, and eventually called the state auto dealers association. The ADA reported that, yes, most dealers charged a doc fee, and that they were doing so, because the Attorney General had stated that he would not prosecute any dealer charging a doc fee, as long as it was below a certain dollar amount.

Now, where I'm from, "legal" and "I won't prosecute you," are two entirely different things. It may well be that dealers won't be on the pointy end of an AG enforcement action as long as they stay below whatever magic number the AG approves, but they will still be exposed to individual and class action civil suits by plaintiffs' lawyers who contend there's no legal basis for the charge.

Second, customers tend to get annoyed by the "nickeling and diming," and when they get annoyed, they look for reasons to challenge the dealer's actions. The doc fee can provide such a reason, so it increases the dealer's risk of litigation, especially in those states where there is no clear authorization for it.

Plaintiffs' lawyers can get very inventive when they challenge dealers' practices. A recent case dealing with doc fees shows just how inventive they can be.

An Arkansas dealer was hauled into court by a plaintiff's lawyer who contended, among other things, that a dealer who charged a fee (even though expressly permitted by law) for completing legal documents such as the retail installment sale contract, disclosure statements and buyers order, was engaged in the unauthorized practice of law.

Say what? Arkansas, like most states, doesn't want just any ol' body practicing law, so they have a law saying that you can't do legal stuff without a license. The plaintiff's lawyer argued that filling in the blanks on standard car purchase and finance forms and charging for it was lawyering without a license as prohibited by the statute, and the court agreed.

The decision is by a trial court, and we understand is not controlling, even for other trial courts, and we are told that the decision may be appealed. We also understand that there's a bill pending in the legislature that will finesse the issue and permit a doc fee in some amount. So doc fees in Arkansas aren't history—yet.

*[**Editor's note:** The Arkansas legislature enacted a fix for his problem. We'll see if it holds up.]*

We've warned you before that the plaintiffs' lawyers have an electronic grapevine that permits stuff like this to get around instantly. Watch for this theory to pop up in other states.

Palasack v. Asbury Automotive Group, Inc., CIV No. 2002-012712 (Circuit Court of Pulaski County, Ark. November 20, 2006).

Thoughts from Vegas

March 2007

By Thomas B. Hudson

Three thoughts from Vegas, where the 2007 National Auto Dealers Association annual meeting has come and gone.

Thought 1

The Vegas strip is what you would get if the Trailer Trash Army took over the electric utility company.

Thought 2

I stayed in a pricey hotel. OK, I was there on a group rate, so it wasn't as pricey as it usually is, but it was pricey. It was the sort of place that calls its customers "guests," and trains its staff to make the "guests" feel at home and pampered. But when I reached for the phone to make a local call, I noticed a sign near the phone that said local calls were $1.

Now, I don't know how it is at your house, but Lily Grace and I don't charge our guests for phone calls. Perhaps we should—it would make the 12-wide a little easier to pay for.

Thought 3

You were wondering when I was going to get to some car stuff. Here it is.

I was the keynote speaker for the National Association of Motor Vehicle Boards and Administrators, and after the planned part of my talk, we had a Q&A session. One of the questions dealt with document fees; the questioner wanted to know what I thought of charging doc fees when the state statute was silent on the topic.

I first pointed out some basics, such as the warning that doc fees should be the same for cash deals and for financed deals. A doc fee charge should never include a charge for preparation of any of the financing or lien perfection documents. If a dealer charges more for doc fees in a financed deal than in a cash deal, the difference is a finance charge for federal Truth in Lending purposes. Thus, the charge must be disclosed as such, must be part of the calculation to determine the APR, and may have to be treated as a prepaid finance charge in the retail installment contract's itemization of amount financed.

I then turned to the question actually asked. I explained that while federal law dictated the way that doc fees had to be disclosed, the *amount* of the doc fee charge was a matter of state law.

So, what's the maximum amount a dealer can charge when the state retail installment sales act and motor vehicle laws are silent on the issue? That depends. (Did I tell you that I went to law school for four years—OK, I admit it, I went to the evening division at Georgetown, and it takes four years—not three—so I could say, "That depends?")

State laws are set up in different ways. Some state laws essentially say, "You can charge any fees and charges not prohibited by this law." Call these Permissive Laws. Other state laws say, "You can charge only the fees and charges set forth in this law." Call these Prohibitive Laws. Still other state laws don't have a clear philosophy one way, or the other. Call these Muddled Laws.

In a state with a Permissive Law, you can probably charge a document fee in a reasonable amount. In a state with a Prohibitive Law, unless you can find express permission in the law for a doc fee, you are out of luck. The states with Muddled Laws are a crapshoot. Which gets me back to the $1 phone calls.

In my view, charging a $45 doc fee in connection with the sale of a $20,000, $30,000 or $40,000 car is nickeling and diming the customer. If the state law clearly lets you charge the fee, then there's little risk in doing so. I guess, if I were a dealer, I'd probably charge it.

But if there's risk involved—if you are in a state with a Muddled Law—why take that risk? Why not simply charge $45 more for the car (remember, you need to charge the additional $45 on both cash and credit deals)? You come out with the same number of dollars, and you completely eliminate the risk that some class action plaintiffs' lawyer will get you in his or her gun sights.

This analysis isn't limited to doc fees, by the way. Dealers regularly charge a variety of fees, and some of them are not clearly permitted by the laws under which the dealer operates. The dealer's choice is clear: He or she can charge the customer for the fee as a separate line item, or could, instead, charge an equivalent additional amount for the car. The first adds a risk to the transaction; the second eliminates it.

A Doc Fee by Any Other Name is Still a Doc Fee

May 2007

By Shelley B. Fowler and Alicia H. Tortarolo

In his March 2007 article, "Another Reason to Dislike Doc Fees," Tom Hudson mentioned that an Arkansas court had decided that when a dealer completed documents such as the retail installment sale contract, disclosure statements and buyers order, and subsequently charged the buyer a documentary fee for those services, the dealer was engaged in the unauthorized practice of law. Tom noted in that article a bill was pending in the Arkansas legislature to "finesse the issue and permit a doc fee in some amount."

Well, on March 19, the Arkansas Governor signed into law House Bill 1718, which had been introduced less than a month earlier, and which became effective on the date the Governor signed it. The bill repeals the Arkansas Code sections which allowed new and used motor vehicle dealers to charge a documentary fee for "preparing, handling, and processing documents relating to, and closing a retail installment transaction involving" a motor vehicle. That fee was required to be charged to all purchasers, disclosed on the buyers order as a separate itemized charge, and accompanied on all written documentation by a conspicuous notice that the fee is not an official fee, is not required by law, and may be charged for handling documents and performing services relating to the closing of a vehicle sale.

In place of those sections, the bill, now known as Act 366, adds provisions allowing a dealer to fill in the blanks on standardized forms in connection with the sale or lease of a new or used vehicle, if the dealer does not charge the buyer or lessee for the service of filling in the blanks, or otherwise charge for preparing documents. In place of the previously allowed documentary fee, the new law allows dealers to charge a "service and handling fee" for the handling, processing and storage of documents and other administrative and clerical services and expressly extends the right to impose this fee on lessees as well as purchasers. The bill notes that the fee may be charged to allow cost recovery for dealers, and a portion of the fee may result in profit to the dealer.

The law gives the Arkansas Motor Vehicle Commission the authority to determine by rule the amount of the service and handling fee, which cannot exceed $129. Although the MVC is working on proposed rules, the most recent version we have seen still has the allowed amount of the fee left blank. However, we understand that the MVC intends to propose the maximum amount of $129.

As with the documentary fee, the service and handling fee must be charged to all retail customers and disclosed on the retail buyers order as a separate itemized charge. Similarly, as with the old fee, the new fee must be accompanied on all written documentation by a notice in type that is bold-faced, capitalized, underlined, or otherwise conspicuously set out from the surrounding material. The new notice must state:

> A SERVICE AND HANDLING FEE IS NOT AN OFFICIAL FEE. A SERVICE AND HANDLING FEE IS NOT REQUIRED BY LAW BUT MAY BE CHARGED TO THE CUSTOMER FOR PERFORMING SERVICES AND HANDLING DOCUMENTS RELATING TO THE CLOSING OF A SALE OR LEASE. THE SERVICE AND HANDLING FEE MAY RESULT IN PROFIT TO THE DEALER. THE SERVICE AND HANDLING FEE DOES NOT INCLUDE PAYMENT FOR THE PREPARATION OF LEGAL DOCUMENTS. THIS NOTICE IS REQUIRED BY LAW.

The most recent version of the MVC's proposed rules also adds a requirement that a dealer prominently post a sign with the amount of the service and handling fee it charges along with the above notice.

Now, I don't know about you, but I think Shakespeare foreshadowed this Arkansas debacle in Romeo and Juliet when he wrote, "[A] rose by any other name would smell as sweet." I realize the legislature had no choice but to get rid of the documentary fee and provide that a dealer may fill in blanks and prepare documents as long as it doesn't charge the customer for those services. But allowing dealers to charge a fee for similar services, with merely a different name, may just give the plaintiffs' lawyers another bone to pick (and more legal fees in their pocket).

As Tom said in his article, "Customers tend to get annoyed by the 'nickeling and diming,' and when they get annoyed, they look for reasons to challenge the dealer's actions." The Arkansas legislature may have just created a new annoyance.

Chapter 8

Warranties

As Uncle Buster said, "Ain't nothin' simple." You sell a car, and you want to assure the buyer that you will stand behind it. Then you discover that the feds have a law, the Magnuson-Moss Warranty Act, which regulates what your warranty must say. Maybe there's a state law that applies as well. Then you find out that if you want to sell a car "as is," disclaiming so-called "implied warranties" under the Uniform Commercial Code (UCC), those same warranty laws may prohibit you from doing so, if you sell a service contract within 90 days of the date of the sale.

And you have to pay close attention to those disclaimers to make sure that they are enforceable. Some states prohibit them, or prohibit as-is sales entirely, while other states' versions of the UCC require that an attempt to disclaim implied warranties has to use certain words and be "conspicuous."

Are you sure you don't want to go to law school?

Auto Leasing and Federal Warranty Law

May 2006

By Maya Hill

Leases are making a comeback. Whether it's because interest rates are rising, or people are increasingly concerned with maximizing their cash flow, or because changes in federal law have made leases more attractive to lessees—whatever—the result is the same: More and more consumers are opting for leases. Along with the increase in automobile leasing, come the issues of lessor/lessee rights and responsibilities—particularly the issue of whether a consumer lessor is afforded certain protections under various state and federal laws. This is the issue in the case we discuss here...

Bill Parrot leased a Jeep Cherokee from Pitre Chrysler

Plymouth. Pitre Chrysler assigned the lease to Chrysler Financial Company, LLC, but retained title to the vehicle (the court offered no explanation why Pitre retained title to the vehicle). The Jeep came with DaimlerChrysler's standard limited warranty.

Parrot claimed he took the Cherokee at least 13 times to various dealerships for repairs. Dissatisfied with the repair work, Parrot sued DaimlerChrysler, alleging the manufacturer had breached its written limited warranty. The trial court granted DaimlerChrysler's motion for summary judgment. Parrot appealed.

The intermediate appellate court reversed, concluding that Parrot was a consumer, subject to protection under both the federal Magnuson-Moss Warranty Act and Arizona's lemon law. The Arizona Supreme Court granted DaimlerChrysler's petition for review, because the applicability of the MMWA and the Arizona lemon law to lessees was an issue of "first impression." (That's pointy-headed legal speak for, "We haven't decided this issue before.")

The Arizona high court found that Parrot was not a consumer subject to protection under the MMWA or the Arizona lemon law and reversed the appellate court's decision. A cause of action under the MMWA requires that a person (1) be a consumer; and (2) have a written warranty as defined by the MMWA. The MMWA creates three categories of consumers, each of which requires that a "qualifying sale" of a vehicle occur to trigger consumer status. A "qualifying sale," for purposes of the MMWA, is one in which a person buys a consumer product *for purposes other than resale.* The MMWA defines "written warranty" as any written affirmation or promise made in connection with the sale of a product regarding the nature of the product, which becomes part of the basis of the bargain between a supplier and a buyer *for purposes other than resale* of the product.

The high court found that Pitre Chrysler bought the vehicle from DaimlerChrysler for the purpose of resale, noting that the only sale of record was the sale between these two parties. Accordingly, the only sale was for the purpose of resale, and, consequently, no written warranty existed for purposes of the MMWA. Thus, Parrot could not maintain a cause of action under the federal statute.

The high court also found that the Arizona lemon law definition of "consumer" parallels the definition in the MMWA for two of the three categories, but declined to comment on Parrot's status as a consumer under the remaining category, because the limited remedies afforded by the lemon law extinguished Parrot's claim. Specifically, the court found that the remedies (replacement of the vehicle, or return of the vehicle, and refund of the purchase price) both assume that the consumer has the right to transfer the vehicle title back to the manufacturer. Because the vehicle owner, or titleholder, is the only one who may transfer title to the vehicle, and Parrot was a lessee without title, Parrot had no legal right to transfer title back to DaimlerChrysler. Accordingly, the court ruled that Parrot could not maintain a cause of action under the Arizona Lemon Law.

Parrot v. Daimler Chrysler Corp., 2006 WL 625531 (Ariz. March 14, 2006).

The Arizona Supreme Court isn't alone in taking this position; other courts have held that the MMWA and corresponding state lemon law provisions, for one reason or another, do not apply to leases. See, e.g., *Tarantino v. DaimlerChrysler Corporation*, 2001 WL 1834158 (N.Y. App. Div. April 1, 2002); *Alpiser v. Eagle Pontiac-GMC-Isuzu, Inc.*, 389 S.E.2d 293 (N.C. App. March 20, 1990).

And yet, while some courts uphold the lease exemption, there is no consensus on this issue in all courts. *Cohen v. AM*

General Corporation, for example, was decided the opposite way. We first reported on *Cohen* in May 2003; see "Federal Magnuson-Moss Warranty Act: Courts Disagree On Whether Act Applies to Lease" (***Spot Delivery***®, May 2003).

In the *Cohen* case, Mark Cohen and First Choice Medical leased a new American General Hummer from Naperville Hummer Jeep. Mister Leasing Corporation bought the Hummer. The plaintiffs had the option to buy the Hummer at the end of the lease. Mister Leasing maintained that the purchase of the Hummer was for the purpose of leasing it to the plaintiffs and that it would not have otherwise bought the vehicle. Mister Leasing transferred its rights in American General's factory warranty to the plaintiffs. The plaintiffs claimed they had many problems with the Hummer. Pursuant to the warranty, the plaintiffs tendered the vehicle to authorized Hummer dealers, who serviced it at no cost. In July 2002, the plaintiffs traded in the vehicle, receiving $49,000.

The plaintiffs filed suit in Illinois state court, alleging, among other things, breach of warranty. The defendants removed the case to the U.S. District Court for the Northern District of Illinois and sought to have the claim dismissed. The defendants argued that the plaintiffs were not entitled to enforce the warranty under the Magnuson-Moss Warranty Act, because the federal Act does not apply to leases, and, therefore, the MMWA does not allow the plaintiffs to enforce the warranty, because there was no "sale" to "a buyer other than for purposes of resale."

The court disagreed. The court explained that the factory warranty delivered to Mister Leasing was a written warranty as defined by the MMWA. "Sale," as defined by the MMWA, the court said, "is not limited to transactions between the warrantor and the ultimate consumer." Mister Leasing purchased the vehicle for the purpose of leasing it to the plaintiffs, not for resale (though the court recognized that it could sell the vehicle later, perhaps even to the plaintiffs, at the end of the lease term). The court qualified its conclusion with the following statement:

> This is not to say that all lessees of automobiles should be entitled to enforce the manufacturer's warranty. Each lessee gets the rights that he bargains for. In situations like this, however, where the sale of a vehicle is merely to facilitate a lease, the issuance of the warranty accompanies this sale, and the lessor explicitly transfers its rights in the warranty to the lessee—the Magnuson-Moss Act protects the lessee.

Cohen v. AM General Corporation, 2003 WL 1203613 (N.D. Ill. March 11, 2003). See also *Peterson v. Volkswagen of America, Inc.*, 697 N.W.2d 61 (Wis. May 27, 2005); *O'Connor v. BMW of North America, LLC*, 905 So.2d 235 (Fla. App. June 22, 2005).

Given the disagreement in the lower courts, coupled with the increasing popularity of automobile leases, the issue of whether the MMWA and state lemon laws apply to leases seems to be ripe for Supreme Court attention. When the Court might grant *certiorari*[2] in an appropriate case is anyone's guess, but Spot will keep checking the docket. In the meantime, you may want to talk to your lawyer about the ins and outs of leasing. Whether it is your state's lemon law, UDAP provisions, MMWA, insurance laws, or other consumer protection provisions, lease-related claims are bound to surface.

---

[2] The Supreme Court isn't required to take all appeals. When it takes one it isn't required to take, lawyers say it has "granted cert," with "cert." shorthand for "certiorari."

Arizona Dealer *Almost* Off the Hook for MMWA Lawsuit

June 2006

By Catherine Brennan

In a decision bound to cause Arizona car dealers to sigh in relief, the Arizona Supreme Court has ruled that neither a service contract nor an application for the service contract constitutes a "written warranty" under the Magnuson-Moss Warranty Act, because the buyer paid additional consideration for the service contract not included in the purchase price of the car.

Brenda Johnson bought a used Kia Sportage from Earnhardt's Gilbert Dodge Inc., in May 2000. The sales agreement expressly limited the implied warranty of merchantability on the car to the earlier of 15 days or 500 miles, as permitted under Arizona law. At the time Johnson bought the car, she also applied to buy a service contract from DaimlerChrysler, the Kia Sportage's manufacturer. Both Johnson and the dealer signed the application for the service contract, and Johnson paid an additional fee for the contract.

After the sale of the car, Daimler issued the service contract to Johnson. The car experienced mechanical problems, and Johnson ultimately attempted to revoke acceptance of the car nearly a year after the purchase.

Earnhardt's refused to accept the car's return, and Johnson sued, claiming that Earnhardt's breached the implied warranty of merchantability in violation of the Magnuson-Moss Warranty Act. Earnhardt's argued to the trial court that it did not enter into the service contract with Johnson and that it lawfully limited its warranty to the earlier of 15 days or 500 miles. The trial court agreed with Earnhardt's, and granted the dealership's summary judgment motion. Johnson appealed, and the appellate court reversed the trial court's decision, holding as a matter of law that Earnhardt's entered into the service contract with Johnson and made a written warranty in connection with the sale when it signed the application for the service contract—acts that prohibited Earnhardt's from limiting the implied warranty of merchantability. See *Johnson v. Earnhardt's Gilbert Dodge*, 2005 WL 775413 (Ariz. App. April 7, 2005). Earnhardt's appealed.

In an almost-complete victory for the dealer, the Arizona Supreme Court reversed the appellate court decision. The high court found that neither the service contract nor the application for the service contract constituted a written warranty. Under Magnuson-Moss, a written warranty includes an undertaking in writing in connection with the sale of a consumer product that becomes part of the basis of the bargain between a supplier and a buyer. In contrast, a service contract is an agreement that calls for some consideration in addition to the consumer product's purchase price. Accordingly, the high court concluded, the service contract Johnson bought could not also constitute a written warranty, as Johnson paid additional consideration for the service contract that was not included in the purchase price of the car. Therefore, the high court ruled in favor of Earnhardt's on this claim.

Johnson also claimed, however, that Earnhardt's faced liability, because it was a party to the service contract. Under Magnuson-Moss, a used car dealer that enters into a service contract with the purchaser at the time of the sale or within 90 days later cannot limit the implied warranty of merchantability. The high court found that a fact issue remained as to whether Earnhardt's was a party to the service contract and remanded the case to the trial court for further proceedings on that issue.

The Earnhardt's decision tracks the Federal Trade Commission's advisory opinion (www.counselorlibrary.com/

alerts/alerts_02242005040241_599.pdf) on when dealers may disclaim implied warranties. The FTC opined that when a dealer sells the customer a service contract (at time of sale or within 90 days) as the agent of a third-party service provider, without the dealership itself incurring any obligations to perform repairs or pay for repairs under the contract, the dealer may in fact disclaim implied warranties under the MMWA. Thus, if Earnhardt's can show that it was not a party to the service contract—and had no obligation to make repairs to Johnson's car under the contract—it should escape liability.

So, while Earnhardt's is not completely out of the woods, Arizona car dealers can take comfort in the fact that if they can document that they are not a party to a service contract issued by a car's manufacturer, Arizona courts aren't likely to apply Magnuson-Moss against them.

Johnson v. Earnhardt's Gilbert Dodge, 2006 WL 1071875 (Ariz. April 25, 2006).

Arizona High Court Addresses Federal Law on Limitation of Implied Warranties

June 2006

By Catherine Brennan and Teresa Rohwedder

---

*[**Editor's note:** The preceding article deals with an intermediate appellate court's decision; the one below is a discussion of the same case on appeal to the Arizona Supreme Court.]*

The federal Magnuson-Moss Warranty Act governs written and implied warranty claims and is often invoked by car buyers in lawsuits against dealers. In a recent decision, the Arizona Supreme Court ruled on issues under the federal Act that apply to all car dealers, regardless of jurisdiction. The high court found that a manufacturer's service contract was not a "written warranty" for purposes of the Magnuson-Moss Act, where the buyer paid separate consideration for the service contract not included in the purchase price of the car. Perhaps of even greater value is the high court's view of a dealer who sells a manufacturer's service contract or extended warranty. There are a couple of issues that arise with respect to written warranties, which bring into play a dealer's right to disclaim implied warranties in a car sale. Let's take a look...

Brenda Johnson bought a used Kia Sportage from Earnhardt's Gilbert Dodge Inc., in May of 2000. The sales agreement expressly limited the implied warranty of merchantability on the car to the earlier of 15 days or 500 miles, as permitted under Arizona law. When Johnson bought the car, she also applied to buy a service contract from DaimlerChrysler. Both Johnson and the dealer signed the application for the service contract, and Johnson paid an amount for the contract, in addition to the purchase price of the vehicle.

After the sale of the car, Daimler issued the service contract to Johnson. Johnson experienced mechanical problems with the car and ultimately attempted to revoke acceptance nearly a year after the purchase. Earnhardt's refused to accept the car's return, and Johnson sued, claiming that Earnhardt's breached the implied warranty of merchantability in violation of the federal Magnuson-Moss Warranty Act.

Earnhardt's argued to the trial court that it did not enter into the service contract with Johnson and that it lawfully limited its warranty to the earlier of 15 days or 500 miles. The trial court agreed with Earnhardt's and granted the dealership's summary judgment motion. Johnson appealed, and the intermediate appellate court reversed the trial court, finding that Earnhardt's "entered into" the service contract with Johnson as a matter of law and made a written warranty in connection with the sale when it signed the application for the service contract. These actions prohibited Earnhardt's from limiting its implied warranty of merchantability to 15 days or 500 miles; thus, the attempted limitation was deemed ineffective. See *Johnson v. Earnhardt's Gilbert Dodge*, 2005 WL 775413 (Ariz. App. April 7, 2005). Earnhardt's appealed.

In a near-complete victory for the dealer, the Arizona Supreme Court reversed the intermediate appellate court decision. The high court found that neither the service contract nor the application for the service contract constituted a written warranty. Under the Magnuson-Moss Act, a written warranty includes an undertaking in writing in connection with the sale of a consumer product that becomes part of the basis of the bargain between a supplier and a buyer. In contrast, a service contract is an agreement that calls for some consideration in addition to the consumer product's purchase price.

The high court concluded that the service contract Johnson bought could not also constitute a written warranty, as Johnson paid additional consideration for the service contract that was not included in the purchase price of the car. Therefore, the high court ruled in favor of Earnhardt's on this claim.

Johnson also claimed, however, that Earnhardt's could not disclaim implied warranties because it was a party to the service contract. Under Magnuson-Moss, a used car dealer that "enters into" a service contract with the car buyer at the time of sale or within 90 days of the sale cannot limit the implied warranty of merchantability. The high court disagreed with the appellate court's conclusion as a matter of law that Earnhardt's "entered into" and, therefore, was a party to, the service contract. Instead, the high court found unresolved factual issues as to whether Earnhardt's was a party to the service contract, so it remanded the case to the trial court for further proceedings on that issue. The Arizona high court had the following to say with regard to whether a dealer selling a manufacturer's service contract or extended warranty is a party to that contract:

> We agree that a service contract that merely obligates a third party to provide services has not been "entered into" by the dealer, even when sold by the dealer. We also assume that to be the case even if the third party (such as DaimlerChrysler) has contractual arrangements with the dealer requiring the dealer to provide the service.

The above-quoted language is a valuable clarification of the law concerning dealer sales of manufacturer warranties. In the Arizona high court's view, a dealer is not a party to a manufacturer's extended warranty or service contract (and therefore may limit the implied warranty of merchantability) even when the dealer is obligated to provide the service that the manufacturer pays for under that service contract or extended warranty.

In this case, however, the high court determined that it was unclear, both because of language in the contract documents, and because of evidence outside of the documents, whether the dealer was a party to the service contract.

> In this case, language in the documents comprising the transaction, combined with parol evidence, both supports and undermines the conclusion that Earnhardt itself entered into the service contract. This evidence raises a question of fact as to whether Earnhardt was a party to the service contract.

The Federal Trade Commission has issued an advisory opinion on the subject of when and under what circumstances a dealer may disclaim implied warranties. The FTC states that when a dealer sells the customer a service contract (at time of sale or within 90 days) as the agent of a third-party service provider without the dealership itself incurring any obligation to perform repairs *or* pay for repairs under the contract, the dealer may in fact disclaim implied warranties under the Magnuson-Moss Act.

In this case, Earnhardt's was obligated to make repairs to Johnson's car under the service contract. However, it was unclear whether Earnhardt's obligation to make those repairs was a promise to Johnson or a promise to DaimlerChrysler. This was the unresolved factual issue identified by the high court. The FTC advisory letter seems to indicate that if the dealership is obligated to either pay for repairs *or* perform repairs, then it *cannot* disclaim implied warranties (presumably because the dealership would be deemed a party to the contract). The Arizona high court takes a different position, indicating that a dealership obligated to make repairs under a manufacturer's service contract is not necessarily a party to that contract.

Earnhardt's is not completely out of the woods. Its job on remand to the trial court will be to prove that its obligation to make repairs to Johnson's car arises out of an agreement with DaimlerChrysler and not out of the service contract Johnson entered into with DaimlerChrysler (and perhaps Earnhardt's). It's a very subtle distinction. Earnhardt's will argue that it did not enter into the service contract, even though it signed the application for that contract. We'll be keeping an eye on this case. After the trial court resolves the issue, we could see another appeal. Although this is an Arizona case, it deals with federal law that applies to all dealers in every state. This is an important case no matter what state you're in.

Johnson v. Earnhardt's Gilbert Dodge, 2006 WL 1071875 (Ariz. April 25, 2006).

Let's Get Something Done!

June 2006

By Thomas B. Hudson

I like mowing the lawn. I think it's because I can actually see the result of my work as the chore progresses. Unlike the paper shuffling I do at work, I actually get a feeling of accomplishment.

If you're a dealer, I'd like to provide you with a compliance chore that you can actually do yourself, without a whole lot of effort. Pick up the buyers order and retail installment sale agreements that you use, and follow along.

The Uniform Commercial Code (UCC), a version of which is the law in your state, says that when a merchant sells goods, the goods come with two "implied warranties." Implied warranties are those that arise even when nothing is said or written regarding them. The two implied warranties are, the warranty of merchantability (fit for the ordinary purposes for which such goods are used, among other things); and the warranty of fitness for a particular use. (This arises when the seller, at the time of sale, knows of a particular use and the buyer is relying on the seller's skill and judgment to select goods that can be used in such a way.)

The UCC, as enacted in most states, allows sellers to "exclude" these implied warranties. If you live in such a state, your buyers order, and, probably, your retail installment sale contracts have language that attempts to exclude these warranties. I say "attempts" because you have to follow the UCC rules if you want to exclude these warranties. If your attempt to exclude the warranties doesn't follow the rules, it won't be effective. Many dealers (or dealers' lawyers) don't follow the rules, and end up giving warranties they thought they had successfully excluded.

An exclusion of implied warranties must be in writing; an exclusion of the implied warranty of merchantability must mention the term, "merchantability;" and (this is where a lot of folks do it wrong) the exclusion must be "conspicuous;" that is, as the UCC describes, in part, as "in larger or other contrasting type or color." The UCC says that if the exclusion is not conspicuous, then it isn't enforceable.

How does this work in real life? Let's take a look at a recent case in which the issue arose.

Walter and Julie Schultz bought a recreational vehicle manufactured by Damon Corporation from General R.V. Center. The Schultzes financed the purchase through Fifth Third Bank. Unhappy with their purchase, the Schultzes sued Damon, General R.V., and the bank, alleging that Damon sold them the RV in a defective state; that the RV was out of service for various repairs on at least five occasions during the first four months of ownership; and that the RV continued to be in a defective state.

The Schultzes asserted a number of claims, including breach of express and implied warranties of merchantability under Michigan law, revocation of acceptance, breach of implied warranties in violation of the Magnuson-Moss Warranty Act, and violation of the Michigan Consumer Protection Act. General R.V. and Damon moved for summary judgment.

General R.V. argued that it was entitled to judgment on the Schultzes' breach of warranty, revocation of acceptance, Magnuson-Moss, and Michigan Consumer Protection Act claims, because it effectively disclaimed all express and implied warranties in the purchase agreement.

The U.S. District Court for the Eastern District of Michigan rejected General R.V.'s argument. The court found that General R.V.'s disclaimer was unenforceable, because it was not conspicuous. The purchase agreement was a two-sided document with the disclaimer language on the second page; it was single-spaced and not entirely in capital letters. The court contrasted another case where it found a disclaimer to be sufficiently conspicuous. The court stated that the key difference between the disclaimer in this case, and the enforceable disclaimer in the other case, was that the buyer in the other case signed an additional document titled "AS IS DEALER WARRANTY DISCLAIMER."

We see buyers orders all the time that contain these implied warranty exclusions in a type size and font that is no different from the surrounding text. Take a look at your documents, and see whether or not the language excluding warranties is conspicuous.

Is it in all caps if placed in a section that is otherwise "regular" type? Better yet, is it in all caps and bold-faced? If the exclusion language appears in a paragraph that is all caps, is it distinguished from the surrounding text in any way, such as by appearing in bold-faced type, in a different color, or underlined? If you can answer any of these questions affirmatively, than your warranty disclaimer language will stand out and should be considered to be "conspicuous" in a court of law.

If your exclusion language is "conspicuous," give yourself (or your lawyer, trade association, or forms company) an "A." If it isn't, get it fixed.

There. You actually accomplished a compliance chore. Feels about as good as finishing the mowing, doesn't it?

Schultz v. General R.V. Center, 2006 WL 901684 (E.D. Mich. April 3, 2006).

Chapter 9

Spot Delivery

The National Consumer Law Center (NCLC) provides legal resources for plaintiffs' lawyers around the country to use when they sue creditors, including car dealers. The NCLC staff is very smart, and they produce some very good stuff. With it, a second-year lawyer from some backwater town can file a complaint, discovery requests, motions and memos supporting those motions that are first-class work (albeit the tone can be a bit shrill), and he or she can do it quickly and cheaply.

For that reason, I pay particular attention whenever the NCLC lawyers look like they are particularly interested in something. A few short years ago, one of their newsletter articles caught my eye.

The article dealt with spot deliveries and how to successfully attack them. The NCLC, calling spot deliveries "yo-yo" deals, had evidently determined that they were inherently unfair and deceptive. The NCLC asserted further that dealers regularly used the technique to put buyers in a car on terms they knew no financing source would honor, just so the dealers could drag the consumers back to the bargaining table to jack up the price of the car or the credit.

That may happen in some dealerships; but, in my experience, the vast majority of spot delivery transactions go off without a hitch. The dealer rolls the car, the finance source approves the deal, the customer takes his or her new wheels home to show off to the neighbors, and everybody's happy.

But I digress. The NCLC folks don't share my benign view of the practice, and I was surprised to see all the ways they came up with to attack it. From titling issues to temporary, dealer tag issues; from tax problems to federal odometer law issues; from unfair and deceptive acts and practices claims to Truth in Lending problems; it seemed as if it was not possible for a dealer to engage in a legal spot delivery transaction.

So what's going on here? Are the NCLC people chasing their tails, inventing legal problems where there are none? Or have the dealers who use spot deliveries really done their homework and figured out ways to keep spotting cars without running afoul of all of the snags identified by the NCLC?

I don't really have an answer for those questions, but I have a guess and a prediction.

My guess is that most dealers really haven't thoroughly scoped out their spot delivery procedures to determine whether they could withstand these NCLC-type charges, and they have been flying under the radar, hoping that no one looks too closely at their practices. The prediction is that this will be an area of heated litigation over the next few years.

A Spot Delivery Gone Bad; Lessons To Learn

May 2006

By Thomas B. Hudson

If you want to institute a spot delivery procedure that is an invitation to a lawsuit, just follow this handy-dandy example...

Jeremiah Mann and DeeAundrea Cartier entered into a purchase contract and a retail installment sale contract with Brown Credit Lot for the purchase of a 2001 Saturn. Both documents purported to be "the entire agreement" between the parties.

The buyers gave Brown a $500 cash down payment and traded in a 1993 Honda Civic valued at $500. The buyers were allegedly told before they left Brown that their financing through Household Auto Finance was approved. However, Household declined to buy the contract.

At some point, Brown told the buyers that financing was not approved and that new documents would have to be signed.

Unhappy, the buyers asked for the return of their trade-in and down payment. Brown told the buyers that the Honda had been sold and refused to return their down payment.

According to Brown's finance manager, the buyers' financing fell through when Household found a 9-month gap in Mann's employment between his current and former jobs, and did not find this information reflected on Mann's credit application. In fact, the credit application did not ask for employment dates and had no questions that would identify a gap in employment.

The buyers sued Brown, alleging that Brown's representation that financing was approved, when such was not the case, was unfair, deceptive, and unconscionable in violation of the Ohio Consumer Sales Practices Act.

The Ohio Municipal Court characterized the transaction as a "yo-yo deal" that was a "variation of the classic bait-and-switch." The court had no difficulty concluding that the following acts by Brown were unfair or deceptive:

- The demand on the buyers to return the vehicle when Household declined to buy the contract;
- The representation that financing was approved when it was not;
- The failure to provide the buyers with a copy of the retail installment sale contract;
- The delivery of the vehicle pursuant to a sale subject to financing without a written agreement setting forth the parties' rights and obligations; and
- The sale of the buyers' trade-in vehicle before the deal was finalized.

Limited by its small claims court maximum jurisdictional amount, the court awarded the buyers three times their actual damages of $1,000, or $3,000, plus costs. In a court other than a small claims court, the dealer would have faced the possibility of a much larger hit.

What are the lessons here? There are several, and at least some of them have appeared before in these pages.

Lesson 1

A dealer entering into a retail installment sale agreement with a car buyer is extending credit. If a dealer does not have some sort of "unwind agreement" permitting the dealer to rescind the deal if he cannot assign the agreement to a finance company or bank, the dealer must hold the agreement and collect the payments. He has no right to unilaterally cancel the deal. He cannot repossess the car if the customer is not in default. If you want to paint a big bulls eye on your dealership, try to unwind a deal in the absence of an unwind agreement.

Lesson 2

A dealer should not sell the buyer's trade-in vehicle until the assignment of the buyer's agreement to an assignee is complete, even if state law permits it and the dealer's buyers order permits it. Judges and juries don't like the practice, and they will try to find some way to punish dealers who engage in it.

Lesson 3

Dealers should be careful as to what they tell their customers about the finality of the financing for their cars. It is possible that in this case, Household's communications with the dealer about these buyers led the dealer to believe, in good faith, that the financing was final. If the possibility exists, however, that a bank or finance company could kick a deal back to a dealer after some delay, the dealer should be open with its buyers about that possibility.

Lesson 4

If the sales finance companies and banks to which your dealership assigns contracts require a continuous period of employment as a condition of approving deals, make sure that your credit application is set up to elicit that information. If it isn't, your people should be trained to inquire about such gaps.

Spot deliveries are under attack by consumer advocates, and they have gotten the attention of state regulators and state legislators. There are sometimes-dicey federal and state law problems with spot deliveries. If you haven't had your spot delivery procedures reviewed by your lawyer recently, you need to put that on your "to-do" list.

Cartier v. Brown Credit Lot, 2005 WL 3867414 (Ohio Mun. April 4, 2005).

Court Muffs Ohio Spot Delivery Case

April 2007

By Thomas B. Hudson and Catherine C. Worthington

Most courts don't see Truth in Lending Act cases very often, so it isn't unusual that when they do, they manage to drop the ball in deciding them. A federal judge in Ohio, confronted with a garden-variety spot delivery transaction, fell victim to this common tendency to make bad TILA law. Let's take a look at what happened...

Brian and Jennifer Patton went to Jeff Wyler Eastgate, Inc., to trade in their car and buy a used 2003 Ford Windstar minivan. In connection with the purchase, the Pattons signed a retail installment sale contract which identified the Pattons as the "Buyer and Co-Buyer" and Wyler Eastgate as the "Creditor-Seller." Under a section titled "Federal Truth in Lending Disclosures," the contract listed the financing terms and stated that the Pattons were agreeing to pay the "Creditor-Seller...the Amount Financed and Finance Charge according to the payment schedule."

The installment contract contained a "merger clause." That's lawyer talk for a provision that stated that the installment contract was the entire agreement between the parties and that any changes to it must be in writing.

In addition to the installment contract, the Pattons signed a "Purchase Spot Delivery Agreement," stating that the Pattons were taking possession of the minivan before approval of financing, and that Wyler Eastgate could demand return of the minivan, or have the Pattons pay the balance due, if it was unable to obtain third-party financing, or if it could not assign the contract to a third party within a certain period. The Spot Delivery Agreement and the installment contract did not contain language incorporating the terms of one agreement into the other.

More than a month later, Wyler Eastgate demanded that the Pattons return the minivan because of its inability to obtain financing. Wyler Eastgate gave the Pattons their old car back, once the minivan was returned to the dealership. Later, the Pattons sued Wyler Eastgate for violating the federal Truth in Lending Act and Regulation Z, claiming that the Spot Delivery Agreement rendered meaningless and illusory the installment contract's facially valid disclosures. The Pattons moved for summary judgment.

Wait a minute. Think about that. The TILA disclosures were "facially valid." That sounds like they were accurate, doesn't it? So what could be wrong? Keep reading.

In opposing the motion, Wyler Eastgate tried to argue that it was not a "creditor" under TILA. If you are a ***Spot Delivery®*** reader, you know that this argument has "loser" painted all over it. The court quickly (and accurately) made mincemeat of the dealer's argument on this point, concluding that Wyler Eastgate satisfied both requirements in the TILA definition of "creditor," which are (1) someone who regularly extends consumer credit; and (2) someone to whom the debt is initially payable, based on the face of the obligation.

Wyler Eastgate argued that it was not a "lending institution" and did not usually finance its own retail sales. (Hint for Wyler Eastgate's lawyer: Read the retail installment sale contract—you will find that it is an agreement *to sell a car on credit.*) However, the court found that Wyler Eastgate did, in fact, regularly extend credit to its customers to finance car purchases. In support of this finding, the court noted that Wyler Eastgate required (1) all buyers who financed their car purchases to sign installment contracts listing Wyler Eastgate as the creditor; (2) requested that monthly payments be made to it; and (3) included a finance charge. As such, Wyler Eastgate was obligated to provide financing to the Pattons by the terms in the installment contract, until the contract could be validly assigned to a third party or cancelled.

The court also found that Wyler Eastgate satisfied the second requirement in the statutory definition of a TILA creditor because it expressly identified itself as the Creditor-Seller on the installment contract to whom the Pattons were obligated to pay both the amount financed and the finance charge.

Having concluded that Wyler Eastgate was a creditor under TILA, the court went on to determine whether Wyler Eastgate violated the Act by using the Spot Delivery Agreement. Wyler Eastgate argued that the TILA disclosures on the installment contract were valid when made and that other federal courts have upheld the spot delivery practice.

The court distinguished other federal cases that have upheld the spot delivery practice, stating that, in this case, the Pattons' installment contract only provided Wyler Eastgate—not the Pattons—with the ability to cancel the contract, if financing could not be obtained. The court didn't address why this made any difference in its analysis and conclusions, and, for the life of us, we can't figure why it should. If both parties had the right to rescind, would there have been no TILA violation?

In addition, the other federal cases did not address the Pattons' argument that the Spot Delivery Agreement rendered the installment contract disclosures illusory. The court found that the language in the Spot Delivery Agreement, "Financing for your purchase has not been finalized," directly contradicted the language in the installment contract that disclosed the TILA financing terms and identified Wyler Eastgate as the Creditor-Seller to whom payments were due. The court found that the installment contract's representation that Wyler Eastgate was providing credit for the Pattons' minivan purchase on the financing terms stated in the contract was rendered meaningless by the Spot Delivery Agreement's language, which permitted Wyler Eastgate the authority to cancel the purchase. Therefore, the court concluded that Wyler Eastgate violated TILA by using a spot delivery agreement to rescind the terms of a fully integrated retail installment contract.

The court's analysis is almost certainly wrong. TILA is a disclosure statute. TILA doesn't tell a creditor what the terms of the credit offering must be; rather, it tells the creditor how it must disclose those terms.

TILA and Reg. Z say that TILA disclosures must be based on the terms of the contract between the parties. In this case, the parties agreed on financing terms, but they also agreed that if the dealer couldn't assign the contract, the contract would be rescinded. If financing ended up being provided under the contract, the disclosures describing the transaction were accurate.

Is the court saying that a credit contract that can be rescinded violates TILA and Reg. Z? If so, that will come as a surprise to all those creditors that make real estate loans that contain a 3-day right of rescission. Do all of those transactions violate TILA and Reg. Z?

Meanwhile, what's an Ohio dealer (or dealers in other states who don't want to see this result) to do?

First, the dealer should sit down with his or her lawyer and review the terms and conditions of the buyers order, the retail installment sale contract, and any other documents (like the "Purchase Spot Delivery Agreement" the dealer used in this case) that address any aspect of the "spot" part of the transaction. The documents need to be internally consistent with each other; they also may need to be incorporated as one document by adding appropriate language.

This analysis should give some thought to the terms of the spot delivery arrangement. We've seen spot deliveries done at least three ways.

- Some dealers use a bailment agreement, in effect, lending the car to the buyer until the dealer has located a source willing to purchase the buyer's retail installment contract. When that financing source is found, the dealer has the buyer come in and sign the documents for the sale and financing of the car.
- Some dealers use documents that say, in effect, "You, the buyer, and we, the seller, have signed all the necessary

documents, but we agree that the deal isn't done until we assign your contract." This is a "condition precedent," in lawyer talk, which says, in effect, that there is no deal before something (the assignment) happens.

- Some dealers use documents that say, in effect, "You, the buyer, and we, the seller, have a final deal when all the documents are signed, but we agree that the deal can be rescinded, if we are unable to assign the contract." This is a "condition subsequent," in lawyer talk, which says there is a deal, but if something (the inability to assign the contract) happens *afterward*, the deal goes away.

We've seen spot delivery agreements that seem to take parts and pieces from each arrangement described above. That's a mistake—the agreements should reflect a consistent approach to one of the three arrangements.

Whether the dealer's spot delivery agreements reflect a bailment, a condition precedent, or a condition subsequent will depend on state retail installment sales, titling, and other laws, the treatment of the arrangement under TILA and Reg. Z, the dealer's tolerance for risk, and the advice the dealer's lawyer provides.

One more thing to worry about.

Patton v. Jeff Wyler Eastgate, Inc., 2007 WL 756709 (S.D. Ohio March 8, 2007).

'Yo-Yo' Deals? I Don't Think So

May 2007

By Thomas B. Hudson

If you listen to the true believers at the National Consumer Law Center (these are the folks who provide legal support for consumer advocates and plaintiffs' lawyers around the country), they will tell you that dealers regularly write retail installment contracts with customers knowing that they will be unable to sell the contracts to financing sources. According to NCLC, dealers do this with the intent of calling the consumers back to the dealership to write deals that require larger down payments, higher APRs, or that, otherwise, disadvantage the customer. NCLC calls these "yo-yo" deals.

I don't believe that such practices are as common as the NCLC would have you think. Actually, until recently, we had not encountered such practices in any of our dealer audits. Last summer, for the first time, we found a dealer who cheerfully reported that he contracted with everyone whom he could convince to sign a retail installment sale contract. He said that he did it in order to "take the customer out of the market." He stopped the practice when we told him that, at the very least, it probably constituted an unfair and deceptive trade practice under state and federal law.

Although some states prohibit, or limit, the practice, many do not, and conditional deliveries, or spot deliveries, as they are sometimes called, are commonplace in most states. Let me stop for a minute, though, and define these terms.

A conditional delivery, or spot delivery, occurs when a dealer takes a credit application and determines, from the information provided by the buyer and from a credit bureau report, that he can sell the customer's retail installment contract to one of his regular financing sources. The dealer then has the customer sign the deal documents and take the car home. The vast majority of spot deliveries go off without a hitch. The buyer has provided complete and accurate credit data, and the finance source buys the contract. These are not "yo-yo" deals.

Sometimes, though, the train comes off the track. The buyer

forgets about the fact that, say, she just lost her job, or she misstates her income, or forgets how long she has lived at her current address. The buyer no longer falls within the credit criteria of any source the dealer uses. Now, assuming that the dealer has had the foresight to have the buyer sign an "unwind agreement" of some sort, it's time to drag the buyer back to the dealership to see if the deal can be salvaged. Sometimes it can, sometimes it can't. These also are not "yo-yo" deals.

Then there are those (in our experience) rare cases of actual misconduct or fraud by the dealer. Either the dealer thinks, like the one we encountered, that it's OK to "take everyone out of the market." Or, maybe, the dealer has a crooked F&I operation that provides false credit information on behalf of the buyer in an effort to sneak a deal past the financing source. These are "yo-yo" deals. In our experience, very few dealers actually engage in such transactions.

The relative rarity of these transactions doesn't faze the NCLC, or, for that matter, the press. They know a good, catchy (and loaded) headline phrase when they hear one. So, they call every conditional delivery transaction a "yo-yo" deal. And judges sometimes even erroneously adopt the incorrect terminology.

Plaintiffs' lawyers have attacked conditional deliveries for some time now. They claim federal Truth in Lending violations, unfair and deceptive trade practices, fraud, violations of state titling and registration laws and regulations, and other causes of action. How can you shield your dealership from these claims?

- Have your lawyer review your conditional delivery procedures to determine, first, whether the laws in your state permit the practice, and, if so, whether the practice is regulated.
- If state law permits you to engage in conditional deliveries, have your conditional delivery agreement reviewed by

your lawyer, as well. Make sure your lawyer knows what your dealership's actual conditional delivery procedures are, so that the agreement matches those procedures.

- Institute practices that are fair to the buyer. Don't, for example, sell the buyer's trade-in vehicle while you are trying to assign her contract.
- Don't make the conditional delivery process a profit center by attempting to charge a daily or mileage charge for the use of the vehicle, if the deal has to be unwound. Make sure you can recover for actual damages, but absorb the other charges as simply the occasional cost of doing these sorts of deals.
- Check your state's titling and registration rules to make sure that your conditional delivery process complies with such requirements.
- Check your arbitration agreement to make sure that it applies to a conditional delivery and that it survives a terminated deal.
- Go over your conditional delivery process with your insurance company—you don't want to wait until your buyer has plowed into a school bus with a car you have out on conditional delivery to determine what your potential liability might be.

When you have all your ducks lined up, you can do conditional deliveries with a minimum of risk. And you can also correct all those media types, when they ask you if you do "yo-yo" deals, by saying, "No, we do conditional deliveries."

Chapter 10

Internet Sales and Electronic Commerce

These days, there seems to be no end to the din when it comes to "how to" sell cars over the Internet. Every industry conference that I attend has at least one session on Internet sales. Every dealer publication I read seems to have an article or two on the topic. What I never see is a presentation or article on legal problems relating to Internet sales and how to solve them. *(Note to self: That may be a profit-making opportunity.)* And from where I sit, most dealers need that kind of help.

So far, the only lawsuits that we have seen dealing with Internet sales involve (1) the question of where—meaning which state, his? Mine?—an Internet seller can be sued; or (2) issues that are simply variations on print media advertising claims.

The first category of cases—to address the "where" question—can be illustrated like this: A dealer in Kansas sells a car on eBay to the buyer, who lives in Arizona. When the buyer has a problem with the car, or the deal, she sues in Arizona. The dealer screams, "You can't do that! The Arizona courts don't have any jurisdiction over me because I don't do any business in that state." Of the six or eight opinions we've seen on this issue, the courts seem to be pretty evenly divided on whether the dealer can be sued in the buyer's state; likewise, we find there is not much consensus among the courts about the facts that control their deliberations.

In the second category of cases, a car is advertised as having particular equipment or features. When it doesn't have the features described, the unhappy buyer sues.

The tough cases haven't shown up yet, but I'll bet they are coming. Disgruntled buyers will claim that the selling dealer wasn't licensed to sell cars in the buyer's state; that the selling dealer violated advertising, disclosure, usury, simple language, or other laws of the buyer's state, which the dealer never intended to obey; and that the selling dealer's activities (you guessed it) violated the unfair and deceptive acts and practices laws of the buyer's state.

Those cases are on the way. They won't be fun to watch, but I guarantee you they will be interesting.

State 'Long Arm' Laws and Internet Sales

November 2005

By Thomas B. Hudson

When you sell cars over the Internet without limiting who can buy those cars, you had better be prepared to show up in court in any state in the country when problems arise with the sale. What? you say. Yeah, I'm about to tell you what. But first, let me ask you a couple of rhetorical questions...

- Is it reasonable for a buyer in a state you've never set foot in to haul you into court when that buyer has a grievance about the sale?
- What if you've never sold any cars in that state, with the exception of the car you sold to this one buyer?

For answers, let's take a look at what a court in Virginia had to say on this subject in 2003.

Prestigious Motor Sales, Inc., a car dealership located in Connecticut, advertised a 1995 BMW 530i on eBay. Joseph Malcolm, a Virginia resident, submitted the winning bid of $12,450.

The parties exchanged information over the phone and by e-mail, and Prestigious arranged to have the car shipped from California to Virginia. Malcolm claimed to have discovered a defect in the car and attempted to rescind the purchase. Prestigious refused to rescind the sale, so Malcolm sued the dealership, along with two of its agents, in Virginia state court.

Neither the dealership nor the individual defendants maintained an office in Virginia or transacted business there. Aside from the sale to Malcolm, the dealership had never sold a car to anyone in Virginia.

The defendants entered a special appearance to contest the court's exercise of jurisdiction over them. The Circuit Court of Virginia ruled that it had jurisdiction over the defendants based on the single sale transaction over the Internet.

Every state has what is called a "long-arm statute," under which the courts in that state assert jurisdiction (bring persons into their courtrooms) over non-residents who engage in some type of activity within the state's borders. The state's exercise of jurisdiction must also be permissible under the Due Process Clause of the United States Constitution.

The Virginia court found that the sale contract for the BMW was formed in Virginia. The terms of the eBay sale mirrored Virginia law regarding auctions. The court explained, "In the case of an auction without reserve, the announced terms of the sale constitute a continuing offer by the owner, subject to acceptance by the submission of a bid. *Each bid is the consummation of a contract,* subject only to the receipt of a higher bid."

Thus, the court found that the parties formed a contract in Virginia the moment Malcolm placed his bid. The Virginia long-arm statute, the court observed, is "a single act statute requiring only one transaction in Virginia to confer jurisdiction." The court found that the exercise of jurisdiction satisfied "due process" requirements under the U.S. Constitution as well.

A "due process" analysis gets into a lot of legal nitty gritty, but suffice to say, the defendant must have "minimum contacts" with the state attempting to exercise jurisdiction. One element of the analysis is the defendant's ability to foresee the possibility of being sued in the forum state. In this case, the court concluded that the defendants could "reasonably foresee" being hauled into court in Virginia, based on their conduct in selling the vehicle to a Virginia resident.

The court did note, at that time, that the few courts, which had addressed the question of jurisdiction in the context of eBay transactions, "generally declined to exercise personal jurisdiction" over non-resident defendants. Note in this regard that state long-arm statutes differ. In Virginia, the long-arm statute provides for jurisdiction based on a "single act" within the state. Consequently, in deciding to exercise jurisdiction, the Virginia court noted the following factors:

- The defendants were commercial sellers of automobiles and were represented as "power sellers" on the eBay Web site.
- The defendants represented that they had local, national, and international eBay customers.
- The defendants foresaw potential transactions with non-resident buyers, based on the "winning bidder" e-mail it sent to Malcolm.
- The product in this case is an automobile, to be delivered to, and driven in, Virginia.
- Under the terms of the sale, the choice of the buyer was beyond the defendants' control.

Given all these factors, the court found that the defendants must have foreseen the possibility of being sued in a court outside of Connecticut.

Malcolm v. Esposito, 2003 WL 23272406 (Va. Cir. Ct. December 12, 2003).

Now, fast-forward two years. A Virginia trial court, again,

faced the same issue. Well, not quite the same issue. This time the seller set a reserve on the car being offered. Did that one little fact make a difference? You betcha.

Wagner Zone, Inc., an Illinois corporation, listed a 2003 Subaru Legacy Wagon for sale on eBay's Web site as an item "with reserve." Under eBay rules, a seller is not obligated to sell an item to any buyer, if the reserve price has not been met; furthermore, the winning bid must meet the reserve price and represent the highest bid on the item.

Irving, a citizen and resident of Virginia, contacted Wagner Zone through the Web site's e-mail server, bid the required reserve amount, and was the accepted buyer of the vehicle. After transporting the vehicle from Illinois to Virginia, as required by the purchase and sale contract, Irving determined that the Subaru was defective, so he sought rescission of the contract with Wagner Zone.

When Wagner Zone refused to rescind the transaction, Irving sued the company in Virginia state court. Wagner Zone contested the Virginia court's exercise of jurisdiction.

The Circuit Court of Virginia agreed with Wagner Zone, concluding that it did not have *in personam* jurisdiction over the company. The court explained that where an auction sale is conducted with reserve, a contract between the buyer and seller only forms upon the seller's acceptance of a buyer's bid. As such, the contract was consummated at the time of Wagner Zone's acceptance of Irving's bid—in Illinois—not Virginia. Thus, Irving failed to allege a business transaction occurring within Virginia, which was necessary to invoke Virginia's long arm jurisdiction.

The court also rejected Irving's argument that Virginia's long arm statute should apply, because Wagner Zone used a computer or computer network located in Virginia. The court explained that Wagner Zone did not "manifest an intent to target and focus on Virginia[n]" buyers, and that Wagner Zone stipulated on the Web site that Illinois pick-up was required. Consequently, the court concluded that the exercise of jurisdiction was inappropriate. In other words, if Irving wants to sue, he'll have to go to Illinois to do it.

That's one state's take on whether an Internet seller can be subject to suit in the buyer's state. Expect to see cases going both ways on this issue, depending on what the state's "long arm" law looks like, and how the courts interpret it.

Irving v. Wagner Zone, Inc., 2005 WL 2242814 (Va. Cir. Ct. June 6, 2005).

Internet Sales—One Question, Two Answers

July 2006

By Thomas B. Hudson

What happens when a brand-new concept like Internet car sales runs into legal principles that are literally centuries old? Sometimes, it ain't pretty.

The new stuff is eBay sales activities. The old stuff is something called "personal jurisdiction." The legal issue involved is whether a court in state A, where the eBay buyer lives, can exercise its authority over the selling dealer, located in state B. These types of cases are becoming more and more frequent. Take, for example, this one...

A Virginia dealership sold a car on eBay to a South Carolina resident. When the unhappy South Carolina buyer later sued, the defendants said, "Wait just a cotton-picking minute! This South Carolina court doesn't have any say-so over us." Let's look at how the court handled the dealer's objection to jurisdiction.

HBL, LLC, is a dealer organized under Delaware law, with its principal place of business in Virginia. HBL contracted with Auction 123 to list a black Porsche Carrera GT for sale. Auction 123 listed the vehicle on eBay as a new vehicle. Patrick Driscoll, an HBL employee, was listed as the contact person for the Porsche. Robert Gossett, a South Carolina resident, was the high bidder at $380,000. The parties agreed to substitute a silver Porsche for the black one listed on eBay.

After receiving the Porsche, Gossett heard it making a knocking noise (usually not a good sign) and sued HBL, Driscoll, Robert Penske (also a member of HBL), and United Auto Group. The U.S. District Court for the District of South Carolina dismissed Gossett's claims against both HBL and Driscoll for lack of personal jurisdiction. Gossett moved for reconsideration, and Penske moved to dismiss for lack of personal jurisdiction.

The court denied Gossett's motion for reconsideration. The court found that HBL's listing on eBay was not sufficient to subject HBL to personal jurisdiction in South Carolina because HBL conducted only isolated activities there and did not direct its activities at South Carolina. Thus, the court concluded that it lacked personal jurisdiction over HBL.

Similarly, the court found that Driscoll and Penske, as HBL employees, did not purposefully avail themselves of the privilege of conducting business in South Carolina. Thus, Driscoll and Penske lacked the "minimum contacts" to South Carolina necessary to support personal jurisdiction. As such, the court concluded that it lacked personal jurisdiction over Driscoll and Penske.

Gossett v. HBL, LLC, 2006 WL 1328757 (D.S.C. May 11, 2006).

So, are we clear? A dealer selling on eBay to a buyer in

another state isn't subject to the jurisdiction of that state's court.

Got it? Keep reading.

Michael Tindall, a Michigan resident, bought a 1973 Mustang in an eBay Motors auction. The seller was Guthrie, Inc., and the car was listed on eBay for Guthrie by Dan Cunningham. Both Cunningham and Guthrie were located in California. The Mustang arrived with no title and was not, according to Tindall, as described on eBay. Tindall sought rescission of his purchase and tendered the car for return to Guthrie and Cunningham.

Unsuccessful in his rescission attempts, Tindall sued and obtained a default judgment against Cunningham and Guthrie. The defendants then moved to set aside the default judgment, arguing that the U.S. District Court for the Eastern District of Michigan lacked personal jurisdiction over them. Sound familiar? We know what's coming next, don't we? Maybe not.

Interpreting Michigan's long-arm statute as broadly as due process considerations would permit, the court concluded that it had personal jurisdiction over the defendants.

Tindall v. One 1973 Ford Mustang, 2006 WL 1329168 (E.D. Mich. May 16, 2006).

So, two courts, same facts, more or less, different conclusions. What's a dealer to do?

First, unless you are selling on eBay to buyers in South Carolina, Michigan, or the two or three other states whose courts have addressed this issue, assume that there is real risk of your getting hauled into court in your buyer's state. Second, talk to your lawyer about this topic, because the courts have so far only scratched the surface of the many questions raised by interstate Internet car sales.

Like what, you ask? Well, like what about at least the following:

- Does the buyer's state require you to be licensed to sell cars to its residents?
- What advertising laws of the buyer's state apply to your Internet activities?
- What sales laws of the buyer's state (such as a prohibition of "as-is" sales) apply to your sales?
- What credit laws of the buyer's state apply to these sales, and what contract do you use to evidence a credit sale to the buyer?

And there are more, limited only by the lack of imagination of plaintiffs' lawyers. Many, many dealers are using eBay and other Internet sales avenues to sell cars. There are ways to engage in these activities that will increase your chances of winning not only an argument like the one raised by the buyers in these cases, but also, the arguments likely to be raised by such buyers in the future. If you haven't had a thorough review of your Internet sales practices, it's time for a session with your lawyer to review them to make sure that they are designed to give you as much protection as possible. She will appreciate it—she has a boat payment coming up shortly.

Some Courts are Miles Apart: Personal Jurisdiction and Internet Vehicle Sales

September 2006

By Maya P. Hill

Depending on where you start and where you want to go, California and Georgia are about 2,517.4 miles apart. And depending on what issue you're looking at, it's possible that the California and Georgia courts are that far apart as well. Take, for example, the issue of personal jurisdiction—the issue of what state can force you into its courts if you live in one state, and the person or company you're suing (or the person who is suing you) is located in another state.

Recently courts in both states each heard a case in which the defendant, an Internet seller of a motor vehicle, raised a defense of "lack of personal jurisdiction." This is like the seller saying, "Dear Court, thanks for thinking of me, but you have no right to bring me into your court." The California court held that it lacked personal jurisdiction over the seller, but the Georgia court held the opposite way. Why the difference? Let's take a look at both cases to figure out what actions will trigger a finding of personal jurisdiction. But first, let's run through the fundamentals of personal jurisdiction. I promise, it'll be brief.

A court can exercise personal jurisdiction over a defendant when the jurisdiction comports with the law of the state in which the court sits and with the requirements of "due process." Due process requires that a defendant have certain minimum contacts with the forum state (that is, the place where legal remedy can be sought), so that allowing the suit would not "offend traditional notions of fair play and substantial justice."

In other words, a defendant's conduct and connection with the forum state must be such that the defendant would reasonably expect being brought into court there. There are two types of personal jurisdiction: general and specific. General jurisdiction exists when a defendant has substantial or continuous and systematic contacts with the forum state. This is a pretty high standard and can sometimes be difficult to meet. So, a plaintiff always has the option of seeking specific jurisdiction. Although the elements might vary from state to state, specific jurisdiction generally means that even a defendant whose activity in the forum is sporadic, or consists only of a single act, may be subject to the jurisdiction of the forum's courts, when the cause of action arises out of that activity or act.

Paul Boschetto, a California resident, bought a 1964 Ford Galaxy from Jeffery Hansing, a Wisconsin resident, via eBay. According to Boschetto, the car was advertised on the site as an "R Code," in "awesome condition," "recently rebuilt" and "ready to be driven." Boschetto claims that he relied on this description when submitting a bid.

Boschetto won the auction, and after he paid for the car, Hansing instructed him by e-mail that he would pick up the car from Frank Boucher Chrysler Dodge Jeep, the Wisconsin dealership where Hansing worked. Boschetto hired a delivery company to transport the vehicle to California. Upon delivery, he discovered that the vehicle was defective and not an "R Code" as advertised. Boschetto sued Hansing and the dealership in the Northern District of California for breach of contract and fraud. Boschetto moved to dismiss the case based on lack of personal jurisdiction.

Boschetto argued that the court would have general jurisdiction over Hansing, if Hansing previously sold cars to other California residents, and argued that the fact that Frank Boucher Chrysler Dodge Jeep maintained a Web site might be enough to establish general jurisdiction. If that argument sounds pretty weak to you, it's because it is. The court found that there was no evidence that Hansing or the dealership had "continuing or systematic" contacts with the state of California. Even if Boschetto could have shown previous sales to California residents, the court explained that those occasional sales would have been insufficient to create general jurisdiction.

Like we said, general jurisdiction is a pretty high standard. So, Boschetto turned to specific jurisdiction. He claimed that Hansing contracted to sell a car to a California resident, an action which subjected Hansing to personal jurisdiction. But once again, the court found these arguments unpersuasive. Boschetto didn't purposefully direct his actions toward California—he happened to sell a car to a California resident. The court noted that auction sales on eBay are "attenuated" and that the choice of the highest bidder is beyond the control of the seller. No negotiations took place in California—everything was done online. The court further noted that Hansing's contacts with California were not repetitive or comprehensive. The relationship between Hansing and Boschetto was not intended by either party to be ongoing in nature, but was rather a "one-shot affair."

The court also commented on the nature of personal jurisdiction in connection with Internet sales. Assume an eBay seller was subject to personal jurisdiction simply by placing an item for sale on the site that is eventually bought by someone in a galaxy far, far away. The court predicted that such a rule would cause a friction on e-commerce that would slow the flow of transactions, perhaps in a crippling manner.

From *Boschetto*, then, we learn that, at least in California, personal jurisdiction over an Internet seller in one state, in a case brought by a resident buyer of another state, might not typically be found when the following criteria apply:

- No negotiations take place in the forum state;
- There are no continuous and systematic contacts between the defendant and the forum state;
- The defendant's actions are not purposefully aimed towards the forum state; and
- The defendant's actions in connection with the forum state are not repetitive or comprehensive, but, rather, a "one-shot affair."

So you think you've got personal jurisdiction down pat, right? Think again. The Court of Appeals of Georgia recently heard a similar case, but ruled the opposite way. Why, you ask? Let's find out.

While perusing through the eBay Motors auction Web site, Gordon Grieves, a Georgia resident, saw a 2001 BMW offered for sale by Aero Toy Store, a Florida company. Grieves began making e-mail inquiries to Juan Almeida, the individual listed as the seller's agent on the site. Almeida responded to Grieves with several e-mails. Grieves claimed that, based on Almeida's promises and representations regarding the car's condition and warranty, he calculated his winning bid. After that, Almeida faxed copies of the purchase agreement to him, which he signed and faxed back, and mailed a check to Aero for the purchase price.

Grieves later brought suit in a Georgia state court against Aero for allegedly making material misrepresentations about the car. Aero filed a motion to dismiss the case for—you guessed it—lack of personal jurisdiction.

Aero provided the following support for its motion: (1) It did not have any agents, representatives, employees or officers in Georgia; (2) It did not own or rent property in Georgia; (3) It did not maintain an office in Georgia; and (4) It had no subsidiaries or business affiliates in Georgia. Aero also provided the language from the back of the purchase agreement evidencing the sale. That language stated that the contract was made in Florida, that it would be governed by Florida law, and that any action or proceeding would be litigated only in a Florida court.

Grieves argued that he never agreed to the Florida provisions, and produced e-mails between himself and Almeida demonstrating that, although the purchase agreement made reference to the information on the back of the contract, Grieves had never received that information. There was some dispute over whether Grieves ever received the language on the back of the contract.

Aero further maintained that since its formation in 2002, it had only made two Internet sales to persons in Georgia, with revenues totaling less than one-half of one percent of its gross revenues for the years 2002 through 2004. Through some handy detective work, Grieves found evidence showing that from November 2003 until February 2005, at least 11 people from Georgia had submitted winning bids on cars offered by Aero on eBay. Aero responded that no more than two of those sales were ever consummated.

The trial court denied Aero's motion to dismiss. In so doing, it found that Aero purposefully transacted business in Georgia when its agent conducted business negotiations with Grieves, who lived in Georgia, and when Aero delivered the vehicle to Grieves in Georgia. These actions, the court found, were sufficient to establish minimum contacts with Georgia so as to establish personal jurisdiction over Aero in Georgia. Aero appealed, but unfortunately for the Florida seller, the appellate court agreed with the trial court.

In making its ruling, the appellate court explained that to establish personal jurisdiction, there must be some act by which the defendant purposefully avails itself of the privilege of conducting business in the forum state. The court found that Aero operated an interactive Web site through which it reached out to, and did business with, persons in Georgia. The court took notice that the transaction was worth thousands of dollars (just under $32,000) and involved shipment of an automobile to be operated in Georgia. The car was shipped into Georgia by the nonresident seller (Aero), and not by a carrier acting as the resident buyer's agent. The court also concluded that although the revenue Aero derived from goods sold in Georgia was not substantial in relation to Aero's overall revenue, Aero regularly solicited business in Georgia through the Internet, and the revenue it derived from shipping cars to persons in Georgia was substantial enough to establish sufficient minimum contacts with Georgia.

From *Aero*, then, we learn that, at least in Georgia, personal jurisdiction over an Internet seller in one state, in a case brought by a resident buyer of another state, might be found when the following conditions apply:

- The seller reaches out to persons in the forum state;
- The seller does business with persons in the forum state;
- The seller gains revenue from doing business with persons in the forum state; and
- The nonresident seller, as opposed to the resident buyer, ships the vehicle into the forum state.

If you're confused, it means you've been reading carefully. It seems that *Boschetto* and *Aero* present similar facts, but the courts arrive at opposite conclusions nonetheless. The key differences seem to be that in *Boschetto*, only one car was sold in the forum state, whereas in Aero, two were sold, and 11 "high bids" were submitted from persons in the forum state. Additionally, in *Boschetto*, the resident buyer shipped the car into the forum state, whereas in *Aero*, the nonresident seller shipped it into the forum state.

But of course, as is often the case with judges and courts, nothing is black and white. Courts are coming down on opposite sides of this issue, and it is likely that cases like *Aero* and *Boschetto* are just the beginning.

Look for cases on this topic in your state. The variance between states on this issue just might mean that the topic of personal jurisdiction in Internet sales is ripe for Supreme

Court attention. Ah, those lucky Supremes—they get to have all the fun.

Boschetto v. Hansing, 2006 WL 1980383 (N.D. Cal.July13, 2006). *Aero Toy Store, LLC v. Grieves*, 631 S.E.2d 734 (Ga. App. May 23, 2006).

Maryland Buyer, South Carolina Seller—Where Does an Internet Deal Occur?

March 2007

By Thomas B. Hudson

My wife and I have a place at Pawleys Island, South Carolina. By the time both Golden Retrievers and both humans make all the required pit stops, it's an 8-hour haul to Pawleys from our house in Maryland. For two years, we made the trip in our normal-sized wagon, but I had to strap one of those rooftop carriers to the top and load and unload the thing using a stepladder. 'Twas a real pain all the way around.

So when gas prices rose, and used SUV prices dropped, I started thinking about getting myself a fairly new "Pawleys Hauler." I asked a very good friend for help—he manages the used car operations for one of the mega-dealers.

He sent me to his Web site, and I found exactly what I was looking for.

About a week later, a huge, white 2004 Yukon XL (that's "extra long," Bunkie) that looks something like an industrial freezer shows up in my driveway in Maryland, followed by another car and driver that would return my driver home to the selling dealership in South Carolina.

The delivery person has me sign a slew of papers, and, after I direct him to my favorite local barbeque place, he heads south with his buddy. Deal done. Neat, huh?

Well, the car (OK, truck) ran great, the dealership called to make sure we were happy with it, and everything was going swimmingly, until my wife took the beast to the local MVA to title it. "No can do," says the MVA. "You don't have a safety inspection certificate."

Oops. So off she goes and gets the truck inspected. Back to the MVA for the title and registration. Everything's cool. But that got me thinking. In Maryland, a used car seller is obligated to obtain the inspection certificate. This dealer, in South Carolina, hadn't done so.

The questions began to circle my head like a spiral of hawks...

In the brave new world of Internet used car sales, does that Maryland requirement apply to the South Carolina dealer? How about other Maryland requirements dealing with the sale of used cars? Do they apply to my transaction?

Does the South Carolina dealer need a used car dealer's license to sell cars to Maryland residents? Must the dealer have a place of business in Maryland, as required for Maryland used car dealers? Must the dealer use a buyers order that complies with Maryland law? Must the dealer's retail installment sale contract comply with Maryland law? How about Maryland advertising requirements? Can the dealer disclaim implied warranties (Maryland law says no)? The questions went on and on.

Now, I reasoned that the South Carolina dealer would protest that this deal is a South Carolina transaction; after all, I contacted him through the Internet at his place of business, right? That contact would be one of the "indicia" (lawyer talk for "clue") that the deal was a South Carolina deal.

But what about that delivery? Two nice guys I had never heard of, who had been hired by the dealer, delivered the Yukon to my residence in Maryland. When courts look at a transaction and try to figure out the controlling law, the place of delivery is another clue.

Yet another clue is the place where the documents were signed and accepted. I signed the sale documents at my kitchen table in Maryland, and, as far as I could tell, the delivery person (hired by the dealer, remember, and arguably the dealer's agent) accepted them. What should a dealership do to refute these arguments that its home state laws don't apply? How can the dealership "load the dice" to boost its chances if the deal is ever challenged?

Well, some of the facts recited above are within the control of the dealer. The dealer could have arranged for me to hire my own delivery folks (he could have recommended someone), and then could have "delivered" the car to "my" delivery company at the dealer's location. I could have signed the documents in Maryland, but the documents could have contained a statement that they were not complete until "accepted" by the dealership at its South Carolina address. In other words, just by structuring and papering the deal differently, the dealer, if challenged, would have given himself a fighting chance to successfully argue that the transaction was a legal South Carolina deal and not a perhaps illegal Maryland deal.

My friend will probably be chapped that I'm writing about the transaction, but I'm hoping that the free legal advice will partly thank him for helping me out. I'd give him, and the dealership, a top-flight CSI rating, and I'm about to buy another car from him. Over the Internet.

CHAPTER 10

Reasonable Attorneys' Fees?

August 2007

By Thomas B. Hudson

Many contracts have a provision that requires the losing party in litigation to pay "reasonable attorneys' fees" (many business people I know would say that this phrase is an oxymoron). Whether it makes sense or not, though, the phrase crossed my mind recently when I was discussing with a North Carolina dealer a particular jam in which he found himself.

It seems that the dealer had decided he could no longer ignore the Internet, so he decided he would begin selling his cars on eBay. Now, selling cars on eBay, or through any other Internet site, can be dicey, especially when a dealership determines that it is willing to do business over the Internet with buyers from other states.

When the seller is from one state and the buyer is from another, a lot of interesting issues arise. You start worrying, for instance, about whether the laws of the buyer's state that deal with licensing, advertising, buyers orders, warranties, safety inspections, and other aspects of the transaction, might apply to the dealer. Usually, the laws don't expressly address these questions, and there have been very few cases so far that have dealt with these issues. That sort of uncertainty is enough to make a plaintiff's lawyer drool.

Now, the North Carolina dealer didn't ignore the risks imposed by these unanswered questions. Nosiree, he did some homework, and put together an Internet sales program that included pretty much every precaution that we urge dealers to take.

His documents expressly stated that North Carolina law would apply to the transaction. They also said that the deal wasn't final, and didn't become a deal, until the dealer signed the documents in North Carolina. The dealer also did not ship cars out-of-state but, instead, told the buyer that the buyer had to pick the car up in North Carolina or arrange to have the car picked up there by the buyer's transportation company. This gave the dealer a good argument that "delivery" had taken place in North Carolina.

So, you ask, if the dealer did all of those things, why was he in a jam?

Well, it seems that the dealer sold a car to a California buyer. The buyer's transportation company picked the car up from the dealership's lot in North Carolina and trucked it to the Left Coast.

Two weeks (yes, two weeks) after the car landed in the buyer's driveway, the buyer decided that the car had been damaged. He made his claim to the North Carolina dealer, who denied that the car had been damaged when it left his lot. The transportation company also denied any knowledge of the damage. You know what comes next. The California buyer sues the dealership—in California.

"Wait a minute," says the dealer. "I'm not in California—you can't sue me there."

Unfortunately, just saying those words won't make the lawsuit disappear. The dealer now has to hire a lawyer to go to court and file a motion contesting the court's jurisdiction over the dealer. His chances of making the suit go away are pretty good, though. There have been a number of cases addressing the issue of whether a court in the buyer's state has jurisdiction over an Internet seller, and while the cases have gone both ways, one of the courts finding no such jurisdiction was a California court.

That's where I got involved. The dealer had spoken to a California lawyer about representing him in the matter, and the lawyer had responded that he would be glad to do so, but that he needed a retainer of $5,000 to do so. The dealer was not happy with the prospect that he'd have to fork over that much loot in order to hire a lawyer.

I wasn't at all shocked by the lawyer's request (and yes, I've heard the lawyer joke about sharks and professional courtesy). First, the dealer isn't known to the lawyer, so he wants a substantial amount of up-front cash. If the lawyer has some experience and is any good, the chances are that his billing rate is $400 to $500 per hour.

That translates into 10 to 12 hours of work. When you consider that he will need to talk with his client, review the paperwork, do some research, prepare a motion and a supporting memorandum, travel to court, argue the matter and then report to his client, 10 to 12 hours isn't out of line.

When the dealer and I last spoke, he had not decided to hire the lawyer. It's possible that he was discussing settling the matter directly with the buyer—the $5,000 would likely go a long way toward fixing whatever damage the car might have sustained.

The story illustrates one of the perils of Internet sales. A selling dealer can find himself in litigation with a dissatisfied buyer far from home. Litigating in the local courthouse can be burdensome enough, but trying to litigate in a courthouse 3,000 miles away, where no one knows who you are, can really be a problem. Even "reasonable" attorneys' fees can be very painful for the selling dealer.

Until the courts provide us with some more guidance on Internet sales and jurisdiction, dissatisfied out-of-state buyers will be holding the upper hand. And the matter of "reasonable attorney fees" will remain a current discussion.

Chapter 11

Advertising

You've heard of "low-hanging fruit"? That's the stuff that's so easy to harvest, you don't need to waste time getting out the ladder or climbing the tree. Well, there isn't much fruit that hangs lower for Attorneys General than dealer advertising violations.

Wherever I travel, I like to pick up the local paper and check the car ads. Usually, I can spot half-dozen problems in each ad that I think the state's AG would pick up on. And the AGs have plenty of incentive to pursue advertising violations.

Not long ago, a Midwest state AG nailed a dealer for a $250,000 fine for advertisement violations. You can bet your last dollar that at the next National Association of Attorneys General, that AG stood up and crowed about his triumph over evil. And 50 other AGs went home thinking, "I think I'll go get me some of that."

And aside from the easy stuff, there are other advertising issues that dealers really need to think about. Many dealers assume that because the Internet is new, all those old advertising laws and regulations that applied to print, TV, and radio don't apply to the dealer's Internet activities. But, dealers, beware: Tricky issues arise in many vendor-designed "one day sale" programs. Depending on the facts, sometimes state lottery, sweepstakes, door-to-door sale and other laws apply.

As Monk says, "It's a jungle out there."

Trader Magazine Ad Hauls Dealer Out of State

January/February 2006

By Teresa Rohwedder

The case discussed below should trigger some thought about how you deal with out-of-state customers, and what provisions would protect you, if one of those customers sued you in a remote venue. Whether you advertise and do business over the Internet, in Trader magazines, or other types of advertisement, one thing you may not give much thought to is what happens if one of your out-of-state customers is unhappy.

This case involves a dispute between a dealership and an out-of-state customer who purchased ATVs and accessories. Before a case gets off the ground, the defendant may challenge the court's right to exercise jurisdiction, and that is exactly what happened here. The question was whether a Tennessee trial court could properly exercise jurisdiction over two Michigan corporations for alleged violations of the Tennessee Consumer Protection Act. Let's get started...

Troy Noles, a resident of Lafayette, Tennessee, bought an *Ohio Valley Circle Trader* in Indiana while traveling for business there. Although the court *does not* specifically discuss the circulation of the *Trader*, the title, and the fact that Noles picked it up while in Indiana, suggests that the circulation included more than one state, and was, perhaps, regional. The court *does* say that the magazine was not available to Noles in his home state of Tennessee.

Noles focused on a deal for two Yamaha all-terrain vehicles, plus trailer and accessories. He initiated contact with Champion Powersports by calling the toll-free number listed in the advertisement. Several phone calls followed, including those where the Champion representative contacted Noles at his home in Tennessee. The representative eventually told Noles that he did not qualify for the advertised financing, but he said that Michigan Powersports might be able to provide an alterative arrangement.

Champion and Michigan Powersports are separate entities, both located in Michigan. They rely on different financing resources but often refer customers to each other. Noles eventually arranged for an acceptable ATV package with the original representative. The ATVs were delivered to Noles in Tennessee, and he accepted delivery.

Noles later sued the two Michigan companies. The court's opinion does not reveal what his complaint was about, so we cannot speculate. However, we know that the defendants moved to dismiss the case for lack of personal jurisdiction. The trial court denied the motion but recommended that the defendants appeal the issue. The Tennessee Court of Appeals concluded that the trial court properly exercised jurisdiction under Tennessee's long-arm jurisdiction statute.

The Tennessee long-arm jurisdiction statute allows Tennessee courts to exercise jurisdiction to the extent of the Fourteenth Amendment to the U.S. Constitution; that means, unless the exercise of jurisdiction deprived the corporations of due process of law, then the court could properly exercise jurisdiction. Some state long-arm statutes impose more stringent requirements, before their courts may exercise jurisdiction over a foreign (out-of-state) defendant, but many state long-arm statutes defer to the Fourteenth Amendment due process requirements, as this one does. The defendants argued that they were not registered to do business in Tennessee; that they did not maintain an office or a sales force in Tennessee; and that they did not focus their advertising and promotions with the intent of attracting Tennessee customers.

The appellate court concluded that the defendants "purposely availed themselves of the privilege of conducting business within the state of Tennessee by knowingly entering into a contract for the sale of goods with a Tennessee resident after numerous telephone conversations and after delivering the ATVs and trailer to Noles in Lafayette, Tennessee." The appellate court noted that the defendants made no argument regarding any inconvenience they might experience if forced to litigate in Tennessee.

The key facts in this case that lead the court to its conclusion are (1) delivery of the vehicles in Tennessee; and (2) phone calls by the defendants' representative to Noles at his home in Tennessee. Even though it may have been a one-time sale to a Tennessee resident, the defendants knew they were selling to a Tennessee resident.

The next time you advertise to attract out-of-state customers, think about these things.

Noles v. Michigan Powersports, Inc., 2005 WL 2989614 (Tenn. App. November 7, 2005).

Dealer Gets Lucky

March 2006

By Thomas B. Hudson

This is a tale about a lucky dealer. One of the dealer's customers sued the dealer, alleging advertising violations, and won.

Hold on, Tom, I thought you said the dealer was lucky.

I did, read on.

John Wherry, Jr., drove to Showcase Isuzu, Inc.'s showroom to negotiate the purchase of an Isuzu Rodeo advertised in the newspaper the previous day. Wherry told the salesman he wanted to buy the "special purchase" 2000 Rodeo LS 4 X 4 with an MSRP of $27,779, minus the $9,000 savings as advertised.

The parties agreed that Wherry's trade-in was worth $4,000. Wherry concluded that the remaining purchase price, after the discount and the trade-in, should be $14,779.

At this point, the salesman told Wherry that the Rodeo was used or previously leased. Referring to the advertisement, Wherry complained that he had not negotiated the purchase of a used car, but a new one.

The salesman responded that "anybody knows" that "special purchase" means the vehicle was previously leased (we all know that, right?). Wherry unsuccessfully appealed to the sales manager, then drove to a Kia dealership and bought a Sportage. Wherry later sued Showcase, alleging advertising violations.

The trial court determined that Showcase violated two Attorney General regulations by running the advertisement and then refusing to sell the vehicle as advertised to the consumer, referring to the event as a "classic bait and switch."

Applying a variation of the "benefit of the bargain" rule, the trial court awarded Wherry $9,000. Concluding that the violations were "willful and knowing" [sic], the trial court doubled that amount and added attorney's fees and costs.

Showcase appealed the trial court's decision. Showcase did not dispute the determination that it had violated the advertising rules, but contested the damages award. The Massachusetts Court of Appeals affirmed the trial court's judgment, rejecting Showcase's arguments that the UCC governed damages; that Wherry's post-breach purchase prevented him from pursuing a benefit-of-the-bargain remedy; and that Wherry was limited to "cover" damages.

So the dealer is out $18,000, plus attorney's fees and costs. The amount of attorney's fees wasn't mentioned in the opinion, but it isn't unusual for fees in these cases to exceed the amount awarded to the plaintiff for damages. Let's guess that the plaintiff's attorney's fee number is $25,000, and let's guess that the dealer paid his own attorney the same amount. So we're looking at a hit of something approaching $70,000, if our guesses are right (and I'll bet they're conservative).

OK, Tom, the dealer's billfold is lighter by $70,000, and you say he's lucky? I have two questions. What are you smoking, and where can I get some?

Let me explain. A customer, who brought a private lawsuit seeking damages, sued this dealer. What if the state's Attorney General had sued the dealer?

AGs across the country are aggressively targeting dealers' advertising, sensing a "target-rich environment." And when an AG takes the trouble to come calling, it usually takes a lot more than $70,000 to encourage him or her to leave. One AG advertising challenge last year resulted in a $250,000 settlement, and the scuttlebutt among lawyers who represent dealers is that such large sums are typical of AG demands in advertising enforcement actions in many states.

I'd really like to be around when someone tries to explain to an AG that "anybody knows" that an off-lease car is a "special purchase" used car and not a new car.

Wherry v. Showcase Isuzu, Inc., 2006 WL 163331 (Mass. App. January 23, 2006).

Parle Vous Dealerese? Ditch the 'Dealer-Speak' in Your Ads

July 2006

By Emily Marlow Beck

We in the car business speak our own language. This is the type of thing we might take for granted, particularly if, like me, you grew up in the car business. However, dealer-speak can get you in trouble if a customer doesn't understand you. This is particularly true in the case of dealer advertising.

For example, a few months ago, a dealer in Massachusetts lost a case to a customer who claimed that the dealer violated state law by advertising a vehicle as a "special purchase" vehicle. What the dealer meant, and the customer failed to understand, was that the car was not new. It was a "special purchase," and, by that, the dealer meant, "used," a fact he failed to tell the customer until after the price was negotiated. The salesperson defended the dealer's ad, saying that "anybody knows" that "special purchase" means that the vehicle was previously leased. Apparently "anybody" isn't "everybody," and the dealer lost.

The case made me wonder how often dealers write car ads using words and phrases that just don't compute with customers. So, I decided to conduct an informal experiment. I pulled out a bunch of dealership print ads that I gathered while traveling throughout the country (yes, I need to get a life), and strong-armed some friends and acquaintances of mine to go over them with me. For the most part, these friends were college-educated, young professionals in the Washington, D.C., area. Most had bought cars from dealers before. None had experience in the car business.

I asked these friends to point out to me the words that they didn't understand. I also asked them if they knew what certain words meant. Not surprisingly, many of the ad disclosures got lost in translation.

For the most part, my "guinea pigs" didn't know the meaning of words like "special purpose" or "program car," and some totally missed the meaning of "O.A.C." ("on approved credit") or "W.A.C." ("with approved credit"). (Someone actually thought "W.A.C." meant "with air conditioning.") Many other abbreviations and disclosures, they just simply didn't understand.

This "experiment" frustrated me. I don't always take sides with state regulators and Attorneys General, but my crude little "experiment" supported what the state regulators and Attorneys General have been on their soapboxes screaming about for year—that advertising disclosures should be made in consumer-friendly, commonly understood language.

State advertising laws applicable to dealers reflect these AG and regulator concerns. For example, many states restrict a dealer's use of abbreviations, such as "W.A.C.," unless the abbreviations are commonly understood by the public. Advertising guidelines put out by the Illinois Attorney General's office go a step further, expressly listing "W.A.C." as an "abbreviation not commonly understood." Other states prohibit the use of abbreviations unless the abbreviations are also "spelled out" in the ad. (However, it's notable that in Arkansas, the advertising regulations expressly list "W.A.C." as an acceptable abbreviation because it is a commonly understood abbreviation.)

State laws also have something to say about the proper way for a dealer to disclose that a particular vehicle is used. In Virginia, for example, the fact that a car is used must be clearly and unequivocally expressed by the term "used," unless the dealer uses another word that is commonly understood to mean, "used."

The Virginia law goes on to say that "special purchase" or "program car," by itself, is not a satisfactory disclosure and gives this advice to dealers: When in doubt, just use the word "used." There are a few clarifications I should make about my "experiment." First of all, I used print ads from multiple states, but I did not review those ads for state law compliance. For all I know, the ads very well may have been in technical compliance with their states' laws. Secondly, it is quite possible that my friends are just dumber than most.

But the bigger issue is this: If your ads are targeted at customers that aren't in the car business, why not make all disclosures as clear as possible, in words that your customers will understand?

Need help? Think about all the people who will read your ads—the college student, the grandma, the neighbor—and consider whether they will understand the terms and disclosures used in the ads. If that doesn't provide you with enough direction (or incentive), think about having to convince a jury that the words and disclosures in your advertisements are commonly understood. Keep your fingers crossed that the guy in the jury box doesn't think "W.A.C." means "with air conditioning."

Oregon Attorney General Slams Dealer for Pre-Approved Credit, Gas Card, and Other Promotions

December 2006

By Thomas B. Hudson

On November 6, 2006, the Oregon Attorney General announced a settlement of claims against several Oregon dealerships for misleading advertising in the areas of credit, free gas offers, and unclear sponsorship of sales. The settlements, outlined in so-called "Assurances of Voluntary Compliance" filed in county courts, involved Carmart, Inc., doing business as Car Mart of Portland, and JKC Automotive, Inc., doing business as Kiefer Kia, Kiefer Mazda, Kiefer Mazda-Kia, Kiefer's Eugene Mazda, Kiefer's Kia, Kiefer's Mazda, and U.S. Auto Wholesale, all owned by John P. Kiefer, president, of Eugene, Oregon. The Assurances of Voluntary Compliance admit no violation of law on the part of the dealerships.

According to the AG's news release, the Oregon Department of Justice staff regularly monitors automobile advertising and marketing campaigns throughout the state (you might point this out to whoever in your dealership is responsible for ads and promotions). The Justice staff found that a direct mail flyer from Car Mart enticed consumers into the dealership with what it alleged was a "false credit offer." Consumers who had filed for bankruptcy were promised "great opportunities" through a pre-qualified certificate, supposedly good for up to $24,995. The Justice staff claimed consumers were not pre-qualified for any credit.

The Justice staff received many consumer complaints involving Car Mart. Most complaints alleged that Car Mart refused to unwind deals, return customers' deposits, and return customers' trade-ins when the company couldn't obtain financing as negotiated. According to the AG's news release, the dealer must do all three under Oregon's "bushing law" or be in violation of the state's Unlawful Trade Practices Act.

The AG also attacked the advertising practices of Kiefer's U.S. Auto Wholesale, a registered "dba" of JKC Automotive, but not a licensed dealership through the Oregon Department of Motor Vehicles. Kiefer allegedly held a "Vehicle Disposal" sale with the Gateway Mall in Springfield as the "exclusive Oregon location" for a "West Coast Auto Disbursement" sale. Since the sale was a Kiefer sale, there was no "exclusive Oregon location" and no "West Coast" sale, according to the AG.

The AG also found fault with a Kiefer "free gas" promotion. An electronic billboard at the entrance to Kiefer's Kia dealership offered consumers "free gas." In newspaper advertisements, Kiefer offered, "Buy a new Kia, get gas for a year." In addition, individual cars were listed as coming with "gas for a year." In "mouse type" under each offer, the company stated that the deal was a "combination offer." Consumers were told in barely readable type to, "Make your best deal on a package price...Gas offer is $500 gas card." The DOJ staff, not surprisingly, found the ads to be unclear and not conspicuous. The staff also alleged that $500 would not cover gas for a year for a typical driver.

Under the Car Mart Inc., agreement, Car Mart is required to comply with the credit repair statutes and the state "bushing" law and permanently close Car Mart of Portland. Kiefer agreed not to open another used car store in the Portland metro area for at least a year and to pay $1,000 to the DOJ Consumer Protection and Education Fund.

The JKC Automotive, Inc., settlement sets several conditions in which Kiefer can advertise, including only selling under names of dealerships licensed with the DMV. For one year, the company must send copies of all advertisements and direct mail flyers to the Justice staff 14 days before publication. Finally, JKC Automotive paid $9,000 to the DOJ Consumer Protection and Education Fund.

Note that the dealerships were able to settle these charges without admitting any wrongdoing, so no one has proven anything yet. But the settlement details will give you a good idea of the sorts of actions that AGs will attack.

The Oregon AG's actions involving dealerships are more the norm these days than the exception. Dealers need to police their advertisements in the same way the DOJ staff here did, asking themselves if every statement in the ad is accurate and fully supportable. They should also fight the impulse to fudge (a $500 gas card will buy gas for a year?) or get cute ("West Coast Sale").

The fines levied by the Oregon AG in this matter were modest—other AGs have been much more aggressive, seeking fines of hundreds of thousands of dollars for advertising violations. Don't think that the dealers here are out of the woods either. It's still possible that consumers could file civil lawsuits, alleging violations of the state laws addressed by the AG.

More State Advertising Enforcement Actions

December 2006

By Thomas B. Hudson

After writing an article about the Oregon Attorney General's actions against car dealer advertisements, I went snooping on the AG's Web site, and found another example of such enforcement actions. Again, the Oregon AG moved against car dealers and marketers for allegedly bad advertisements. An October 2006 news release announced that the AG had filed agreements in two Oregon courts with two car dealerships and a direct marketing company for allegedly luring consumers onto dealership lots with direct mail flyers containing false offers of credit.

The AG's document, called an "Assurance of Voluntary Compliance" (AVC) and filed in one county court, named Hillsboro Automotive Group, Inc., (d/b/a Hillsboro Chrysler Jeep), Larry Miller Chrysler Jeep and Larry Miller Hillsboro Chrysler Jeep and Larry H. Miller Corporation-Oregon (d/b/a Honda of St. Johns), and Larry Miller Honda of St. Johns.

An AVC filed in another county court named Direct Marketing Associates, Corp. (d/b/a www.onlinebkmanager.com), Evergreen Automotive Acceptance, and Evergreen's president, John Rainey. Neither AVC admitted a violation of law on the part of the dealers or the ad companies.

"Both the dealers and marketing company were blatantly violating state and federal laws with so-called, pre-approved offers of credit that consumers never received," AG Hardy Myers said. "Unfortunately, these are the first of many sanctions to come concerning these types of misleading offers. The continuing pattern of dealers and marketers ignoring the law and using these illusory credit offers must be stopped."

What had these dealers and marketers done to get the AG so riled up, you ask?

The Department of Justice legal staff claimed that both the Hillsboro and St. Johns dealers sent out "Vehicle Buyback Notice" direct mail flyers offering to "buy back consumers' current vehicles at 20% of $4,000 over NADA book value." That advertisement, the AG said, violated an Oregon rule that makes it illegal to guarantee a minimum amount that will be paid for a trade-in vehicle.

The Hillsboro dealership flyers also stated that the recipients had been "pre-approved" for loans "of up to $42,988" at a 4.9% interest rate "with no money down." The AG claimed this offer did not comply with the federal Truth in Lending Act.

AG Myers also outlined another allegedly illegal practice used by the marketing company; this one included using an exception to the federal Fair Credit Reporting Act that allows businesses to pull credit information in order to make a "firm offer of credit."

The company used the exception to obtain the mailing lists but was not making firm offers of credit, according to the AG. Flyers stated that the recipients were "approved for an auto loan of up to $23,375.00" through Financial Services. At the bottom of the flyer was a "prescreen and opt-out notice" letting the recipients know that they could stop receiving "prescreened" offers of credit.

"Unfortunately, consumers were being deceived into thinking they were approved for a $23,375 loan through Financial Services, when in reality no offer of credit was being extended," Myers said.

You can't always tell from these self-serving AG news releases what actually went on; the fact is, the AGs tend to report on the things that show how diligent they are at protecting consumers, and don't deal with extraneous stuff. But I'll bet I can make a couple of educated guesses about the facts not reported.

Guess #1

I'll bet that the dealers bought these advertising packages on the assumption that the ad company knew the law and had followed applicable law in crafting the ad packages.

Guess # 2

I'll bet the dealerships involved didn't ask the ad companies for the legal reviews they had commissioned for the advertisements.

Guess #3

I'll bet that the contract between the ad companies and the dealers said something like, "Ad Company's liability in the event there is anything wrong with these ads is limited to the amount that Dealer has paid Ad Company."

I wonder how many of my guesses are right.

We've reported on several enforcement actions dealing with advertisements recently, and if you haven't identified this as a hot compliance topic for your dealership, it's high time you did. Many AGs around the country have their sights set on dealer advertising, and as this enforcement action shows, there is plenty of low-hanging fruit for the AGs to pick.

We've said it before, but here we go again: Your dealership's ads are the responsibility of your dealership. The ad company won't pay your fines or legal fees when the AG comes-a-calling. It will be your dealership that gets its name smeared all over the media for violating advertising rules.

So don't engage in an ad campaign unless you've gotten a

legal review of what your ads will say, and how they will say it. If you've got ad campaigns running that haven't been reviewed, pull them and get them blessed. And don't sign any ad company contracts without doing a due diligence review on the ad company and without having your lawyer review the contract.

Oregon Attorney General Announces Settlement of Advertising and 'Bushing' Claims

January/February 2007

By Nicole F. Munro

We've said it before and we'll say it again, Attorneys General have their hair on fire over dealer advertising. This time, it's the Oregon AG, whose press release contains a couple of worthwhile lessons for dealers.

Oregon Attorney General Hardy Myers filed a second major court action in less than four years against Asbury Automotive Oregon, LLC, doing business in Oregon as Thomason Autogroup, along with all of their affiliated Oregon dealerships. The AG charged Autogroup and their affiliates with (1) violating a 2001 agreement concerning misleading advertising; and (2) circumventing the state's anti-bushing laws. The dealership entities entered into an "Assurance of Voluntary Compliance" agreement with the AG. The agreement admits no violation of law.

The AG's press release said, "Just because Asbury is one of the biggest in the automobile industry doesn't mean it can willfully ignore Oregon's consumer protection laws. When we caught Asbury/Thomason Autogroup in 2001 selling cars to consumers for thousands of dollars more than the advertised sale price, we were surprised at their brashness, but frankly, we were shocked to find that not only were Asbury's dealerships ignoring our earlier agreement but were committing new violations of the Unlawful Trade Practices Act." Thomason paid more than $1.5 million in restitution as well as $300,000 to the Justice Department Consumer Protection and Education Fund. As part of the 2001 agreement, Thomason dealerships also were required, when financing for a vehicle was not available, to return the buyer's trade-in and refund the down payment before entering into any negotiations for different financing terms or a different vehicle.

After the dealerships agreed to change business practices in the 2001 agreement, the AG's staff evidently kept an eye on their advertising and business activities. In 2003, Justice investigators learned that Thomason Toyota of Gladstone was not in compliance with the court agreement by having customers sign an acknowledgement of the possibility of renegotiation if financing fell through, at the inception of the transaction rather than when financing was actually denied.

The AG also alleged that the dealer wasn't offering a full rescission and termination of the original contract when financing fell through, before trying to talk consumers into signing a new deal, mostly with higher interest, a practice known as "bushing."

So here's lesson number one. If the AG has alleged that you were misbehaving, and you've agreed not to do any more of whatever it was you claimed you didn't do in the first place, it's a real good idea to abide by your agreement.

Here's lesson number two. Don't get cute with your advertising.

In March 2004, a Thomason Honda dealership advertised in large, bold print "35 PERCENT OFF MSRP (Manufacturer's Suggested Retail Price) ON ALL HONDAS IN STOCK!!"

Yikes! What a bargain!

But in very small type above the offer, the dealership posted "Dealer Installed Options Discounted" *(Note to the dealership manager: This just wasn't smart.)* According to the AG, large numbers of angry customers arrived to buy a new Honda at a 35% reduction, only to find the discount was for dealer installed options. The dealership closed its doors early that day and remained closed the next day. A number of consumers filed complaints with the Justice Department about the alleged fraudulent ad.

After lengthy negotiations concerning the defendants' "bushing" and advertising violations, Asbury and Thomason agreed to pay $250,000 to the Justice Department Consumer Protection and Education Fund.

In addition, the dealership group agreed to comply with the Unlawful Trade Practices Act and the terms of the prior court order, especially in the area of "bushing." The defendants agreed to designate an employee to ensure legal compliance of all of their advertising and promotional materials before publication, and they must offer "35 PERCENT OFF MSRP" on any new Honda to the 23 consumers who complained to the AG concerning the misleading ads.

The Oregon AG would probably have come down pretty hard on these defendants just for the advertising claims, but it really didn't help that the dealership group had violated an earlier agreement to walk the straight and narrow.

So, keep your promises, and don't get cute with your advertising.

What Happens When a Plaintiff's Lawyer Examines Your Direct Mail Piece?

May 2007

By Thomas B. Hudson

Once again, I received a direct mail piece from a dealer. It arrived in my home mailbox. My hobbies are fishing, gardening, and reading dealership direct mail pieces. I'm always interested in these things, because I find it simply amazing that a dealer will pay a direct mail company to send out stuff that can expose the dealer to consumer lawsuits or an action by the Attorney General.

For fun, let's pretend that we are plaintiffs' lawyers, or lawyers on the staff of the state AG's office, and that we are looking over this mailer. What'll we find?

First, let's look at the envelope. The upper left-hand corner contains a return address, "CERTIFICATION OFFICE, ABC, Inc., Anystreet, USA 12345."

OK, the name and address are made up for this article. Under the name and address appears the following: CERTIFIED DOCUMENTS ENCLOSED FOR ADDRESSEE ONLY. $2,000 FINE OR 5 YEARS IMPRISONMENT, OR BOTH, FOR ANY PERSON WHO TAMPERS WITH OR OBSTRUCTS DELIVERY; U.S. CODE TITLE 18, SEC 1702. To the right of the address and this warning is what appears to be a green and black bar code, with a 12-digit number printed across the bottom.

If I were attempting to attack this mailer, I'd argue that the use on the envelope of the term "Certification Office," the all-caps reference to a U.S. Code provision that applies to all mail and the green bar code (I will bet both of my Golden Retrievers it's not a real bar code) are all designed to deceive the recipient into thinking that the envelope contains something official, when it doesn't.

Now let's look at the letter inside the envelope. The term "CERTIFICATION OFFICE" is repeated at the top of the page, and just above the text of the letter appears "Notice to the Public. Special Test Market." If I were attacking this mailer, I'd argue that there's nothing "special" about the event that is being promoted, and that there is no "test" of any sort involved in the event.

Now, to the body of the letter itself. Here's the text, interspersed [in brackets, in italics] with some of my suspicions and the sorts of allegations that I'd make if I were a plaintiff's lawyer or the AG.

The firm of ABC will be conducting test marketing pricing and strategy events at various locations in Maryland. *[I would argue that all that is happening is an advertised sale of cars at a dealership, and not a "test marketing pricing and strategy event."]* During these events, new cars, trucks, mini vans, and sport utility vehicles from Ford Motor Company *[I'd argue that this is an attempt to mislead the reader into believing that Ford had something to do with the sale, and, other than the fact that the dealer may be a Ford dealer, I'll bet Ford doesn't have any idea its name is being used.]* will be priced below national averages *[I'd challenge the dealer to prove that the prices are "below national averages."]* to promote immediate product awareness *[I'd argue that the intent is to sell cars, not to promote "product awareness." Do you think I'd be wrong?].*

In addition, our firm has been ordered *[I'd want to know by whom.]* to conduct a three-day Final Close-Out *[Is the sale in fact "final?" Are these cars, or is the dealership, in fact, being "closed out?"]* of over $3,000,000 worth of new vehicles, lease returns, factory program vehicles, executive demonstrators, and dealership vehicles *[I'd ask whether all of these categories of cars were actually included.]*—all marked with test market prices *[Are they really "test market prices," or will discovery show that the prices are no different from any other weekend?]* for this three-day event.

As a recipient of this certification, you are eligible for immediate qualification. *[This meaningless phrase seems designed to make it appear that the recipient is getting some sort of special treatment. If everyone who visits the dealership during the sale is treated the same, whether they received the letter or not, this statement is deceptive.]* Finance and lease representatives will be at the test market site *[The dealership?]* to assist you with financing and arrange for same day delivery. ALL CREDIT APPLICATIONS WILL BE REVIEWED! *[Another meaningless statement suggesting, without saying, that people with bad credit can get credit at the event.]*

It is the desire of Ford Motor Co., to put as many new products as possible in service immediately to gain quick recognition in the communities in which they are sold. *[While no doubt that's what Ford—and every other manufacturer—desires, this statement seems to imply that Ford has some connection with the event. On discovery, I suspect we would find that's not the case.]* This recognition will increase product awareness and subsequent sales. For three days only, we will be conducting one of these tests at a dealership near you. You will not have to negotiate. *[This is an implication that negotiating isn't permitted, which, on discovery, I believe is likely not to be the case.]* All models will be included in this test and factory rebates and discounts of up to $9,000 or special below market financing starting as low as 0.0% A.P.R. up to 60 months. *[OK, bad grammar isn't a crime (more's the pity), but the financing better be "special" and "below market" and not the same old deals the dealership offers the other 362 days of the year.]*

There's more, but I'm getting tired of typing.

If you are a dealer, your first reaction might be, "Why do I care? If these guys get into trouble with this mailer, it's no skin off my nose."

The problem is that I can just about guarantee you the plaintiffs' lawyers and the AG are going to come after your dealership, if they decide to attack this ad. Your dealership contracted with ABC, and ABC will be deemed to be acting on your behalf. If you get into mischief, you might have a claim against ABC, but the contract you signed probably says that you reviewed and approved all ad copy (You did read the contract before you signed it, and you do read all material that's sent out with your dealership's name on it, right? Right?), and even if it didn't, the company may well be so thinly capitalized as to be judgment proof against the typical $200,000 to $300,000 fines being imposed by state AGs for advertising violations, not to mention the damages awards that plaintiffs' lawyers often obtain.

And for the AG or for a plaintiffs' lawyer, this is like shooting fish in a barrel. In the first place, they have mailboxes, too. All they have to do is what I did—open an envelope—and they have a ready-made case. And in the second place, some of these mailers are so bad that they might as well have "SUE ME" stamped on them.

If you're looking for proof that the AGs are going after dealers for their ads, take a look at three more announcements:

Idaho Attorney General Lawrence Wasden announced on April 6 that his office had imposed a $5,000 civil penalty, plus attorneys' fees and costs, on Larry Miller Sundance Dodge to settle claims that the dealer's direct mail solicitations were false and misleading. The envelopes, containing only an ad for a "vehicle liquidation event," bore on the front the words "Extremely Urgent: Please Hand Deliver to Addressee." On the back appeared "Extremely Urgent—Do Not Bend—Priority Delivery." The AG evidently objected that these legends on the envelope attempted to fool the recipient into believing that something other than an ad was enclosed. The AG also objected to a $4,000 "Instant Savings Voucher" on the ground that it violated the state's law against dealer rebates. Finally, the AG alleged that the ad failed to clearly and conspicuously disclose all material terms and conditions of the advertised offers, that it used color contrasts and tiny print that made the text hard to read, and that it used asterisks that confused or contradicted the ad's principal message.

On April 6, New York's AG, Andrew Cuomo, announced a settlement with two dealers regarding their ad practices. One dealer, Poughkeepsie Chevrolet, mailed fliers to owners of GM cars with a headline that read "IMPORTANT—SECOND NOTICE—SAFETY RECALL," complete with a recall number, a warning that their vehicles "may be at risk," and an admonition to call their "designated safety recall center" to schedule an appointment to address the recall. The recall and the recall number were fictitious, and the listed phone number was for the dealer's service center, for which the dealer hoped to increase business. The dealer paid $5,000 in civil penalties.

Cuomo also announced a settlement with Harriman Chevrolet. Harriman had sent a flier offering deals and credit terms that did not exist. Among the terms of the ad the AG objected to were a "guaranteed $3,000 for any trade-in vehicle" the consumer could "push, pull, or tow" to the dealership, financing consisting of $59 down and payments of $129 per month for terms as short as 24 months, and a scratch-off prize giveaway of dubious value. Harriman Chevrolet agreed to stop advertising in this manner, to comply with the AG's Advertising Guidelines for Auto Dealers and to pay $10,000 in civil penalties.

These penalties of $5,000 and $10,000 are at the very low end of the scale for recent AG enforcement actions regarding advertising violations. If you are trying to assess the risks associated with advertising campaigns for your dealership, you should keep in mind the occasions on which the fines have been $100,000, $200,000 or even, in one case, $250,000.

As the Illinois Attorney General said in a late 2004 press release announcing a settlement involving a dealer's ad campaign, "Car dealerships are not allowed to make up whatever they think will lure consumers to the lot."

Words of Wisdom—Dealerese Part Deux

August 2007

By Emily Marlow Beck

I write lots of articles, and I get lots of feedback on the things I write. Some good, some not so good (with time, most lawyers become just as thick-skinned as they are thick-headed). But an article I wrote about a year ago triggered a tsunami of e-mails, the ripples of which still flood my inbox today.

In my article, "Parle vous Dealerese? Ditch the 'Dealer-Speak' in Your Ads," I wrote about my experiment where a bunch of college-educated, "inside the Beltway" consumers couldn't understand the dealer-speak in the car advertisement section of our local rag. Many of my "guinea pigs" did not understand the abbreviations "O.A.C." and "W.A.C." One of my piggies thought that "W.A.C." meant "with air conditioning." The moral of my article was that because ads are targeted at customers that aren't in the car business, dealers should make all disclosures as clear as possible and use words that non-car people will understand.

But, after that article hit print, my mailbox was flooded with one-sentence e-mails that all went a little something like this:

"I've been in the car business for [insert number] of [years, decades, generations], and I have no idea what O.A.C. or W.A.C mean!"

I'll answer these e-mails en masse and (hopefully) avoid a future onslaught of e-mails by explaining that I often see the initials "W.A.C." and "O.A.C" used as "with approved credit" or "on approved credit." I almost always see these abbreviations in print ads, but they sometimes show up on the tube (on a recent ad I saw, a slick five-year-old sported the initials "W.A.C." on the back of his spiked leather jacket before hopping behind the wheel of a Mustang) or other media.

But, I must say that this wave of e-mails put me back a bit. Was I out of touch? Had I been out of the car business too long? Had too many years of legal propaganda rotted my brain? Feeling a little blue and rejected, I immediately hit the streets searching for a little pick-me-up. Once I got to the newsstand (where did you think I was going?), I bought up every newspaper I could find. And, to my surprise, there they were again, spattered all over the car pages: O.A.C. and W.A.C. (Sweet validation!)

But, as the student becomes the teacher, I learned a few big lessons from the barrage of e-mails I received in response to that article. Most importantly, it's not a good idea to go slinging around a bunch of industry slang, assuming that everyone understands what you're talking about. But, it's certainly worth noting that if a big chunk of "car people" reading a "car publication" didn't get my lingo, average consumers most certainly won't. It's also worth noting that my car-dealer father admonished me that I'd receive this wave of e-mails when he read a draft of my article. (Alas, father really does know best!)

But, all those e-mails made me think about how much we car folk risk by living in a lingo vacuum. Because much of the time we speak to and understand people like ourselves, we must realize that it is even more important to have a firm grasp on the federal and state laws that apply to car ads. Even if you think the statements in your ads are fine and dandy and are perfectly comprehensible to you, your state lawmakers may not have shared your sensibilities when drafting advertising regulations, otherwise known as "regs." The state laws that govern advertisements vary from state to state, and some of the restrictions they contain are far from intuitive.

So, here's a tip. Before you go to press with your hot new car ad, grab a copy of the statute or regulation that governs advertising in your state. (Odds are you can find a copy online or from your state association.) Now, hold a copy of the ad in one hand, and hold a copy of the state regs in the other. Does your ad contain everything that your regs require it to? If not, then add whatever is missing. Does it contain anything that is prohibited? If so, then take it out. Now, do the same with the advertising requirements under Reg. Z or Reg. M. Following this tip won't guarantee your ads will fly completely under the radars of Attorneys General and plaintiff's lawyers, but it could help you say au revoir to that AG homing device.

Maybe You'll Get Time Off for Good Behavior

September 2007

By Thomas B. Hudson

Picture the following conversation at a dealership.

"Hey Boss. I got an idea. You've been saying that our Service Department revenue is off a bit, and that you'd really like to increase it, because we don't really make any money on new car sales, and the F&I guys aren't pulling their weight. Let's buy a list of folks who own the make of cars we sell, and then let's mail them a notice that their cars have been recalled. What do you mean, I'm fired? Well, if you don't like it, I'll take it to the dealer down the street."

Couldn't happen, right? No dealer would be dumb enough to launch a fake recall program just for the purpose of getting more customers for the service department. Would they? Would they?

They would. We don't make this stuff up—we aren't that good at fiction.

But a dealer, and a large dealer at that, was recently nailed by his state Attorney General for allegedly faking a recall notice to boost service revenues. The reason I'm bringing this up is to point out that all the advice we have been giving you over the years regarding your sales department applies equally to your service department.

If you've been following our advice, you've done your homework, and you have scoped out all of the state and federal advertising requirements that apply to you. You have checked with your state ADA or IADA to see what they have by way of advertising guidance. You have checked with your state's motor vehicle dealer regulators, consumer protection agencies and Attorney General to see what aids they might have concerning advertising, and you have designated someone in your dealership to check the Web sites of all of these folks regularly. You have reviewed all of the materials on the Federal Trade Commission's Web site. You have a file for each advertising campaign that you have run, and the file contains a checklist of state and federal advertising requirements. Your dealership's compliance officer signs off on each ad you run, thereby taking responsibility for it. When your people in charge of advertising are not certain they are doing things correctly, you have a lawyer that they can go to for clarification and advice, and you've provided a budget for that legal review (remember, no budget means no compliance). You have provided ethics and compliance training for whoever is in charge of advertising.

But mainly, you have infused your organization from top to bottom with a spirit of straightforward dealings with your customers. You have made it clear that lying, cheating, and stealing from your customers, your finance sources, and your suppliers will simply not be tolerated. You, and your ads, always tell the truth.

OK, if you are doing all of that, you are in pretty good shape. The one thing that you might not be doing, however, is making sure your service department folks are firmly in this loop. They will be signing up for promotional programs offered by various vendors and may be coming up with their own programs. These promotions are subject to many of the same restrictions and limitations that apply to your sales programs. Make sure that your training, compliance, and review structures are broad enough to pick them up too.

You don't want to go to all that trouble and expense? I really don't care! But, hey—you'll look good in that jail-orange jumpsuit.

Are Your Mailers UDAP-Compliant?

September 2007

By Thomas B. Hudson

One of my local car dealers keeps me entertained with his direct mail advertising pieces. Every time one arrives in my mailbox, I fantasize about being either the Attorney General or a plaintiff's lawyer.

The latest one actually wasn't all that bad, but it contained plenty of ammunition for someone wanting to attack it. You will recall that the most potent weapon plaintiffs' lawyers can bring to bear is a state "unfair and deceptive acts or practices," or "UDAP," law. Nearly every state has such a law, and Maryland, my home state, is no exception. Plaintiffs' lawyers love UDAP laws because, while they typically ban certain described acts and practices, they usually have sweeping language that prohibits anything that is "unfair" or "deceptive."

With this sweeping language in mind, let's look at what the Honda dealer sent me.

The mailer announced something called the "Extravaganza Savings Event." Supposedly I could buy a car "without negotiation" and "as if I were a supplier" of the manufacturer. The sale was "due to excess inventory," and the cars were "drastically reduced." The offer was "for one day only." Evidently, the sale applied to used cars, as well, since the mailer announced that I was "entitled to obtain [my] new, or previously owned, vehicle at a price that is substantially lower than the retail-selling price." "Finance representatives" were to be on hand to make sure I would be offered "the best terms." The mailer screamed, "$1,000,000 of previously owned vehicles must be reduced from inventory." After the sale date, supposedly, "All vehicles that remain unsold will return to normal market prices (MSRP)."

So, you say, "What's wrong with the mailer? The dealer's having a sale. What's the big deal?"

Here's how I would look at the mailer if I were the AG or a plaintiff's attorney.

First, I'd wonder whether the "without negotiation" language was an attempt to discourage normal price haggling.

I'd be curious as to the level of the dealer's inventory. Was it actually "excess" on the sale day, or was it at normal levels?

Were cars sold on the sale date sold at "drastically reduced" prices, "substantially lower than the retail selling price," or did customers pay about what they usually paid on other days?

Could I have bought a car on the following day at the same price, or was the sale truly for "one day only"?

Who were the "finance representatives"? The term sounds like they are bank or finance company employees, but are they really the dealership's usual finance people, or people employed by a marketing company running the event for the dealer? If I were to be offered "the best terms," does that mean the dealer would not mark up the bank and finance company buy rates on that day?

Who, or what, is requiring that $1,000,000 of used cars has to be reduced from inventory? Will, in fact, the dealer sell cars after the sale date only at "MSRP"?

Remember, the test that the AG will use, or that the plaintiff's lawyer will urge the court to use, is whether each one of these statements is literally true, or even if literally true, is deceptive. Remember also, both the AG and the plaintiff's lawyer will be able to force the dealer to provide detailed information that will permit the AG, or the court, to judge the truthfulness and deceptiveness, if any, of these statements.

Now, it's possible that the mailer's statements would survive an attack by the bad guys. Call me cynical, but I'd bet that at least some of these statements could be successfully attacked.

NADA's Used Car Industry Report, 2007, at page 28, shows that dealers in 2006 spent more than three times as much on advertising as they did on accounting and legal services. Maybe you ought to consider spending a few more bucks having your ads and mailers reviewed by your friendly local lawyer.

Chapter 12

Dealer Operations

The articles that follow didn't fall smoothly into any of our other fairly arbitrary chapter topics, but all seemed to have something of the same theme—daily dealer operations. We decided, for lack of a better term, to call the chapter "Dealer Ops."

It never fails. When I go past a dealership with its gleaming rows of brand new designs, bold colors, mirrored bumpers, and those...those...dreamers—the customers who wander the lots with their hands in their pockets, who pause, look and sigh, pause...look...and sigh. Well, I say to myself, "They have no idea...."

The dealer's life—easy, right? Sell those gleaming beauties; make dreams come true; get kids to college; grandmother to grandchildren; provide that family with a Grand Canyon summer vacation, that four-wheel ride in the Rockies, or that shadowy trail winding a convertible along the Shenandoah River. Selling dreams...the stuff of clouds.

Wrong, Bunkie. Get your head out of the clouds. Of course, car dealers make people happy—that's the fun part. But, like any other occupation—there's the nitty gritty. And, believe me, I know of no realm of daily life that has more of that grit than the business of dealing cars.

You see, I'm a lawyer who represents those diligent guys who carefully line up the beautiful mobile merchandise you view in the car lot. I see behind the showroom scenes. I view the props behind the façade; that is, the forms that back up the handshakes; the contracts that dictate everything from size of type, to copies to keep; the rules and regs that make salesmen sweat and dealers dance attendance against ever-changing federal and state expectations.

I see it all. And some of what I see is not pretty.

When my Hudson Cook colleagues and I do dealer

compliance audits, we come across practices and documents that often have been handed down over the years from one employee to another, and sometimes from one dealership to another. After years of doing the "same-ol', same-ol'," even the veteran employees have lost track of the origins of daily procedures and their requisite forms.

We look over documents that have been cobbled from other forms, cut and pasted as amendments, not attributing the document from which they came or the document into which they are now incorporated. I have seen documents that have print dates that are at least a decade old, indicating that the last time the document was reviewed was in the 20th century. Literally! *(Note to your compliance officer: Laws change.)*

These crazy quilt documents are telling. They are evidence of daily life. Dealers are subject to a thicket of laws, rules and regulations; they are overseen by regulators who often don't understand the laws they enforce; they are surrounded by plaintiffs' lawyers who make their living suing dealers for violations real and imagined.

You might be surprised. A dealer's life is more than meets your fleeting drive-by glance across the tidy showroom lot. Come along. You'll see what I mean...

The Error Ferret

April 2006

By Thomas B. Hudson

When I broke into the practice of law, it was with a fine Baltimore-based firm that did mostly trial work, but that also had a business practice. I had expressed an interest in business law, so that's where I was assigned. Before long, I was doing the sort of stuff that young banking and compliance lawyers do—creating, and carefully reviewing, banking and credit forms. Essentially, I was a glorified proofreader.

Now, the culture of the firm was primarily that of the trial lawyers. They were competitive and cocky, brash and bold. One of my good friends, Charlie Goodell, was one of these fire-eaters, and he was full of war stories about the combat that he and the other trial lawyers constantly faced. When Charlie found out about what I did day in and day out, he promptly nicknamed me an "Error Ferret."

I've told that story often over the years, because in many ways, my practice hasn't changed. We create and review forms that dealers and sales finance companies use to sell and finance cars. Because the first thing that plaintiffs' lawyers do, when they represent consumers against dealers, is to comb through the dealership's paperwork to detect weaknesses to be used to their clients' advantage, we work hard to eliminate, from the outset, any glitches that can form the basis for a complaint.

Over the last couple of years, we've been doing legal compliance audits of dealerships and their documentation. The stuff we see ranges from pretty good to, "Has anyone ever actually read this stuff?" I thought I'd use this article to pass along a few problems that we see consistently, so that you can be your own "Error Ferret."

Take out your buyers order, and see if any of the following problems appear.

The Used Car Notice Isn't Conspicuous

The Federal Trade Commission Used Car Rule requires that the contract of sale contain a certain notice, and that it be "conspicuous." We often see the notice printed in text that is identical to the text surrounding the notice. Plaintiffs, and the

FTC, will argue that the notice is not conspicuous. The FTC can fine you $11,000 per contract, and plaintiffs' lawyers will be after your firstborn child.

The Used Car Notice Isn't Precisely as it Appears in the FTC's Rule

Repeat after me, "When life gives you a free space, take it." The FTC's Rule mandates the precise text of the notice. It should be *precisely* as it appears in the Federal Register. This is not an opportunity for creative writing. Don't add words. Don't subtract words. "Close" doesn't count. If it's exactly as the FTC says it should be, it will be nearly impossible to successfully attack it.

The Used Car Rule Isn't in Spanish

If you negotiate transactions with your customers in Spanish, you must have a Spanish translation of the notice in your contract. We see very few buyers orders that contain the translation, and I'll bet many of the dealers using these buyers orders are negotiating in Spanish.

Disclaimers of Implied Warranties are Not Conspicuous

The Uniform Commercial Code provides that sales subject to the UCC, as car sales are, automatically come with certain "implied warranties." In some states, a dealer can "disclaim" implied warranties (keep an eye on the federal Magnuson-Moss Warranty Act), but any such disclaimer must be worded in a certain manner and must be conspicuous. If your disclaimer looks just like its surrounding text, plaintiffs will argue that it isn't conspicuous and that the disclaimer is ineffective.

Let's Have a Party

I've seen buyers orders that have obviously been created by the "cut and paste" method. When you have one section from one contract, clipped and pasted from a different contract, things can get screwed up (that's a legal term—it means "screwed up") pretty fast. One common problem area involves party identification by the various source contracts. I've seen cobbled forms that refer to the dealer as, "dealer," "we," "us," and "you," and to the car buyer as, "buyer," "purchaser," "you," "I," and "customer," *all in the same document.* Check your buyers order and see how many terms it uses to refer to the parties.

How Many Times do You Have to Say it?

Whoever drafted the buyers order that I just reviewed must have been really concerned about making sure the customer would be obligated for any pay-off amount in excess of the sum the customer claimed he owed on his trade-in. I know this how? *Because the customer agreed in three different places to pay the excess.* Once is enough.

Do You Really Need all These Provisions?

The buyers orders we see in many cases appear to have been around for years. Over time, as dealers faced various problems, the drafters of these documents have added a sentence here, and a paragraph there, to address the problem the next time it arises. Perhaps the problem never arises again, but the added verbiage lives on—and on—and on. If you read through your buyers order, chances are you will find a great deal of text that can safely be deleted. Don't be afraid to do some surgery. Courts like shorter and simpler contracts. Perhaps, you can add a good arbitration agreement in place of the deleted text.

Try it, yourself. Be an Error Ferret. You may be pleasantly surprised by how good your forms are; but then again, maybe you'll be able to correct some obvious mistakes yourself, before you bring in the lawyers.

Dealer May Be Liable For Negligent Sale of Disability Insurance

October 2006

By Thomas B. Hudson and Meghan Musselman

Does your dealership have an obligation to determine whether a customer has preexisting medical conditions before selling the customer credit disability insurance? At least one court thinks so, giving dealers one more thing to worry about. Here's the story...

During April 2000, Wayne Parker and Kenneth Konopinski separately leased vehicles through Klaben Family Dodge. Both Parker and Konopinski bought credit disability insurance issued by Protective Life Insurance in connection with the lease of their vehicles. In the month prior to leasing his vehicle through Klaben, Parker was diagnosed with hip problems, and, within two months after the lease transaction, underwent a total hip replacement. Similarly, within the six weeks prior to leasing his vehicle through Klaben, Konopinski had a heart catheterization and a balloon angioplasty. Three months after the lease transaction, Konopinski underwent triple bypass surgery.

When Parker and Konopinski became disabled as a result of these medical procedures, they sought coverage under their disability insurance with Protective, but were denied coverage under the contractual provision denying coverage for preexisting conditions. Parker and Konopinski sued Klaben and Protective alleging, among other things, negligence, and fraudulent misrepresentation. The claims against Protective were based on the agency theory of *respondeat superior* (Latin for "let the master answer"). The theory, a doctrine in the law of agency, provides that a principal—here, the insurance company—is responsible for the actions of its agent—here, the dealership—in the "course of employment." Klaben and Protective moved for summary judgment.

The trial court found in favor of Klaben and Protective, and Parker and Konopinski appealed. The Ohio Court of Appeals determined that (1) Klaben's failure to ask Parker and Konopinski about their medical conditions; (2) its failure to investigate reasons why coverage might not be available to them; or (3) their failure to make sure they read their respective insurance policies did not amount to a fraudulent misrepresentation. In fact, the appellate court found that Parker and Konopinski were aware of their respective medical conditions and should have been aware that any disability insurance coverage could be affected by such medical conditions. Thus, the appellate court found that Klaben did not fraudulently misrepresent that the insurance policy would cover Parker's and Konopinski's preexisting medical conditions.

However, under a negligence theory, the appellate court found that Klaben did have a duty to inquire into Parker's and Konopinski's medical histories as a seller of disability insurance. The appellate court held that Klaben's conduct fell short of the standard of care expected of insurance agents selling credit disability insurance, because a minimal level of inquiry would have revealed Parker's and Konopinski's medical conditions as well as the likelihood that they would not be covered for those conditions. Thus, the appellate court held that Klaben's actions in the sale of insurance to Parker and Konopinski were negligent.

Because Protective had an ongoing relationship with Klaben, received monthly remittances of premium payments for disability insurance coverage from Klaben, and provided the forms Klaben used, the appellate court found that Protective and Klaben had an agency relationship such that Protective was liable for Klaben's actions.

The lesson here? Well, at least in Ohio, you'd better make some inquiries about your customer's health before peddling disability insurance to him. And you need to consider whether the ruling has implications in the sale of life insurance, GAP, and perhaps other products. Will courts in other states follow this line of reasoning? Quite possibly. Time to go golfing with the lawyer again.

Parker v. Protective Life Insurance Co. of Ohio, 2006 WL 2241590 (Ohio App. August 4, 2006).

Como Se Dice 'F&I'? How Does Your Finance Office Translate?

December 2006

By Emily Marlow Beck

You've heard a lot about how dealers are making money by selling cars to the Hispanic market. You know that there is a ton of money just sitting out there ready to be made, and you can't wait to join the fiesta. So, you go out and find yourself a Spanish-speaking employee and you slap "se habla Español" signs over anything that will stand still. You stock up on Spanish-language Buyers Guides, and by golly, you even post the darned things on your entire used car inventory. (After all, Tom Hudson's been preaching about those stickers long enough.)

You give your prized Spanish-speaking green pea a little

training, but not too much—after all, you hired him to habla Español, and you can't comprende nada. You'll teach him enough to get him started, and then sit back and watch the money roll in. Right?

Not so fast. Just because your employee speaks Spanish doesn't mean he speaks "F&I Spanish." Here's an example.

In a typical dealer audit, I watch the finance employees go through their sales spiels, making sure they are making all the proper disclosures and not saying anything that violates state or federal laws that could get the dealership in trouble. In one particular audit, I asked the Spanish-speaking employee to go through the whole spiel in Spanish (Thanks, Dad, for making me take those Spanish classes!).

To my surprise, the employee didn't know squat about the contract he was explaining to me; he didn't know what GAP was (though, interestingly, he sold a heck of a lot of it); and he made several statements that were just flat out wrong. When I asked the employee some follow-up questions, he told me he wasn't really sure about what he was doing, but he was afraid to ask. Because no one ever corrected him, the employee carried on making various misrepresentations and committing Truth in Lending Act violations, galore.

Believe it or not, that's not the scary part of the story. The part that curdled my blood was that the dealer was standing 10 feet away from him during this process, and he had no way of knowing that his prized Spanish speaker was breaking all the laws in the book. What also bothered me was that the only thing standing between a customer who couldn't understand English and the $24,000 debt he was about to incur were the representations of a gum-chewing, 19-year-old, who was afraid to ask questions and had virtually no training or oversight.

So, what can a dealer do to tighten up the reins and gain control of his bilingual finance office?

Well, for starters, how about handing out a copy of "Entendiendo el Financiamento de Vehiculos" with every deal? This is a Spanish translation of the "Understanding Vehicle Financing" publication that bears the AFSA, NADA, and FTC stamp of approval. While you're at it, I'd include the Spanish-language version as part of the training program for every employee hired to service the Hispanic market. (I'd start with that 19-year-old who's working all your deals for you.)

Also, if translating all your forms into Spanish isn't practicable, one way to help control what information gets communicated to your Spanish-speaking customers is to develop a Spanish-language closing video. The closing video could have a Spanish-speaking "talking head," who would walk the customer through the delivery process, explaining the various forms the customer must sign, and describing the various products that are optional for purchase. Because the dealer and his lawyer could review and approve the script for this video before it's translated into Spanish, the dealer can regain some control over the representations that are being made to Spanish-speaking customers.

But, then again, if you're the "head in the sand" kind of dealer who would rather *not* know what goes on in your finance office so long as your penetration rates are high, just kick back and enjoy the fiesta. Just don't say I didn't warn you when you get "mystery shopped" by a Spanish-speaking reporter from Channel 4, or the Attorney General shows up to burst your piñata.

CHAPTER 12

Is Your Related Finance Company a Little Too Related?

April 2007

By Emily Marlow Beck

It's difficult to talk about the buy here, pay here industry these days without talking about related finance companies. Most buy here, pay here dealers I work with that have related finance companies get the basics right. They've set up a separate corporation. They've got the right license. They keep separate books. But, it's the "sleeper" issues that they always seem to miss. Archie Bunker and compliance lawyers will agree, "Sleeping dogs bark the loudest."

So, what's the sleeper issue that gets me worked up? To be honest, dealerships and their RFCs that are a little too cozy make me uneasy.

Not maintaining separate boundaries between your dealership and its finance arm may have serious consequences. In addition to the bazillion tax and accounting issues that I don't pretend to understand, fuzzy lines between the two entities could have some serious consumer credit implications.

Consider the privacy obligations of the dealership and the finance company. Too often, customers' private information gets passed back and forth from the RFC to the dealership like a bottle of rum on a pirate ship. You'd be surprised how often I see dealerships that have ready access to all of the customer's credit and payment history maintained by the RFC. I've seen everything from sharing customer lists to integrated computer systems that permit sales employees to access the RFC's customer payment and account information.

All this stuff isn't necessarily illegal, but depending on the type of information sharing involved, the dealership's privacy notices and safeguarding policies may need revisions to reflect these practices. And, don't forget that both the dealership and the RFC have their own separate and distinct obligations when it comes to their customers' personal information.

Also, consider the way the dealer and RFC work together to underwrite and originate the finance contracts. The typical auto finance transaction involves two separate transactions—the first, being a credit sale of a motor vehicle by a dealer to the customer pursuant to a retail installment sale contract, and the second, being the assignment of the contract to a finance company. Dealerships and RFCs working too closely together run the risk of blending these two separate transactions together into one transaction.

Why does this matter? Well, because the laws that govern installment sales of vehicles and those that govern direct loans differ. Every now and again, we hear a case where a plaintiff's lawyer argues that the transaction was not an installment sale transaction, but a disguised direct loan transaction, with the dealer acting as the loan broker—we call these "recharacterization" cases. Dealers that don't maintain proper boundaries between their dealership and RFC may be in a worse position to defend recharacterization claims.

So, what steps should a dealer take to make sure it doesn't get too cozy with its finance company? How about taking a look at how your relationship is papered and what procedures are in place?

Ask yourself:

- How do the documents you use portray the relationship between your dealership and your RFC?
- Do you have a written dealer agreement?
- Do your written documents and forms reflect the relationship with the customer and the obligations and responsibilities of the two distinct companies?

- Do you have separate books and records?
- How do you paper and account for the disposition of collateral?

Then, consider the procedures you've implemented in your dealership:

- Are the two companies distinct and separate, or does everything mesh or run together?
- How are the tasks delegated?
- Is it clear who works for your sales arm and who works for your finance arm?
- Who is responsible for repossessions?

In the interest of efficiency, it might be easy to skip a step here, or to consolidate efforts there. But, even the most common sense changes could have legal implications. (After all, since when did the law have anything to do with common sense?) Those short cuts can come back to bite you. And you thought that dog was asleep!

Under the Big Tent

April 2007

By Emily Marlow Beck

My office always gets a tad bit smaller in the spring. It takes a heck of a lot of will power to toil away under the fluorescent lights when the warm sunlight and cool breeze are calling me from the other side of my office window.

So, I can certainly understand when summertime comes, and dealers and their troops bust out of the confines of their bricks and mortar showrooms and head for the call of the "great outdoors." But, there's a whole lot dealers should consider before firing up their hot dog and popcorn machines and relocating their sales operations for special sales events. If your dealership has visions of setting up a tent sale at the local Piggly Wiggly, parking a car in the local mall, or showing off some wheels at the local fair, this article is for you.

For starters, if you're considering venturing away from your sales lot, you should familiarize yourself with the nuances of the laws of the states where you do business. Some state laws require dealers to go through all sorts of hoops before holding sales or displaying cars away from their normal places of business. For example, some states will let dealers hold off-premise sales only if they're limited in duration, or if the dealer obtains advance approval. Other states let dealers hold off-site sales only if the dealer invites all its local competitors to the party.

Some little state nuances can have a big impact on customers' rights and dealers' responsibilities with respect to the sale transactions. For example, even though dealers are exempt from the federal "door-to-door" sales rule when they hold tent sales or when they sell cars from some other temporary place of business, some state laws may not exempt such activities and may require a "cooling off" period when sales occur at an off-premise spot. Some of these same state statutes require additional disclosures or changes to the dealership's usual forms when selling cars away from the usual place of business.

Don't forget to take the time to educate yourself about any local ordinances or permits that might be required before leaving the confines of your showroom. Things that are perfectly acceptable on your own lot could possibly get your local law enforcers all worked up. Sometimes bad blood with the local cops or your neighbors can linger long after your last balloon has shriveled up and died.

Keep on guard for fly-by-night marketing schemes. Too often I'll hear stories about dealers that sign up with some marketing outfit offering some sales gimmick, only to later be stuck holding the bag when the outfit doesn't walk the line. I've seen all sorts of things: such as, dealerships having to pay fines and penalties, because the marketing outfit failed to obtain the necessary permits; or dealerships facing class action lawsuits because of non-compliant marketing materials. In too many of these cases, the marketing outfit won't come to the rescue and will be long gone when the sheriff or Attorney General comes knocking.

Don't forget the fundamentals of advertising in the fun and fast summer months. While it's tempting to play loose in the heat, the same basic principles of sound advertising will apply, whether you're selling a car from your own lot or from the cow-pie tossing booth at the county fair. It goes without saying that your dealership should be able to substantiate every claim in every advertisement. Don't claim to offer special prices unless you could actually prove that the prices are really special if you had to. Don't claim that you are giving "top dollar" for trade-ins unless you really are, and you can back up that claim. Don't claim that you have "lost your lease" unless, in fact, that is really happening. Don't hold a "going out of business" sale unless you are (gulp) going out of business. In other words, "tell the truth." Got it? Now, go grill some hot dogs and sell some cars. And don't forget the sunscreen.

Credit Card Receipts: Is Your Slip Showing?

June 2007

By Jean Noonan

Can you imagine accepting a customer's credit or debit card for a $30 oil change and winding up owing the customer $1,000? That nightmare is threatening to be real for scores of businesses from Florida to California that are being sued by customers for providing credit and debit card receipts that contain the card's expiration date.

An often-overlooked provision of the Fair Credit Reporting Act amendments became effective on December 1, 2006. It says that the electronically printed credit and debit card receipts you give your customers must shorten—or truncate—the account information. You may include no more than the last five digits of the card number, and you must delete the card's expiration date. For example, a receipt that truncates the credit card number and deletes the expiration date could look like this:

ACCT: ***********12345
EXP: ****

Most electronic card machines have been modified to truncate the account number. But quite a few merchants are still handing out receipts that include the card's expiration date. That's a violation of the FCRA, say a number of courts that have considered these cases. Attorneys have filed class actions all across the country seeking up to $1,000 per credit card receipt for this mistake. The FCRA allows consumers to receive a statutory damage award from $100 to $1,000 for each willful violation of the Act, and each receipt can be a separate violation.

Congress added this provision to the FCRA in 2003, as part of its effort to prevent identity theft. It was concerned that a consumer's credit card slip could fall into the wrong hands, letting a thief use the account number and expiration date for fraudulent purchases. But this provision was phased in gradually. Merchants using newer machines had to comply by December 2004. Merchants with older machines had until December 2006. Since that time, all merchants using electronic machines have to truncate account information, including masking the expiration date.

In addition to class action and individual suits from customers, dealers also must worry about the Federal Trade Commission. The FTC has hinted that it may bring enforcement actions against companies whose credit card slips are showing a little too much information. When the Feds come calling, the penalties jump to as much as $11,000 per violation.

A few details of this new law are worth noting. First, it applies only to electronic receipts, not to receipts that are handwritten or imprinted. Second, it applies only to the receipt copy you give the customer, not to the merchant copy you retain. Of course, separate federal laws require you to safeguard customers' personal information, including account numbers. So although your copy of the receipt can show the full account number and expiration date, you must keep it secure.

So now is the time to be sure your equipment complies with this law—and that your slip is not showing more than it should.

Don't Sell It If You Haven't Read It

June 2007

By Thomas B. Hudson

Selling and reading go hand-in-hand. That so? you say. You bet. When we advise dealers about ways that they can implement an affordable, practical compliance program for their dealerships, one of the things we suggest is that everyone who deals with customers read every document that those customers might be presented with during the course of a sale or lease transaction. Why do we think that's a good idea?

A couple of reasons come to mind. First, there is the educational aspect of having your representatives knowledgeable about the terms and conditions of the transactions that your dealership enters into on a daily basis. Just as any good car salesperson will know the mechanical and performance specifications of the vehicles he or she is selling, that salesperson should know the characteristics, terms, and conditions of the financing, leasing, and related services that he or she is selling. A salesperson or F&I manager with a firm grasp of the details of the documents to be signed will come across to the customer as more knowledgeable than one who doesn't have a clue.

The second reason to ensure that your people understand all sales documents involves your dealership's liability. A dealer representative who does not know, for instance, about a customer's potential liability for the early termination of a lease, might well tell the customer that he or she can terminate at any time without penalty. That simply isn't true for most leases, and if your representatives make such statements, those statements could form the basis for a consumer lawsuit alleging unfair or deceptive trade practices or even fraud.

Other examples are not hard to find.

We have seen misstatements by dealer personnel who did not know the difference between precomputed retail installment sale contracts and interest-bearing (or "simple interest") contracts, and who have given customers bad information about the effects of prepayment.

In other cases, we have seen lawsuits that allege that dealer personnel actually told customers that they were buying cars when, in fact, they were leasing them. Now, it's more than likely that someone who makes a statement that is that far off the mark is intentionally trying to mislead the customer, but I've been at this long enough to suspect that there are some dealership personnel who think that leasing is just an alternative form of financing. (A colleague of mine who conducts compliance reviews of dealerships tells me that she has seen this misunderstanding first-hand.) That's a mistake that employees probably wouldn't make if, as part of their training, they actually had to sit down and read a lease and a retail installment sale contract, side-by-side, from start to finish.

So, require everyone who deals with your customers to read all the customer documents that your dealership uses. These include the retail installment contract, the lease, the buyers order, the agreement to provide insurance, the arbitration agreement, the GAP agreement, the credit life and accident forms, the "etch" agreement, the "we owe" form, and so on. In short, we stress, *every single document* a customer could see.

If you are smart, you will test your employees on how well they understand what they are selling. If you are really smart, you will require them to undertake this process, not just once, but periodically.

Your folks will learn a lot with this exercise, and you'll gain a smarter workforce and reduced liability. And with any luck, your knowledgeable sales people will pick up on some of those typos, incorrect cross-references, and inconsistent provisions that we see every time we review these forms.

Free-Range Finance Departments

July 2007

By Emily Marlow Beck

I'm an indiscriminate carnivore, and, as far as I'm concerned, salad is what food eats. But, free-range food is all the rage where I live in Washington, D.C. According to Wikipedia, the free-range "principle is to allow [animals] as much freedom as possible, to live out...instinctual behaviors in a reasonably natural way, regardless of whether or not they are eventually killed." I suppose folks feel much better about chowing-down on 10-cent wing night if they know their feathered friends joyfully roamed this planet before meeting the big chicken in the sky.

What's my point, you may ask?

Well, I've been running into a few too many of what I would like to refer to as "free-range finance departments" lately. In these free-range finance departments, dealers keep their hands out of the finance office operations and give their employees as much freedom as possible as long as penetration rates and profits per vehicle retailed are high.

In fact, many of the issues I see in dealerships today have less to do with the dealer's knowledge, and more to do with a dealer's inability or unwillingness to pass that knowledge on to the finance department. You might be very surprised to know how often I meet dealers who are relatively informed about consumer credit laws, but are too disconnected from their finance department to put the knowledge to use.

Take the story of one dealer I spoke with at a recent conference. According to this dealer, he refrained from training his employees about pertinent issues like identity theft, fraud, and privacy laws out of fear that he would give his employees "ideas."

Or, how about the dealer who doesn't investigate why his

finance office boasts over 90% penetration rates selling products such as "etch"? This dealer never learns (or, perhaps ignores) that his employees are selling the product illegally and potentially committing unfair and deceptive trade practices and federal Truth in Lending violations on almost every deal.

Better yet, how about the dealer who purchases a fancy menu program but doesn't provide any financial incentive to make the change and doesn't follow up to make sure his employees are getting the support and encouragement to make the required changes? Only later does he learn that his employees have been "modifying" the menus to engage in menu-disguised payment packing.

So, what can you do to get a free-range finance department under control? Here are a few tips:

First and foremost, you should implement a training program in your dealership and require all finance employees to be trained. Just because you know a particular law or regulation doesn't mean that your employees do. After all—don't you want the people executing paper on your behalf to have the best information possible and to make the decisions you would want them to make?

Second, you should audit, audit, audit your finance department. Periodically pull deal files at random to see if forms and disclosures, including menus, are being used properly. If penetration rates seem "too good to be true," try to figure out why. If you're a dealer who videotapes your finance department, put those videos to use by pulling up some sample footage and taking a look-see. Consider mystery shoppers. Correct the mistakes you discover with the appropriate person, and keep a record of the self-testing and self-repairing you do.

Don't forget to compensate your finance employees for making efforts to comply with the laws. It can be scary for employees who have been using more traditional sales techniques to switch to a compliance-oriented process if they think they'll take a personal financial hit. Make sure they know that you support them through the changes. Consider developing a compensation program that rewards more than just penetration rates and profit. After all, you will likely be the one left holding the bag long after your finance employees fly the coop.

Paper or Profit?

September 2007

By Emily Marlow Beck

You say tomato, I say to-maa-to. You eat potato, and I eat po-taa-to. And, when it comes to special finance and buy here, pay here, you say profit, and I say paper.

After all, isn't it usually the rule that the lower the customer's credit score, the higher the number of trees that will be killed in getting the deal done? From a compliance standpoint, the more paperwork required in a deal, the more chances there are to make paper-related mistakes. And, although the rules that govern automobile finance are the same, regardless of the customer's creditworthiness or the dealership's department, some compliance errors are more likely to show their ugly heads in the special finance or buy here, pay here departments.

Admittedly, there are great opportunities for dealers who go confidently and compliantly into the sub prime auto finance world (I heard you say "profit" after all). So, before you make like Astaire and call the whole thing off, consider tightening up your paper practices. To help you get started, here are some of the biggest mistakes I see when working with special finance departments and buy here, pay here dealerships:

Adverse Action Notices

The less creditworthy your customers, the greater likelihood that you will turn customers down. Most dealers know that federal law requires creditors to send adverse action notices (or "turn down" letters) to customers when they deny credit to a customer. What many dealers don't know is that the definition of "adverse action" includes more than just when a creditor sends a customer packing. For example, even if you (like many dealers) believe adverse action requirements don't apply to you because you "finance everyone if the conditions are right," federal law may view your "conditions" as "counteroffers" that could, in some instances, warrant adverse action notices.

Confused? You're not alone. There's a whole bunch to say about this topic. Check out the recently published NADA Management Guide, *A Dealer Guide to Adverse Action Notices*, for some additional information. You can purchase the guide from the NADA ($30 for NADA members, $60 for non-members), and it contains step-by-step guidance on your dealership's adverse action obligations.

Spot Delivery/Unwind Agreements

Just because your dealership doesn't engage in typical "spot delivery" transactions doesn't mean that you don't need "magic language" in your contract to allow you to unwind transactions that aren't funded. For example, do your transaction documents permit you to unwind a deal if the finance company (related or otherwise) kicks the deal back to you, because it can't verify that Johnny has worked at ACME Corp. for 18 months? Let's hope so.

A Written Warranty (Maybe)

If your cars come with a warranty, are you providing customers with a copy of a written warranty? Federal law requires dealers to provide customers with a written copy of the warranty and sets forth the required contents of that written warranty. Some states have laws that will govern the contents of your written warranty. Marking up the federal Buyers Guide "window sticker" to spell out all the details of the warranty is not enough.

Stips

A typical special finance or buy here, pay here deal will require more stips than other deals. We tell people to treat stips, and other forms of non-public personal information, like toxic waste—once it enters your dealership doors, you've got to make sure it is stored, retained, and ultimately disposed of properly. In these days of identity theft and fraud, this has never been more important.

Side Notes

A special finance or buy here, pay here operation may call for some creative financing solutions, like pick-up payments or repair financing. While it may be tempting to whip out a pen and some paper or grab a retail installment sale contract off the shelf to record this financing arrangement, even the best intended side deal could inadvertently run afoul of federal (and sometimes state) laws that govern credit transactions. I've seen some pretty creative financing arrangements out there, and a few of them were even legal! But, the same creativity that earns you a spirit badge at 4-H camp may earn you a class action lawsuit in Regulation Z-ville. If you're one of those "creative types," it might be best to have a chat with a knowledgeable lawyer who can help you channel that creativity of yours.

Phew! How's that for a good start? Now, you say paper, and I'll say profit, and we'll call the calling off, off.

Chapter 13

Starter Interrupt Devices

No topic is more fun than this one. Everyone has an opinion on why these devices are legal or illegal, a good idea or a bad idea, a great collection tool, or a litigation magnet.

The starter interrupt devices first appeared on my radar screen in 1999. At the time, my initial reaction was, "The dealer put a WHAT on a car?" I predicted that, unless the devices were used with care and with full disclosure to the consumer, we would see many lawsuits challenging the things on a number of grounds.

Didn't happen. Hey, I've been wrong before.

Nope. Over the past eight years, we have seen just a few—three or four cases and opinions—dealing with the devices. All of them involved what my propeller-head son calls, "user error," when I call him to report problems with my laptop.

In a couple of the cases we report on here, creditors muffed the management of the devices when the buyer was in bankruptcy, leading the courts to conclude that there had been a violation of the automatic stay (a bankruptcy rule that restricts certain creditor conduct while the bankruptcy proceedings are pending). In another case, the creditor was using the devices without paying attention to his state's law that gave the customer a right to cure (some states give the debtor a right to cure a default before the creditor may repossess).

Why didn't the devices turn into the litigation magnets that I had feared? For one thing, I think the major companies manufacturing these devices have done a good job of educating their customers; that is, dealers and finance companies, about best practices, disclosures, and other precautions to minimize risk. And, who knows? Maybe everybody has been paying attention to our advice to use an arbitration agreement when employing the devices.

Or maybe those dealers using the devices have just been lucky.

From the Mouths of Babes

August 2006

By Daniel J. Laudicina

Last weekend, I was driving a portion of Maryland interstate highway with my five-year-old niece. Five-year-old nieces apparently come preloaded with more questions than a single human being can possibly answer (though I held my own for a while). Tommy guns don't fire as quickly as my niece hurtles questions in rapid-fire succession.

We approached a weigh station with a long line of 18-wheelers stretched along the shoulder of the road, waiting their turn on the scales.

Niece: "What are those trucks doing?"

DL: "They have to be weighed, and this is a station that weighs them."

Niece: "Why do they have to be weighed?"

DL: "Because the law requires them to be weighed to make sure they are not too heavy." (I know trucks are also weighed for tax purposes, but I wasn't about to bring up the exciting world of taxation with my inquisitive niece.)

Niece: "Why aren't we in line?"

DL: "The law that requires them to be weighed doesn't apply to us."

Niece: "Why?"

DL: "We are not driving a big truck, we are in a little car *[DL drives a Civic]*. Even if the law applied to us, we would be well under the maximum weight the law allows."

Niece: "Not if we had an elephant in the trunk."

She had a point there.

The following week, I was reminded of this conversation when I received a letter from an attorney in South Carolina claiming that a product, sold by one of our clients, violates federal law. Our client sells starter interrupt devices to vehicle dealers and other creditors. The devices aid in ensuring prompt payment of installments under financing plans by providing the creditor with the ability to disable a vehicle's starter, if the consumer fails to make timely payments. The South Carolina attorney was concerned that his client, a buy here, pay here dealer, would violate the federal Fair Debt Collection Practices Act if it were to use one of the devices. My five-year-old niece could have explained why he was wrong.

First, just as the laws requiring weigh stations do not apply to my little Civic, the FDCPA does not apply to typical buy here, pay here dealers. The FDCPA applies only to debt collectors, a term the FDCPA defines to exclude an entity collecting its own debts, or an assignee of an obligation—if, at the time of the assignment, the obligation is not in default. Buy here, pay here dealers hold and collect the paper they originate. Thus, buy here, pay here dealers are not subject to the FDCPA, because their collection activities are limited to collecting their own debts.

Even if the buy here, pay here dealer had a related finance company (many do), and the related finance company buys the obligations from the dealer immediately after the dealer originates them and before they are in default, the related finance company would not be a debt collector. The finance company would have obtained assignment before default, and its collection activities would, therefore, not be subject to the FDCPA. (A word of caution, however: Some states have debt collection laws, and some of these laws apply when the federal law doesn't; you need to check them, too, to make sure you're in the clear.)

Second, my niece would tell the South Carolina attorney that, even if the law applied to his client, his client satisfies the law's requirements—just as my Civic (sans an elephant in the trunk) would always fall well within the legal weight limits at the weigh stations. The particular FDCPA provision the South Carolina attorney cited prohibits, "taking or threatening to take any nonjudicial action to effect dispossession or disablement of property if (1) there is no present right to possession of the property claimed as collateral through an enforceable security interest; (2) there is no present intention to take possession of the property; or (3) the property is exempt by law from such dispossession or disablement."

The buy here, pay here dealer would have a right to possession by virtue of its security agreement, satisfying (1). Assuming that (3) didn't apply, that leaves only (2). However, it seems to me that a creditor using starter interrupt devices will almost certainly plan to pick up a disabled vehicle in the event the customer does not pay; or otherwise, come to an agreement with the creditor to effect the creditor's re-activating the starter. That would seem to supply the requisite "present intent" requirement of (2). Accordingly, there would be no FDCPA violation if the dealer were to disable the starter.

So, the next time you receive a letter from an attorney accusing you of some level of legal malfeasance, remember that in more cases than you might realize, the response may be as simple as the explanation you would provide your five-year-old niece to some unrelated issue. If the response doesn't come immediately to mind, give me a call. I can put you in touch with my niece.

After you've responded to a seemingly endless stream of questions from her, she might just be able to help you.

Failure to Disable 'On-Time Payment Protection System' Results in Violation

October 2006

By Thomas B. Hudson and Teresa Rohwedder

Starter interrupt systems have been around for several years. The devices operate in various ways, but one of the common systems requires a car buyer to enter a code into the device each week or each month. The buyer receives the code after making his or her scheduled periodic payment. Although the devices have not met with much enthusiasm from state credit regulators or consumer advocates, their use has expanded in recent years. With that expanded use, we've started seeing lawsuits. Thus far, the suits have not challenged the general use of the devices, but rather, they have focused on the creditor's responsibilities regarding the devices when a customer files for bankruptcy.

Careful lawyers have told their clients that after a customer files for bankruptcy, the continued use of the devices runs the risk of violating the automatic stay. Careful lawyers have also warned clients that the disabling of a customer's car by a device might constitute repossession under state law. That situation triggers various provisions regulating a creditor's actions after repossession. The case described here addresses both of these issues.

Wanda Dawson bought a 1996 Mustang from J&B Detail, L.L.C., and financed the purchase through J&B. Seven months later, Dawson filed for bankruptcy.

J&B installed an "On-Time Payment Protection System" on the Mustang, allowing J&B to disable the car's starter; in the event of nonpayment, the engine would not start. After Dawson filed for bankruptcy, she asked J&B to remove the system or to give her a new code to enter, so the ignition would not be disabled after the grace period, which expired three days later. Meanwhile, her monthly payment was already late.

Initially, J&B refused her request, but eventually the dealer removed the system from Dawson's vehicle. Dawson later filed an adversary proceeding (that is, a lawsuit inside of the bankruptcy legal proceeding) in her bankruptcy case, claiming that J&B violated the Bankruptcy Code's automatic stay, as well as the federal Fair Debt Collection Practices Act, the Ohio Retail Installment Sales Act, and the Ohio Consumer Sales Practices Act.

The U.S. Bankruptcy Court for the Northern District of Ohio concluded that J&B violated the automatic stay by not disabling the on-time system promptly after being notified of Dawson's bankruptcy filing. The court noted that, "simply having the on-time system operating postpetition without a payment code constitutes a violation of the automatic stay," and the violation is actionable once the creditor receives actual notice of the bankruptcy filing. The court awarded Dawson damages of $500 but left open the issue of the amount of attorney's fees to be awarded, pending the filing of an affidavit of fees and costs by Dawson's attorney.

The court ruled in favor of J&B on Dawson's FDCPA claim, finding that J&B was not a debt collector, because it was collecting its own debt, and that the principal purpose of its business was to sell cars, not to collect debts. With regard to Dawson's claim that J&B violated the Ohio RISA by failing to give her notice after it took possession of the car, the court found that J&B did not take physical possession of the car by disabling it, and, therefore, did not violate the RISA. Finally, the court entered judgment in favor of J&B on Dawson's CSPA claim, finding a lack of evidence of a violation of that state statute.

So, at least in Ohio, our careful lawyers are batting .500. The continuing use of the devices after a bankruptcy violates the automatic stay. However, when the device disables a car after a customer fails to enter a required code, no repossession by the creditor has occurred..

Look for the courts to address these issues in other states. We predict that courts will generally agree with the bankruptcy holding, but we are less certain that other courts will agree with the Ohio court on the repossession issue.

Chapter 14

Litigation

Skydiving. Bomb squad. Alligator wrestling. Mushroom taster. Crafting Michael Vick's public image. All—you might say—dangerous and difficult jobs.

But, I submit, nowhere near as tough as being a car dealer in the first decade of the 21st century.

It isn't an exaggeration to say that if your dealership is of any real size, you, the owner, need to be a lawyer, or at least have a full-time lawyer in your employ to cope with the laws and regulations that apply to you.

I belong to a couple of organizations of lawyers who represent dealers. Until I started attending their meetings, I was focused on my world—F&I and sales and lease practices. I had not given much thought to all of the other legal issues that dealers have to tackle.

Environmental laws, workplace safety laws, labor laws, franchise laws, tax laws, succession planning, general corporate governance issues—these are just a few of the things that I hear the dealer lawyers discussing. The issues are complicated, and the consequences of mistakes, costly.

Even as I say that, though, I can't imagine any area of a dealer's operations that offers the potential "bet the company" risk that is incumbent in F&I and sales practices and procedures. That area of practice attracts class action lawyers, which circle a dealer like a great white shark around a wounded whale. These menaces (also called plaintiffs' lawyers) get up every morning and start the day with the same thought, "How can I sue a car dealer today?"

Because one of the most powerful teeth in a plaintiff's lawyer's weaponry is the class action lawsuit, he looks for numbers. You've got a couple of hundred, or maybe a thousand employees, but how many *car buyers* have you had in the last three or four years? That number is the one that interests such class action predators.

Because class action paydays are lucrative, these lawyers actually take the time to learn—and in some cases, learn well—all those federal and state laws that dealers seldom focus on, until, that is, the suit papers arrive.

Those dealers don't even know they are in dangerous territory until the first lethal strike. Plainly spoken, car dealing is a dangerous and difficult job. Would I choose it? you ask. Well, buddy, given the choice, my answer is, "Pass me that bomb-defusing kit."

Got Some Time on Your Hands? Go Sue Someone!

August 2005

By Thomas B. Hudson

Back when I was a first-year law student at Georgetown (man had not yet discovered fire), we studied a strange case in civil procedure class. It involved a fellow from Pennsylvania who sued the FBI, claiming that the agency had implanted a receiver in his head and that FBI agents were sending him messages to affect his behavior.

The feds had moved to dismiss the case on the ground that the plaintiff "had not stated a claim upon which relief could be granted," or some such phrase. The court refused to dismiss the case, despite how ridiculous the alleged facts appeared, because at that stage of the pleadings, the court was required to assume the truth of the facts pleaded by the plaintiff. The professor had included the case to teach us this: It can be decidedly difficult to get rid of even a patently absurd claim. The case featured in this article reminded me of the FBI's difficulty in getting rid of that silly claim.

Amiel Dabush, a software expert, was the co-owner of a company that developed software and hardware for the telecommunications industry.

Dabush obtained a marketing brochure for a 2000 Mercedes S-Class from a local dealer. The brochure contained a number of statements extolling the capabilities of the navigation system that came as standard equipment on the car. Dabush leased an S-Class from a dealer without test driving it, or trying out the navigation system, or talking to the dealer about the navigation system.

After owning the car for several months, Dabush got lost (contrary to the system's instructions, he had not entered the address of his destination) and dialed a help number, which gave him instructions permitting him to find his destination. After complaining, he learned that the navigation provider had mapped only 60% of the areas that needed to be digitized. Evidently, in many rural areas, only the more substantial routes had been mapped. He and other owners were later provided with updated navigation systems at no cost.

Proving yet again that in the good ol' USA you can sue anyone for anything, Dabush filed a class action lawsuit against Mercedes Benz USA, LLC, alleging breach of contract and violations of the New Jersey Consumer Fraud Act. He claimed the onboard navigation system did not work as described in the advertising brochures.

The trial court, in an attack of sanity, denied Dabush's motion to certify a nationwide class, but evidently slipping into and out of lucidity, lost it and certified a class limited to New Jersey and Connecticut residents. The Superior Court of New Jersey denied Mercedes leave to appeal, as did the New Jersey Supreme Court.

The trial court granted partial summary judgment to Mercedes on the breach of contract claim. The court noted a lack of privity between Dabush and Mercedes (a “lack of privity” means that Dabush bought his car from a dealer and didn’t deal directly with Mercedes) and declared that Dabush failed to establish as a matter of law that the marketing brochure established an enforceable contract. This ruling was not appealed. The court also denied summary judgment as to Dabush’s Consumer Fraud Act claim. After discovery was completed, Mercedes moved to decertify the class and for summary judgment on the CFA claim.

The trial court found a genuine issue of material fact as to whether the brochure’s statements were affirmative representations in violation of the CFA with the capacity to mislead the average consumer. The court granted partial summary judgment to Mercedes anyway, noting that Dabush offered “absolutely no evidence of [Mercedes’] intent to mislead or knowing omission and did not prove with reasonable certainty any ascertainable loss of money or property” as a result of the alleged CFA violation.

Dabush appealed. The Superior Court of New Jersey, Appellate Division, felt no need to resolve the question of whether Mercedes violated the CFA, because it affirmed the lower court’s decision based on the finding that Dabush failed to show “any ascertainable loss of money or property” as a result of the alleged violation.

The end result? A fellow who didn’t deal with Mercedes, didn’t bother to follow the instructions for the navigation system, and didn’t suffer any loss, nevertheless, gets to drag Mercedes up and down the court system at enormous expense to Mercedes. That’s our judicial system. And that’s what can happen, even when a claim strains credulity.

Dabush v. Mercedes-Benz USA, LLC, 2005 WL 1334872 (N.J. Super. App. Div. May 26, 2005).

Where There's Smoke, There's Fire. Or Not.

August 2006

By Thomas B. Hudson

Whenever I see a story in the paper about some dealership agreeing with the Attorney General, or the Consumer Credit Commissioner, or some class action plaintiffs' lawyer to settle a case for megabucks, my first reaction is to think that the dealer strayed over the line a bit. The moment I have that thought, though, I haul myself up short, because, although I don't try cases for a living, I know a bit about how the litigation dance works.

Litigation is expensive in terms of money, the allocation of executive resources, damage to your reputation, and lost business. It's possible to spend hundreds of thousands of dollars on legal fees litigating cases, *even when you win*!

So, be careful how you react to stories like this one.

Recently, in *The Record*, a Hackensack, New Jersey, newspaper, there was the report that Ramsey Auto Group Inc., and its ten dealerships had agreed to pay up to $750,000 to settle charges that it defrauded customers. The $750,000, the story said, would drop to $250,000 in a year, if the company complied with the terms of its settlement with the state.

Ramsey Auto Group, which did not admit any wrongdoing, said it settled the lawsuit to avoid the cost of protracted litigation. That's a common statement made by defendants when large lawsuits settle. Civilians think it's a bunch of baloney. But, people who have been through the buzz saw of litigation are much more likely to nod sagely and say, "Yup."

The company was accused of failing to honor advertised prices, forging customer signatures on documents, charging for after-sale items without consumers' knowledge, overcharging for repairs, failing to credit trade-in allowances accurately, and misrepresenting the condition of used cars, among other things. The settlement required the group to pay $250,000 immediately, with $150,000 going for civil penalties and $100,000 going to reimburse the state for attorneys' fees and investigative costs. Customers will get $156,000 in restitution.

Evidently, the state thought it was going light on the dealerships and announced that it was doing so, because the dealerships cooperated in resolving the matter. Kimberly Ricketts, state director of Consumer Affairs, was quoted in *The Record* as saying the dealerships came "to the table with concrete proposals to change their business practices. Before the division had made any proposals, they had put changes into place."

The dealerships agreed to post a customer's bill of rights in all of the company's showrooms and service areas. The company also agreed to make a "good faith effort" to settle consumer complaints and to arbitrate the ones that couldn't be settled.

The company says it didn't violate any laws and that the complaints represented a small percentage of their deals. So, why agree to pay?

Several possibilities: First, the dealerships may have wandered over the line, and the sheriff got the drop on them. Second, maybe bad stuff happened at the dealerships, despite the dealerships' efforts to run shops that complied with the law, giving the dealerships some defenses against the charges. Third, maybe the dealerships are clean as a whistle, and the credit cops got a burr under their saddles anyway (it wouldn't be the first time that's happened). We're unlikely ever to find out.

I can tell you, though, that after seeing what litigation can do to even the best dealerships, I no longer automatically dismiss the statement, "We settled to avoid the cost and expense of litigation."

Court Imposes Hefty Punitive Damages in Vehicle Replacement Case

October 2006

By Maya P. Hill

The Smiths bought a 2001 Pontiac Montana from the Walker automotive dealership. Shortly after the purchase, the Smiths realized the vehicle had a serious water leak. After many attempts to repair the leak, the Smiths contacted General Motors and requested that the vehicle be replaced. After being informed by GM that the 2001 vehicle would be replaced at no cost, the Smiths were sent a "Settlement Offer" letter stating that the total cost to the Smiths was "$0.00."

The Smiths signed some paperwork at the Walker dealership (the case didn't specify exactly what paperwork was included). They exchanged their defective 2001 vehicle for a new 2002 vehicle. Walker employees transferred the plates from the old vehicle to the new one, activated the OnStar system, and gave the Smiths a spare key. At the time of the exchange, however, Walker did not tell the Smiths that they did not yet own the vehicle and that they would be required to return to the dealership to fill out more paperwork to complete the transaction.

A week later, Walker asked the Smiths to return to complete some paperwork. At the dealership, the Smiths were told that their old loan had been paid off, and that they would be required to sign for a new loan on the 2002 vehicle at a rate of 2.99%, even though their loan on the 2001 vehicle had a rate of 0.9%. They were also told that their original down payment would not be fully credited toward the 2002 vehicle, despite the fact that the total cost of the 2002 vehicle was less than that of the 2001 vehicle.

Unhappy, the Smiths alleged that they had been under the impression, based on the representations of Walker and GM, that they would receive the new vehicle and continue payment for it under the same terms as the original financing. Walker would not let the Smiths leave the dealership with the 2002 vehicle if they did not sign the new finance agreement. Walker also informed the Smiths that the 2001 vehicle was no longer available to them. So, eventually, the Smiths signed.

So, what do you suppose the Smiths did next? They sued Walker and GM, alleging several violations of the Ohio Consumer Sales Practice Act. The Smiths even brought in a well-known expert witness—you may have heard of him—David Stivers? The trial court held against GM and Walker, levying compensatory damages against both, and punitive damages against Walker.

Walker and GM both appealed, although GM appealed only the award of attorneys' fees. We're not talking pennies here, either—just under $4,000 in compensatory damages against GM and $800 against Walker, and a whopping $35,000 in punitive damages against Walker. The attorneys' fee award was more than $55,000.

On appeal, Walker argued (1) that the trial court improperly admitted expert testimony from the Smiths' witness; (2) that the trial court erred in denying its motion for a directed verdict and subsequent motion for a JNOV. (A directed verdict is like the defendant saying, "Hey, Judge, I know we have a good looking jury here, but you've heard the evidence, and you're a smart guy, so, won't you forget the jury, and just rule in my favor?" A JNOV is a "judgment notwithstanding the verdict." It is as if the losing party said, "Hey, Judge, I know that good-looking jury just stuck it to me, but won't you please reconsider?") Walker also argued (3) that the trial court erroneously denied its motion for a new trial; and (4) that the attorneys' fee award was excessive.

The appellate court rejected all four arguments. As to the expert witness testimony, Walker argued that the opinions expressed by the expert concerned matters within the knowledge of a layperson, and, therefore, no expert was necessary. Walker further argued that the expert did not have the specialized skills, knowledge, experience, training, or education to permit him to provide expert testimony. Walker also argued that the probative value of the testimony was outweighed by the danger of unfair prejudice, confusion of the issues, or misleading the jury, and that the testimony was barred because the expert was providing inadmissible character evidence.

In rejecting each of these arguments, the court noted that the expert's testimony was necessary, because he was able to explain various industry-specific terms (like Spot's favorite, "de-horsing") and reveal common industry practices with which laypersons would not ordinarily be familiar. The court further noted that the expert had been employed in the industry for 30 years and had testified in many other cases. The court found that any testimony offered by the expert that was improperly admitted was harmless error, and that there were no specific instances of character testimony as alleged by Walker.

In rejecting Walker's claims regarding the directed verdict and JNOV, the court noted that there was substantial evidence upon which reasonable minds could differ regarding the elements of a fraud claim, thus ruling that the trial court properly denied the motions.

In response to Walker's claim that a new trial was warranted, because the verdict for punitive damages was excessive, the court found that, given Walker's conduct, a large punitive award was appropriate. The court did some advanced calculus and further noted that the ratio of punitive damages to the total actual injury suffered was less than 8 to 1. Walker and GM both argued that the attorneys' fee award was excessive and that it was unreasonable to conclude that the Smiths' attorney spent 170 more hours on the case than did their attorneys. In rejecting this argument, the court refused to limit attorneys' fees to the amount of time spent by the attorney for the losing party.

Smith v. General Motors Corp., 2006 WL 2381873 (Ohio. App. August 18, 2006).

Retail Exposure for Wholesale Dealers

April 2007

By Emily Marlow Beck

Let's say you are a motor vehicle wholesaler, and you wholesale a used car to a dealer on the other side of town. The darned thing's got so much frame damage you wouldn't let your mother sit in it, but you've given the dealer a good price, so you won't lose any sleep over it. After all, you don't deal with consumers, so you don't have to deal with consumer lawsuits, right?

Not necessarily. If you wholesaled that car to a Missouri dealer, you just might.

A recent case coming out of the Missouri Supreme Court held that a customer could sue a wholesaler, even though there was no direct connection between the wholesaler and the customer. In this case, a customer bought a used car from a dealership that had purchased the car from a wholesaler. Later, the customer learned that, before he bought it, the car had been in an accident. The customer sued the wholesaler under Missouri's Merchandising Practices Act, claiming that the wholesaler violated the Act by failing to disclose the prior damage to the dealership.

The wholesaler moved to dismiss the case, claiming that there was a lack of "privity." In other words, the wholesaler argued that the court should toss the case, because there was no direct connection between the customer and the wholesaler. The trial court agreed and granted the motion to dismiss, but the customer appealed.

The Missouri Supreme Court disagreed and kicked the case back to the trial court. The Missouri high court took the view that, because the Missouri Merchandising Practices Act applies to any "persons" acting or using any deception or misrepresentations in connection with the sale or advertisement of any merchandise in trade or commerce, the Act did "not contemplate a direct contractual relationship between plaintiff and defendant." In other words, "privity" was not required to bring a claim under the Act, and the customer could sue the wholesaler, even though there was no direct connection between the two. There are a couple of things readers should note about this situation. First, this case doesn't mean that the wholesaler violated the Missouri Merchandising Practices Act. The customer will still have to prove his or her case in the trial court. Second, what it does mean is that, in Missouri, the customer can sue the wholesaler—even though the wholesaler had no contact with the customer.

This case could impact more than just traditional wholesale dealers. For example, this case could affect retail dealers that wholesale trade-ins, or finance sources that wholesale off-lease and repossessed vehicles. Something to think about before wholesaling your cars to Missouri dealers.

Gibbons v. J. Nuckolls, Inc., 2007 WL 828352 (Mo. March 20, 2007).

'Bad, Bad Leroy Brown'—Not the Only Chicago Worry

April 2007

By Thomas B. Hudson

According to Jim Croce, Leroy Brown was from the south side of Chicago and was "the baddest man in the whole damned town. Badder than ol' King Kong, meaner than a junkyard dog."

My guess is that Jim never met Dan Edelman.

Dan is also from Chicago. I don't know what part of town he's from, but my bet is, it's one of the nicer parts. You see, Dan is one of the most successful, and thus most feared, class action plaintiff's lawyers in the country. In recent years, he has been very active in representing consumers against various types of creditors. If you are a multi-state creditor or a Chicago-area car dealer, the odds are good that you've heard of him, and pretty good that you've been sued by him. The odds are very good that you don't want to hear from him.

Let me digress for a minute. My wife plays a really mean tennis game. She has a room full of hardware to prove it, including gold medals in singles and doubles in the Maryland Senior Olympics from a couple of years ago. I used to go to the courts with her and let her use me for target practice. It wasn't so bad for a while, but then she started calling her put away shots. Just before she'd swing her racket, she'd yell, "Backhand" or "Crosscourt," and then she'd let fly. Even thus warned about what was coming, I usually couldn't get into place, and she'd have another point.

What's that got to do with Dan, you ask? Well, it seems that Dan is now calling his put away shots.

Dan's office has issued a letter setting forth the types of claims that he is interested in asserting against car dealers and finance companies. The letter goes, I believe, to other lawyers who Dan thinks don't want the types of technically challenging consumer credit cases that Dan craves.

Here's Dan's current hit list for the auto sales and finance industry. He wants your case if, using his own words:

- You had insurance premiums added to your balance, because the bank claimed you didn't have insurance.
- You were charged for "VSI" or "vendor's single interest" insurance on a car loan.
- You signed a motor vehicle retail installment contract with a wage assignment.
- A car dealer decided to extend credit to less than all persons that [sic] applied for it and failed to give a written notice of credit denial. This often occurs when a car dealer first requests a cosigner on a transaction and then decides to extend credit only to the cosigner.
- We are looking for collection letters seeking to collect deficiencies for auto leases sent on behalf of companies like Ford Motor Credit. We believe that a substantial portion of such letters misrepresent the actual creditor, which is a Titling Trust.

The letter lists other types of cases that aren't limited to auto dealers and finance companies but that would apply to them. It describes these cases like this:

> We are finding that people who have poor credit or have obtained a bankruptcy discharge are inundated with junk mail concerning vague or illusory offers from mortgage lenders and car finance companies. The senders obtain credit reports or lists of bankrupts and target them. Many of these offers are illegal. You may be entitled to recover $100 to $1,000 per mailing. Send us any credit solicitations you receive.

Some people object to this sort of "trolling" for plaintiffs, but Edelman and others have been doing it for several years, and, whether objected to or not, the practice is here to stay. In a way, though, the solicitation of cases can benefit creditors and dealers when, as here, the solicitation letter becomes public. If Dan's calling his put away shots, you might want to listen.

Can You Produce Electronically Stored Information When Sued?

May 2007

By James Chareq

You've just been served with a complaint that was filed against you in federal district court. You've heard about recent changes to the discovery rules that require you to hand over all your electronic records to the plaintiff's attorney. You've also heard that if you make a mistake, the court will enter a default judgment against you or prevent you from presenting an effective defense to the plaintiff's claims. What should you do to prepare to meet your electronic discovery obligations *before you are sued*? What should you do *when you receive the complaint*? Both are good questions.

Since the 1993 amendments, the Federal Rules of Civil Procedure have required mandatory *initial* disclosures—without waiting for a discovery request from the plaintiff. That obligation required the parties to a lawsuit to provide one another with the name and contact information of individuals likely to have discoverable information that may be used to support a claim or defense. In addition (according to the 1993 amendments), a party was required to provide a copy or description by category of "all documents, data compilations, and tangible things" that may be used to support a claim or defense.

In April 2006, the U.S. Supreme Court approved the 2006 amendments to the Federal Rules, which became effective on December 1 of that year. They substitute the words "electronically stored information" (ESI) for the words "data compilations" when describing a party's initial disclosure obligations. What is ESI? Simply stated, it is any information that can be stored electronically. Yes, the definition is that broad; but, at least with respect to your initial disclosure obligations, it includes only information that may be used to support your claim or defense.

When you consider the categories of ESI that should be reviewed to determine whether they will have to be produced, think about your backup tapes and archived records; e-contracts; current and archived e-mail messages; images used to promote your vehicle sales; presentations you've made; spreadsheets your dealership has developed; voicemail messages and their backups files; and your Web site log files. If you plan on using any of these materials, or other ESI in the case, it likely will have to be provided to the plaintiff as part of your initial disclosures.

Other information—that is, information other than that which may be used to support your claim or defense—need not be produced as part of your *initial* disclosures but may still be requested by the plaintiff's attorney during the discovery process. Remember, you have a duty to preserve evidence at the commencement of the case, during the case, and even before the case is filed, if you "knew or should have known" that the evidence was "relevant to pending, imminent, or reasonably foreseeable litigation." The meaning of the words "knew," "should have known," "relevant," "imminent," and "reasonably foreseeable" could each be the subject of its own article and is not addressed here. It is enough to note that if you believe you will be sued, or are sued, you should consult with your counsel immediately concerning the need to suspend any destruction or deletion of your records under your existing record retention/destruction program.

So, back to our questions. What should you do to prepare to meet your electronic discovery obligations *before* you are sued? You must know (1) what types of electronic records you create; (2) whether those records are retained or archived; (3) whether those records are destroyed or deleted and how often this occurs; and (4) where to find the records. You may need to check the following: computer systems including legacy systems, databases, individual employee computers (e.g., laptops the employees take home), networks, and servers. Electronic information is, after all, just bits of data. It can be almost anywhere.

What should you do when you receive the complaint? You should call your lawyer immediately. It sounds like a cliché, and it is, but "cliché" is often just another word for the "tried and true." With your lawyer's help, you'll identify potential witnesses, documents, ESI, and other things that you might need to prove your claim or defense. These will have to be provided to the plaintiff within just a few weeks of the complaint being served on you. Your attorney will also help you put together a plan to periodically supplement these disclosures and figure out whether and to what extent you should suspend any routine destruction or deletion of your documents and ESI.

The consequences of not meeting your initial disclosure obligations can be severe. Depending upon its view of your actions or inactions, the court could enter a default judgment against you; exclude the information you failed to disclose from the case, and thereby deprive you of an essential defense; enter an order establishing some or all of the plaintiff's allegations as indisputable facts in the case; or impose monetary sanctions for your failure to cooperate in discovery.

The bottom line: The Federal Rules have been amended to make clear that the scope of your initial disclosure obligation touches upon virtually every aspect of your dealership's operations. When you are sued, you'll have to act fast to meet these obligations. Therefore, act now to identify the sources of current and archived ESI that may need to be disclosed. And while you're at it, think about how you'd effectively access the ESI and prepare it for disclosure within a limited time—say a handful of weeks—after a process server walks through your doors.

What's That Gonna Cost Me?

May 2007

By Emily Marlow Beck

It's not unusual for dealers to ask me about the potential costs of not complying with state and federal laws. Sometimes the answers are easy; after all, some penalties are spelled out in the applicable statutes and regulations. At other times, the answer is a bit more complicated. Will the dealer be forced to pay actual damages? Punitive damages? The dealer's legal fees and court costs? The customer's legal fees and court costs? Will the dealer suffer reputational harm? These sorts of costs are often difficult to predict or quantify.

But, a recent press release issued by the Illinois Attorney General's office has caught my attention. It seems that Illinois Attorney General Lisa Madigan had to take out her switch again and filed a lawsuit against the owners and operators of a car dealership in Illinois.

The AG's suit is aimed at a Ford dealership, its parent companies, as well as its corporate owners, alleging that these folks violated the Illinois Consumer Fraud and Deceptive

Business Practices Act. According to the AG's office, the Ford dealership failed to pay off the outstanding credit balance on several trades, leaving each customer with outstanding balances on two separate contracts—the contract for his or her new vehicle and the contract balance left over on the trade-in vehicle.

According to the complaint, the dealership's failure to fulfill its promises to pay off the liens on the trade-in vehicles hurt some of its customers' credit ratings. Also, because the dealership failed in some instances to pay title and registration fees on the vehicles, many customers could not obtain license plates or renewals. Other customers learned that their names were not on the titles of their new vehicles.

So, what punishments are Madigan and her office requesting for these alleged deeds? For starters, the AG's office thinks the dealer should pay a civil penalty of $50,000, with additional penalties of $50,000 for each violation found to have been committed with the intent to defraud. The AG also wants the court to rescind the vehicle sales contracts and order the dealership to pay restitution to consumers and to pay all costs for the prosecution and investigation of the case.

But, that's not all. Madigan's lawsuit also asks the court to prohibit the defendants from engaging in the business of selling motor vehicles in the State of Illinois. In fact, according to *The Southern Illinoisan*, an Illinois newspaper, the AG's office has expressed that its first priority is assuring that none of the corporations or individuals comprising the dealership is ever allowed to engage in the automobile sales business in Illinois. Ouch!

This certainly isn't the first time an AG's office or state agency has put down the hammer and forbidden a dealer from working in the car business or stripped a dealer of its license. In fact, you might be shocked to know how often this sort of punishment is doled out.

But, this Illinois AG claim begs the question: How much is your dealer license worth to you? How much will it cost you to be *persona non grata* in the industry in which you earn your living? If you figure out how to quantify that, let me know.

Buddy, Can You Spare $125,000?

May 2007

By Thomas B. Hudson

Yet another AG has hammered yet another car dealership with a big fine for what the AG asserted were advertising violations. Arizona Attorney General Terry Goddard has announced a $125,000 settlement with Budget Car & Truck Sales, a used car dealership in Tucson, owned by Budget Resale Inc., resolving allegations of deceptive advertising.

Under the settlement, Budget will pay the AG's Office $125,000. The AG will use the money for a serious beer blast (just kidding, the money will go for consumer fraud education, attorneys' fees, and investigation costs). The settlement also requires future Budget ads to be clear, truthful, and non-misleading (which is something all ads should be in the first place).

A consent judgment approved by an Arizona court settled the lawsuit by the AG against Budget. The judgment, as is usual for these enforcement actions, does not constitute an admission of any wrongdoing by Budget.

The suit alleged that between 2003 and 2005, Budget placed various "Public Notice" ads falsely declaring a "Nation Wide Rental Car Disposal Sale." The suit alleged that the Budget ads:

- Falsely claimed that three major rental car companies were "prematurely forced to liquidate thousands of cars" because of a "recent crisis" and a "decline in the national tourism industry";
- Falsely stated that Budget was an "exclusive regional site" for the non-existent "national" sale;
- Deceptively compared their used car sale prices with the original Manufacturer's Suggested Retail Price for the vehicles, a practice that greatly misrepresented the amount of the advertised savings; and
- Claimed big savings ("up to 50% off") by deceptively comparing the used car price to the original MSRP.

In fact, as was noted in the AG's press release, there is no MSRP for used cars. "The current value of a used car is determined by the marketplace or by consulting industry guidebooks such as *Edmunds* or *Kelly Blue Book*," Goddard said. "The type of deceptive advertising alleged here is unacceptable. We are keeping a watchful eye to make sure businesses are being truthful with Arizona consumers."

The consent judgment also prohibits Budget from the following:

- Advertising "Public Notice Sales" or sales based on a purported crisis, national rental car sale or forced liquidation, unless the facts stated as the reason for the sale are true;
- Advertising used vehicles with comparative pricing, unless the comparison is to the "regular" price (the regular price of the dealer or the market price in industry guides like *Kelly Blue Book*); and

- Advertising used vehicles using the MSRP as a comparative price. Budget may include an accurate statement of a vehicle's MSRP in an advertisement, but only if it does not state, directly or by implication, that Budget's price represents a reduction or discount from the MSRP.

How many times do dealers have to be hit with these fines before they begin to consider whether their ads are accurate and truthful? This case illustrates the warnings that we've been giving dealerships for the last several years—ever since the AGs concluded that enforcement actions regarding dealer advertising were like taking candy from a baby.

The warnings?

First, you need to look at every statement in your advertisement to see whether it is, in fact, literally true. When the AG hauls you into court, this is the test you'll have to meet. Second, even if a statement is literally true, you need to give some consideration to whether it might be misleading.

If you heed these warnings, you'll sleep better at night, and you might be $125,000 richer.

Class Action Lawsuits (And Other Not So Mythical Characters)

July 2007

By Emily Marlow Beck

If you've been reading ***Spot Delivery***® long enough, you've heard that class action lawsuits are no joke. You've also heard that class action lawsuits can be crippling and sometimes deadly. But, so are dragons, giants, and other mythological creatures, right? After all, aren't tales of class action lawsuits against car dealers just lawyerly folklore to keep dealers up at night?

Well, how 'bout asking that question to the Missouri dealer who may have to cough up more than $3 million following a class action lawsuit involving the dealer's sale of service contracts.

According to a news report in the *Kansas City Star*, a Clay County jury awarded more than $3.4 million in actual damages against a Missouri Honda dealer, following a class action lawsuit involving a "100% money-back guarantee" that the dealership offered as an inducement to buy one of its service contracts. The "class" was made up of 1,186 customers who bought contracts from January 1, 1997, to December 22, 2003, and who got the money-back guarantees and made no claims under the contracts.

According to the news report, jurors initially awarded $8.4 million (gulp!), but Missouri law adjusted the amount given for punitive (or, "punishment") damages. They also returned two separate verdicts for punitive damages against the dealership in the amount of $5 million. That amount may be reduced when the court enters the judgment; and, according to the news article, the plaintiffs' lawyers will ask for prejudgment interest, attorneys' fees, and a separate amount for the class representatives who filed the lawsuit.

So, what did the dealership do to get into this predicament?

The *Star* reported that the customers who brought the suit bought a service contract from the dealership for $1,335 when buying a used Honda. The customers said that the dealership's representatives told them that if they did not use the service contract during the contract period, the full price of the service contract would be refunded. However, when the customers requested the refund after the contract expired, the dealership told them that the money-back guarantee applied only if the service contract owner bought an additional vehicle from the dealer.

Now, it's important to note that I'm getting the information about this case from a news report, so there's a whole lot I don't know about it. But, I do have a few thoughts and some things about which I'm just plain curious.

For one, I wonder if the dealer used an arbitration agreement containing a class action waiver. Maybe he did. Maybe he didn't. But, I'd bet dollars to donuts that this case would have had a much different outcome, if the dealer had been able to rely on a class action waiver to keep the case as a "one versus one" and not a "one versus 1,186" situation.

I also wonder what the real story is here. Was this extended service contract "money-back guarantee" something marketed by the dealer? Or, was it a little something extra that the employees used to close the sale? Or, maybe this "guarantee" was something marketed by the third-party plan administrator (yes, there are some companies like that out there). I also wonder whether the "money-back guarantee" was in writing, and whether the customers received a copy of the terms before they bought the service contract.

But, regardless of the scenario, the lesson is the same—your dealership should honor any "guarantees," "return policies," or similar programs you offer. It seems simple enough, but you'd be surprised how often we read cases where the opposite happens. Some dealers never intend to honor these promises, others make these promises "gambling" that customers will forget to assert their rights, and other dealers simply forget they ever made these promises in the first place.

If you're offering any sort of return, guarantee, or similar program, consider putting it in writing, including any exclusions or restrictions, and have these materials reviewed by your lawyer (after all, some such programs are regulated under state law). Or, you may learn the hard way that class action lawsuits are all too real.

Electronic Copies of Collection Notices? Prove It

August 2007

By Catherine Carter Berkeley and Thomas B. Hudson

A question we get a lot deals with whether a sales finance company needs to keep paper copies of various documents, such as collection letters and notices sent to delinquent customers. We generally advise that retention of the paper copies isn't required, as long as the creditor can prove, if necessary, the content of the document and that the document was sent. This case illustrates the problems that can arise when the creditor doesn't produce the necessary proof.

Lula Stoval bought a car and financed it through General Motors Acceptance Corporation. Stoval defaulted on the contract. GMAC sued Stoval, asserting claims for replevin (a court action by a creditor to recover its collateral) and breach of contract. Stoval voluntarily surrendered the car. GMAC then sold it at public auction. GMAC dismissed the replevin claim with prejudice and sued Stoval for breaching the contract.

At trial, Mike Pappas, a GMAC account collection manager, testified that, after GMAC repossessed Stoval's car, it sent her a notice, generated by GMAC's automated billing and collections software, informing her of its plan to sell the car at public auction. Pappas also testified that he did not have a copy of the notice sent to Stoval and had not seen one prior to testifying. Pappas further asserted that GMAC sent Stoval a post-sale deficiency letter after it sold the car.

Stoval claimed that she did not receive a notice from GMAC regarding its plan to sell the car, but conceded that she received a deficiency letter for the balance GMAC claimed she owed on the car after it was sold. The trial court found in favor of Stoval.

In reaching its determination, the trial court held that the

Uniform Commercial Code Section 9-611 "notice of a plan to sell repossessed collateral" requirement applied to the case, and GMAC could not prove it complied with that requirement without presenting a copy of the notice sent to Stoval. The trial court further held that, as a result of its failure to provide the required notice, GMAC's ability to collect a deficiency balance from Stoval was limited, as a matter of law, to the money it collected from the sale of the car.

GMAC moved to reopen the evidence to introduce a copy of the "notice of plan to sell" sent to Stoval. The trial court denied that motion. GMAC appealed.

The Appellate Court of Illinois affirmed in part and reversed in part the trial court's decision. GMAC argued that the UCC Section 9-611 notice requirement did not apply to replevin actions like the present case. The court rejected GMAC's argument.

The court noted that GMAC voluntarily dismissed the replevin action and had also raised a breach of contract claim. The court stated that Illinois law governing motor vehicle retail installment sale contracts provided that, unless otherwise limited, the parties to such contracts have the rights and remedies under UCC Article 9 regarding default and the disposition and redemption of collateral.

The court also noted that it previously had held that buyers and sellers subject to Illinois law governing retail installment sale contracts have the rights and remedies provided in Article 9. Therefore, the appellate court concluded that the trial court properly determined that UCC Section 9-611 applied. The appellate court also stated that Article 9 allowed a secured party to repossess collateral with or without judicial process and, therefore, its application was not limited to situations where self-help was used to repossess collateral.

The court also considered GMAC's argument that the trial court incorrectly found that GMAC could not show that it complied with UCC Section 9-611 without producing a copy of the notice of plan to sell it sent to Stoval.

The court stated that under UCC Section 9-611, a secured party that sells repossessed collateral must send the debtor notice of the disposition of the collateral, and bears the burden of proving that it has done so. The court noted Pappas's testimony that GMAC sent the notice of plan to sell to Stoval and Stoval's assertion that she never received such a notice from GMAC. The court stated that, although Pappas testified that the notice sent to Stoval was generated automatically by GMAC's billing and collection software, GMAC failed to present either a copy of the notice or evidence regarding its contents. Therefore, the appellate court concluded that the trial court correctly determined that GMAC failed to prove that it sent the notice required by UCC Section 9-611.

All was not lost for GMAC, however. The appellate court also concluded that the trial court had incorrectly found that GMAC was barred from receiving a deficiency balance from Stoval because of its failure to send the required notice. The court noted that the Illinois Supreme Court had held that the failure of a secured party to give the UCC Section 9-611 notice created a rebuttable presumption that the amount received from the sale of the repossessed collateral equaled the amount owed by the debtor.

The court further noted that the Illinois Supreme Court also had held that none of the UCC provisions barred a secured party from receiving a deficiency balance because it failed to provide the debtor with the required notice. Accordingly, the appellate court concluded that the trial court applied the incorrect standard when it determined the consequence of GMAC's failure to provide Stoval with the notice required by UCC Section 9-611, and reversed the trial court's determination to that effect.

So, GMAC ended up in pretty good shape, but only after going through an expensive appellate process. You can bet that next time GMAC's collection folks testify in a collection action, they will be armed with the electronic text of the notices in question, proof from GMAC's computer systems that the notice was generated and sent, and everything else that GMAC's lawyers can think of to meet GMAC's burden of proof.

General Motors Acceptance Corp. v. Stoval, 2007 WL 1880705 (Ill. App. June 29, 2007).

Small Claims Can Cost You

August 2007

By Thomas B. Hudson and Clayton C. Swears

OK, your dealership gets sued for violations of your state's consumer fraud act and consumer protection act. The judge awards the customer a paltry $453. Your reaction is that an award like that is almost as good as a win for you, until the judge tells you that you have to pay the customer's $20,240 legal fee bill, plus $719.69 in court costs. Yikes!

So, you ask the judge to rethink the attorney's fees in light of the chump change the customer got for actual damages. Wonder of wonders, the court does so, and vacates the attorney's fee award. Whew!

But the fat lady hasn't sung yet. The customer appeals. That's what this case is about.

Evelyn Rivera bought a Toyota Corolla from Dependable Motors, Inc. The car was sold "as is" with no warranties. Shortly after the sale, the car had problems. Then Rivera learned that the dealer failed to tell her that the car had been in an accident.

Rivera sued Dependable under various New Jersey consumer protection acts. After the trial court granted judgment to Rivera for $53 under the Consumer Fraud Act and $400 under the Truth-in-Consumer Contract, Warranty and Notice Act, Rivera moved for attorney's fees and costs.

Dependable failed to respond to the motion. The trial court granted Rivera attorney's fees and court costs. *(Note to Dependable's lawyer: Responding to motions is one of those things they teach in law school and is highly recommended.)* At that point, Dependable moved to have the fees vacated, and Rivera moved to have additional fees awarded. The trial court reversed itself and set aside its previous grant of attorney's fees. This time, the court reasoned that an award of less than $500 in statutory damages did not warrant attorney's fees. The trial court found the low damages to be evidence that the case should not have been filed. Rivera appealed.

The Superior Court of New Jersey reversed the trial court's decision and reinstated the award for attorney's fees. The court noted that both statutes required a defendant to pay reasonable attorney's fees and court costs to a successful plaintiff. The superior court found that the purpose of such a statute was to allow a consumer to pursue legitimate, small-dollar consumer fraud actions without experiencing financial hardship.

In addition, the court found that no law requires proportionality between the damages awarded and the attorney's fees awarded. The superior court remanded the case to the trial court for a determination of appropriate attorney's fees and court costs. It instructed the trial court to consider the reasonableness of the attorney's hourly rates, whether the time expended on the case was reasonable, and whether the fees should be reduced, because the prevailing party achieved only limited success in relation to the relief that was sought.

What now? The trial court will contemplate its navel and, after applying the factors set forth in the appellate opinion, will come up with a second attorney's fee award. We're betting that it won't be a whole lot less than the first one.

Rivera v. Salerno Duane, Inc., 2007 WL 1790723 (N.J. Super. App. Div. June 22, 2007).

Sometimes It Doesn't Pay to Fight

August 2007

By Thomas B. Hudson

This case illustrates the point that, when it comes to litigation, the first check you get a chance to write is probably for the lowest amount. Here's what happened.

Mathew Van Eman bought a car with an odometer reading of 125,850 miles. Van Eman also paid $500 for a C.A.R.S. Protection Plus, Inc., Power Train Value Limited Warranty, which was good for three months or 4,500 miles.

The warranty listed the specific parts that it covered. The warranty explicitly stated that items not covered included diagnostic charges and damage that resulted from the failure of a non-covered component.

The car malfunctioned before the warranty expired. North Hill Marathon determined that one of the engine's lubricated parts had broken and pierced the oil pan, which was a covered part. North Hill Marathon determined that the damage rendered the engine irreparable.

North Hill Marathon reported its conclusion to C.A.R.S.,

which ordered additional tear down and diagnosis to discover exactly which engine parts had broken. North Hill Marathon conducted further tear down and found that the damage was caused by lack of oil pressure. A faulty oil pump, an obstructed oil channel, or Van Eman's failure to put oil in the car could have caused lack of oil pressure.

In North Hill Marathon's experience, a faulty oil pump, a covered part, usually caused a lack of oil pressure. North Hill Marathon also reasoned that the low oil pressure was not likely caused by Van Eman's negligence, because Van Eman owned the vehicle for only three months, and the oil should not have receded to a damaging low level within that time.

North Hill Marathon reported its findings to C.A.R.S., which ordered North Hill Marathon to disassemble the entire engine to find out exactly what caused the damage. The estimated cost to disassemble the engine was $1,500. Van Eman believed that C.A.R.S. had no intention of honoring the limited warranty and would continue to demand additional tear down and diagnosis until the warranty was rendered valueless.

Van Eman paid North Hill Marathon $478 for the diagnosis and had the car towed to another facility that repaired the engine for $4,047. Van Eman then sued C.A.R.S. under the Michigan Consumer Protection Act.

The trial court awarded Van Eman damages in the amount of $4,047 and $43,538 in attorneys' fees. C.A.R.S. appealed to the Michigan Court of Appeals, arguing that the trial judge erred in denying C.A.R.S.' motion for summary disposition, erred in denying C.A.R.S.' motion for directed verdict, abused its discretion in issuing a permanent injunction, erred in instructing the jury, impugned judicial impartiality, and abused its discretion in the award of attorneys' fees. C.A.R.S. also claimed that the judge's mother was ugly (just kidding).

The appellate court rejected all of C.A.R.S.' claims. The appellate court reviewed the record and found that the trial court properly denied C.A.R.S.' summary disposition and motion for directed verdict because of the existence of genuine issues of material fact. The appellate court found that a grant of injunctive relief was not an abuse of discretion, because Van Eman introduced evidence that C.A.R.S. had a pattern of violating the MCPA and that a real and imminent danger of irreparable injury existed to support the grant of injunctive relief.

Before denying C.A.R.S.' claim that the trial court erred in instructing the jury, the appellate court read the jury instructions as a whole. The appellate court found that, although there were some imperfections, C.A.R.S. had not established plain error regarding the jury instructions.

The appellate court also found that the trial court had not impugned judicial impartiality and had not unduly influenced the jury. Finally, the appellate court found that the trial court had not abused its discretion in the award of attorneys' fees, because the amount awarded was within the range of reasonable attorneys' fees as opined by C.A.R.S.' expert witness.

To make matters worse, the appellate court remanded the case for an award of Van Eman's appellate attorneys' fees.

So, on day one, C.A.R.S. could have stroked a $4,047 check for the reworked engine, but decided on a different course. It ended up paying the $4,047 anyway, along with $43,538 for the customer's legal fees through the trial stage, an unspecified additional amount for the customer's legal fees in connection with the appeal, plus, of course, the fees of its own lawyers for the trial and appeal. Assuming that C.A.R.S.' legal fees were as much as the customer's through trial, and assuming that both parties spent $10,000 on their lawyers for the appeal, C.A.R.S.' ultimate tab probably topped $100,000.

Van Eman v. C.A.R.S. Protection Plus, Inc., 2007 WL 1491814 (Mich. App. May 22, 2007).

Chapter 15

Arbitration

Some things are too good to last, and arbitration is probably one of them. For the previous decade or longer, many dealers have been requiring their sales, finance, and lease customers to sign mandatory arbitration agreements as a condition of engaging in a vehicle sale or lease transaction.

When the trend started, plaintiffs' lawyers went nuts, because arbitration agreements eliminated two of their biggest threats against dealers—class action suits and out-of-control juries. They responded by coming up with every argument they could muster to convince judges that the arbitration agreements their clients had signed should not be enforced.

For a while, they scored some successes. Dealers' lawyers were new to crafting arbitration agreements, and they were slow to realize that, unlike other agreements drafted for their dealer clients that were heavily biased in the dealer's favor, arbitration agreements needed to be balanced and fair, or courts wouldn't enforce them.

The lesson sank in quickly, however, and now it is fairly rare for a court to refuse to enforce a well-drafted arbitration agreement. When a court does refuse to enforce an arbitration agreement, it's usually because the dealer's lawyer has done a poor job of drafting it, or because there is "user error"—the dealer forgets to sign it, for example.

As we go to press, there is a bill in Congress designed to eliminate the ability of dealers and other retailers and creditors to require arbitration in their agreements. I'd say that it has a pretty good chance of success in a Democrat-controlled Congress. Until that bill passes, the benefits of requiring arbitration outweigh the disadvantages, in my humble opinion. You'll see that point of view reflected in the pages that follow...

Have You Thanked Your Arbitration Agreement Lately?

March 2006

By Thomas B. Hudson and Cathy Brennan

One of the best ways a dealership can protect itself from devastating class action lawsuits is to ensure that each one of its retail installment sale contracts and buyers orders includes a fair and balanced arbitration agreement. Consumer class action lawyers don't like these arbitration agreements much, because they cut into their bottom line.

But, for dealers, the agreements have advantages. When well drafted and fair, an arbitration agreement can keep your customer happy and can ensure that your business survives to continue making customers happy. Recently, the highest court in the country, the U.S. Supreme Court, looked again at arbitration agreements and came out with a result that ensures the continued viability of arbitration agreements—and the continued profitability of your business.

Buckeye Check Cashing, a payday lender in Florida, adopted a credit agreement that included a provision that the borrower and Buckeye would agree to arbitrate all disputes arising out of the transaction. After obtaining payday loans, several borrowers sued Buckeye in Florida state court, claiming that Buckeye charged usurious rates, and that the credit agreement violated various Florida laws, rendering it criminal.

Buckeye moved to compel arbitration, but the trial court denied the motion, holding that a court, rather than an arbitrator, should resolve a claim that a contract is illegal and void from its inception. The Florida Supreme Court ultimately agreed, reasoning that enforcing an arbitration agreement in a contract challenged as unlawful would violate Florida public policy and contract law.

The U.S. Supreme Court agreed to review the Florida high court decision and reversed it, holding that, regardless of whether a party brings a lawsuit in federal or state court, a challenge to the validity of a contract as a whole, and not specifically to the arbitration clause within it, must go to the arbitrator, not the court. The high court noted that the Federal Arbitration Act embodies a national policy favoring arbitration and places an agreement to arbitrate on a footing with all other contracts. A challenge to such an agreement can be divided into one of two types: one specifically to the arbitration agreement, or one to the agreement as a whole, including the arbitration agreement.

The Supreme Court noted that it previously held that the Federal Arbitration Act does not permit federal courts to consider claims of "fraud in the inducement" of the contract generally, and that, as a matter of substantive federal arbitration law, an arbitration provision is severable from the rest of the contract. Accordingly, unless the challenge is to the arbitration clause itself, the arbitrator, and not the court, considers the issue of the contract's validity in the first instance. The high court also confirmed that the Federal Arbitration Act applies to challenges brought in state as well as federal courts.

Based on its previous decisions, the Court ruled that, because the allegations in *Buckeye* challenged the agreement, and not just its arbitration provisions, the arbitration provisions were enforceable apart from the rest of the contract, and an arbitrator, not a court, should consider the challenge. The Court rejected the customers' assertion that this rule does not apply in state court.

So, keep bending over backwards to make sure your arbitration agreement is fair and balanced. At a minimum, it should name several arbitration organizations from which the consumer may choose; it should state that arbitration will occur in the county or town of the consumer's residence; it should not put the consumer in a position of having to arbitrate all disputes, while the dealer is not obligated to arbitrate any; and it should make the dealership bear the majority of the expenses related to arbitration to the extent possible. These are suggestions regarding the fairness of the arbitration agreement. You should also ensure that the arbitration agreement protects you by, for example, expressly invoking the Federal Arbitration Act and expressly precluding class relief.

Make sure your lawyer is knowledgeable about arbitration, and then have him or her review your arbitration agreement to make sure it is fair and balanced. The next time a consumer tries to take you to court, likely, you'll be rewarded for your efforts.

Buckeye Check Cashing, Inc. v. Cardegna et al., U.S. Supreme Court (No. 04–1264), February 21, 2006.

Consumer's Challenge to Arbitration Agreement Fails

April 2006

By Thomas B. Hudson

Every rare now and again I read a court opinion packed with good, old-fashioned common sense.

Let me set the stage: Plaintiffs' lawyers have discovered that car dealers and finance companies are easy pickings when it comes to suits by consumers. Car dealers and finance companies have discovered that arbitration agreements are a very potent first line of defense against such suits, particularly against class action lawsuits. However, plaintiffs' lawyers don't just roll over and play dead when they encounter an arbitration agreement. No siree! They try every trick in the book to convince the court that the arbitration agreement their client signed should not be enforced.

That's what this opinion involved.

Sharon Battle and Tamara Johnson were the named plaintiffs in a putative (not yet certified by the court) class action lawsuit against Nissan Motor Acceptance Corporation. They alleged claims under the federal Equal Credit Opportunity Act, the Wisconsin Deceptive Trade Practices Act, and the Wisconsin Consumer Act, as well as claims for strict liability and intentional misrepresentation.

NMAC moved to compel arbitration and stay proceedings, based on arbitration clauses contained in the retail installment sale agreements that the plaintiffs signed when they bought their cars. The court granted NMAC's motion as to Johnson, but denied it as to Battle, after concluding that Battle's contract did not contain an arbitration provision. *(Note to dealership manager: Time to throw away those old forms.)*

In granting NMAC's motion as to Johnson, the court rejected Johnson's arguments that the arbitration agreement was not supported by consideration, violated the Wisconsin Consumer Act, and was procedurally and substantively unconscionable.

Let's look at each of these challenges.

There's a concept in contract law that a contract has to be supported with consideration. That means that each party to the contract has to do, or promise to do, something it isn't otherwise obligated to do. Or, alternatively, each party has to refrain from doing, or promise to refrain from doing, something it would otherwise be entitled to do. The consideration does not have to be of any great value—law school professors often use the example of a "peppercorn" in exchange for a promise as consideration.

Johnson argued that there was no consideration to support her agreement to arbitrate. "Wait," said Johnson. "There has to be separate consideration—apart from the consideration supporting the contract of sale—to support the agreement to arbitrate."

The court wasn't buying that argument. It ruled that no separate consideration was required for the arbitration agreement, because the consideration relating to the purchase transaction supported the arbitration provision as well. Anyway, the court said, the parties' mutual promises to arbitrate constituted sufficient consideration. This, I submit, is the correct analysis of this issue.

Johnson next argued that the state laws under which she was suing provided her access to the courts to redress her grievances; she claimed that state law prohibited the waiver of that right. The court wasn't buying this one either, explaining that the Federal Arbitration Act trumps any state laws that would prohibit arbitration of disputes. (The concept the court was enunciating is called "federal supremacy.")

Next, Johnson dragged out one of the most frequent challenges that we see from plaintiffs seeking to avoid arbitration; that is, unconscionability. What a plaintiff is saying when she argues that a transaction or an agreement is unconscionable is that it is grossly unfair. Courts usually say that an unconscionable agreement must be both "procedurally" and "substantively" unfair. "Procedurally" indicates that something leading to the formation of the agreement made it unfair. "Substantively" unfair means that something in the terms of the agreement is so overbearing, it shouldn't be enforced.

Johnson's procedural unconscionability claim was that she and the dealer were in unequal bargaining positions. Her substantive unconscionability claim was that the contract required her to forego a court or jury trial of her claims and waive class action remedies, while preserving to NMAC a judicial forum for small claims actions and the right of repossession.

The court rejected Johnson's procedural unconscionability claim, noting that she was free to buy a car and find financing from many sources. It also rejected her substantive unconscionability claim, noting that the arbitration agreement provided that, in exchange for her giving up her class rights, NMAC would pay a part of her arbitration costs and would arbitrate in her federal judicial district.

Good grief, Charlie Brown. A sensible judge renders a thoughtful and well-analyzed opinion. What's the world coming to?

Battle v. Nissan Motor Acceptance Corporation, Case No. 05-C-0669, (E.D. Wis.) March 9, 2006.

New Jersey Does?—Does Not?—Like Class Waivers in Arbitration Agreements

July 2006

By Thomas B. Hudson

Why do you care about arbitration developments in New Jersey? Because, my friend, the courts in your state can issue opinions just like the ones we handle here. Read on.

We have followed arbitration developments for several years now, as dealers and finance companies have turned to mandatory arbitration agreements as a shield against class action lawyers and hostile courts. The response of lawyers who represent car buyers has been fierce. They have come up with every reason imaginable to argue to courts that arbitration agreements shouldn't be enforced.

Because dealers and other creditors principally use arbitration agreements to stop dangerous class action claims, well-drafted arbitration agreements always contain a prohibition against class proceedings in arbitration. Plaintiffs' lawyers call this so-called "class waiver" unconscionable, and they argue to courts that arbitration agreements containing class waivers should not be enforced.

That argument has failed to gain traction in most courts, but the traditionally consumer-friendly California courts have agreed that, in at least some circumstances, class waivers are unconscionable and unenforceable. Now, New Jersey's Supreme Court has agreed with the California courts. Our friends at the Philadelphia law firm of Pepper Hamilton, LLP, have alerted us to two recent decisions by the New Jersey Supreme Court in which it determined the enforceability of class-arbitration waivers. Just to keep everyone guessing, the court decided, in the first case, that class waivers couldn't be enforced, and in the second case, that they could. Your tax dollars at work, at least if you live in New Jersey.

In *Muhammad v. County Bank of Rehoboth Beach, Delaware*, the plaintiff obtained a $200 unsecured loan from County Bank of Rehoboth Beach; in the process, he signed loan documents containing a class-arbitration waiver. The plaintiff brought a putative class action against the Bank for violating state consumer protection laws and New Jersey's RICO statute. The trial court granted the Bank's motion to compel arbitration, and the appellate court affirmed. The New Jersey Supreme Court reversed, concluding that the class-arbitration waiver was unconscionable, because due to the low value of her claim, it prevented the plaintiff from enforcing her statutory rights in the absence of a class action.

In *Delta Funding Corporation v. Harris*, another class-arbitration waiver case, decided on the same day, the high court clarified that class-arbitration waivers are not unconscionable *per se* under New Jersey law, noting that the unconscionability determination is a fact-sensitive analysis. The court's *Delta Funding* decision was based, at least in part, on the court's conclusion that the borrower in that case had a claim that was substantial and worth pursuing in a venue other than a class action court case.

What's a New Jersey car dealer or finance company to make of these two cases? It's probably too soon to tell, but it looks as if the enforceability of the class waiver in an arbitration agreement will turn, at least in part, on the magnitude of the consumer's complaint against the dealer or finance company. Class waivers won't be enforced as to little claims, but they will be enforced as to big claims.

How little is little, and how big is big? We don't know, and we'll have to wait for more court decisions to find out.

What's a dealer or finance company to do until the courts finally decide? We'd suggest huddling with your lawyer and making an informed decision, but we think the smarter call is to keep on using arbitration agreements. After all, if a court decides not to enforce the arbitration agreement because the consumer's claim is too small, you're probably no worse off than you would have been had you never used an arbitration agreement in the first place. This assumes that your arbitration agreement provides, as it should, that the arbitration agreement goes away if the class waiver is unenforceable. And if you are using an arbitration agreement in New Jersey, you'll need to pay particular attention to the Supreme Court's pronouncements on how the arbitration agreement treats fees and charges imposed on the consumer. You also should assess how well your arbitration agreement would hold up under scrutiny.

Muhammad v. County Bank of Rehoboth Beach, Delaware, 2006 WL 2273448 (N.J. August 9, 2006). *Delta Funding Corporation v. Harris*, 2006 WL 2277984 (N.J. August 9, 2006).

W. Va. Court Rejects Attacks on Arbitration Agreement

November 2006

By Thomas B. Hudson and Michael Goodman

Occasionally, a court decision involving mortgage lending deals with issues that are equally applicable on the auto sales and finance side of the consumer credit business. This is one of those decisions.

The decision is noteworthy for a couple of reasons. The court is the U.S. District Court for the Southern District of West Virginia. Courts in West Virginia have shown some hostility to arbitration provisions, and this decision upholds the enforceability of such a provision. Also, the decision deals with a wide-ranging attack on an arbitration agreement. It includes most of the arguments commonly asserted by plaintiffs' lawyers around the country, rejecting them one by one. All in all, it's a fun read.

Borrowers James and Kathy Miller sued lender Equifirst Corporation of WV and others for alleged improprieties associated with the marketing, brokering, and closing of a mortgage refinance transaction. Five counts of the Millers' complaint challenged the validity of the arbitration clause included in the transaction documents.

Equifirst moved to compel arbitration and stay judicial proceedings or dismiss the Millers' complaint. The U.S. District

Court for the Southern District of West Virginia granted Equifirst's motion to compel arbitration.

First, the court considered the Millers' argument that the arbitration agreement was an unenforceable unconscionable contract of adhesion. The court stated that contracts of adhesion, if not unconscionable, may be enforceable. A finding of unconscionability hinges on both the relative bargaining positions of the parties and the existence of unfair terms in the contract. The court found that the Millers could not show their arbitration agreement was unconscionable. The court was especially persuaded by the Millers' level of education, their opportunity to review the terms of the arbitration agreement, and the relatively balanced terms of the agreement.

Second, the court turned to the Millers' claim that the arbitration entity selected in the agreement was unfairly biased in favor of lenders. Note that this is why you often see arbitration agreements that permit the consumer to select the arbitration organization from among a list of two or three organizations. The court rejected this claim as well, finding that the arbitration entity's code of procedure contained adequate checks and balances to protect against bias and to uphold the neutrality of the process.

Third, the court considered the Millers' claim that the arbitration agreement improperly barred them from seeking remedies available in litigation, such as declaratory, injunctive, and class action relief. The court found that declaratory and injunctive relief were available in the arbitration process, and that parties could, by contract, waive the availability of class action relief. Thus, the court rejected this claim as well. The decision regarding class relief is in sharp contrast with courts in California and New Jersey, which have called into question class action waivers in arbitration agreements.

Finally, the court determined whether other defendants—non-parties to the arbitration agreement between the Millers and Equifirst—could require the Millers to arbitrate claims against them. The court applied the "intertwined claims" test, which considers whether allegations against a non-party concern substantially interdependent and concerted misconduct. The court found that this test was satisfied and concluded that the Millers' claims against Community Home Mortgage, a non-party to the arbitration agreement, must proceed in arbitration. This decision provides strong support for the enforceability of arbitration agreements, and, in the process, dashes many of the most popular attacks on such agreements. The fact that it comes from West Virginia, a very consumer-protective state, is just icing on the cake.

Miller v. Equifirst Corporation of WV, 2006 WL 2571634 (S.D. W. Va. September 5, 2006).

The Devil Is In the Details

November 2006

By Thomas B. Hudson

When I speak to dealers at industry events, there is almost always a Q&A session following my talk. Nearly always, I speak of the benefits dealers get from using a mandatory arbitration clause or agreement. As a result, one of the frequent questions from dealers is, "Do those things really work?"

I answer that question by saying that my best guesstimate is that dealers and finance companies win challenges to mandatory arbitration provisions about 80% of the time. And when they don't win, it's because someone has done something boneheaded. I frequently reference, as a "boneheaded" example, a case decided a year or so ago, in which a dealer failed to sign the arbitration agreement. The dealer was unsuccessful in convincing the court to enforce its unsigned mandatory arbitration agreement. So, when I started reading the facts of the case discussed in this article and saw that, not only had the dealer failed to sign the arbitration agreement, but also that he failed to date it as well, I was certain the court would find the dealer's arbitration provision unenforceable.

That's not how the case came out, however. Much to my surprise, the court enforced the undated agreement that the dealer had not signed. Here's what happened.

Wade McMahan sued Rizza Chevrolet, Inc., alleging violations of the federal Truth in Lending Act, arising from the way Rizza disclosed McMahan's trade-in negative equity. Rizza responded to the suit by moving to compel arbitration, attaching to the motion an undated arbitration agreement that the dealership had not signed. The arbitration agreement stated that it was "incorporated into and made a part of any and all agreements or contracts executed on or about the date shown above."

Predictably, McMahan argued that the document was not valid, because it was not dated and signed. The court determined that lack of a signature did not preclude a finding of mutuality or consideration, and that Illinois law did not require a signature. The court rejected McMahan's argument that a lack of a date on the agreement should preclude its enforcement, pointing out that the agreement was attached to McMahan's purchase documents. Thus, it granted Rizza's motion to compel arbitration.

Make no mistake—this dealer dodged a very large bullet. Many courts don't think arbitration provisions in consumer transactions are appropriate, and they look hard for ways to find them unenforceable. You want to avoid giving such courts an inviting set of facts.

In summary, I'd suggest that you break out your deal documents and look them over carefully. Then go over your procedures, and teach your folks that signatures and dates are critically important. My take is that very few courts would come out the way this court did.

McMahan v. Rizza Chevrolet, Inc., 2006 WL 2560883 (N.D. Ill.), August 31, 2006.

Federal Court Upholds Class Waiver in Arbitration Agreement

March 2007

By Thomas B. Hudson

For years, we have been advising our dealer and finance company clients that they should consider using arbitration agreements in connection with their sales and lease transactions. We advocate arbitration agreements, because, when properly drafted to expressly exclude class relief, they can serve as a very effective first line of defense against class action lawyers.

Lately, plaintiffs' lawyers have convinced a few courts that requiring a consumer to waive class relief is "unconscionable," and reason enough for courts to refuse to enforce the arbitration agreements. This case illustrates the value of an arbitration clause in blunting a class action; it shows what happens when the plaintiffs' lawyer's "unconscionable" argument is made to a thinking judge.

Artemio Ornelas sued Sonic-Denver T, Inc., a dealership, and Toyota Motor Credit Corporation, alleging that the defendants induced him into executing lease, rather than purchase, documents for a Toyota Camry because of his inability to understand the all-English documents he signed. As a result of his inability to understand the documents, Ornelas alleged that the purchase price of the car was higher, and the financing terms were less favorable, than he had negotiated. Ornelas claimed that he found out he had leased the car when he asked if he could payoff the loan early and was told he could not do that, because he had leased the vehicle for a fixed period of time. Ornelas contended that when he informed TMCC that he had been deceived into a lease rather than a purchase, TMCC merely prepared documents for the outright purchase of the leased car. Ornelas apparently did pay the "payoff price" to buy the car, but he claimed that it was significantly more than the purchase price he had originally negotiated. Ornelas brought a class action suit on behalf of "[a]ll racial or ethnic minority individuals whose principal or first language is other than English, and who, since 15 February 2002, have leased a new or used motor vehicle from Sonic-Denver."

Ornelas alleged that Sonic had a pattern of inducing Latinos and other non-white consumers, particularly those with a limited ability to understand written or spoken English, into leasing cars instead of buying them, even when Sonic knew the consumers wanted to buy the cars. Ornelas claimed that TMCC knew about this discriminatory pattern, profited from it, and did nothing to stop it. Ornelas asked for actual damages, treble actual damages under the Colorado Consumer Protection Act claim for the defendants' bad faith conduct, punitive damages as allowed by law, attorneys' fees and costs, and pre-judgment interest. The defendants moved to compel arbitration pursuant to the arbitration provision in the Lease Agreement, which contained a class action waiver.

Ornelas argued that the arbitration provision was unenforceable for several reasons. Ornelas claimed that no contract was formed between the parties, because he did not understand the documents he was signing; that the parties lacked mutual assent to the essential terms of the Lease Agreement; that the class waiver provision was "contrary to law" and, therefore, pursuant to the language of the arbitration provision. He further claimed that the entire arbitration arrangement should be declared null and void, and that the issue of enforceability of the arbitration provision was solely an issue for the court, and not the arbitrator, to decide.

The U.S. District Court for the District of Colorado rejected all of Ornelas's arguments. It granted the motion to compel arbitration to the extent it sought to compel arbitration of Ornelas's individual claims on an individual basis. Finding that Ornelas challenged the validity of the Lease Agreement, and not the arbitration provision itself, the court concluded that the arbitration provision was enforceable, and that the validity of the Lease Agreement was an issue for the arbitrator. The court also concluded that the provision prohibiting class-wide arbitration did not render the arbitration provision unenforceable and did not effectively preclude Ornelas from pursuing his claims individually, because he claimed substantial damages, treble damages, punitive damages, interest, attorneys' fees, and costs. The court also noted that the bar to class-wide arbitration was not unconscionable.

So, at the risk of repeating ourselves, if you aren't using an arbitration agreement, you should consider doing so. You may hear some lawyers claim that courts will not enforce the class waiver provision that we recommend. While it is true that some may not, this case makes it clear that some courts will.

Ornelas v. Sonic-Denver T, Inc., 2007 WL 274738 (D. Colo. January 29, 2007).

CHAPTER 15

Maryland and South Carolina High Courts Nix Binding Arbitration for Magnuson-Moss Warranty Act Claims

April 2007

By Thomas B. Hudson

I was born in Alabama, and raised in Georgia, but my adoptive state, at least for the nonce (or "the time being" as we say in the South) is Maryland. (State motto: If you can dream it, we can tax it.) I also hang out a lot at our vacation place in South Carolina. People often ask me how I rank the states when it comes to the business climate for car dealers and those who do business with them. Until recently, I've generally given the states of Maryland and South Carolina a more or less neutral score.

That will change, though, if we get any more boneheaded decisions like the ones I include here. One is by Maryland's highest court, the Court of Appeals, and one is by the South Carolina Supreme Court. Both deal with one of my favorite topics, arbitration agreements.

The Maryland case involved a buyer named Raymond Calvin Lobach and a car dealership, Koons Ford of Baltimore, Inc. It dealt squarely with the question of whether a car buyer can be forced to submit a claim under the federal Magnuson-Moss Warranty Act to binding arbitration. The MMWA contains language that allows those offering warranties to establish an "informal dispute settlement procedure" in order to encourage the settlement of disputes in a manner other than through lawsuits.

The Federal Trade Commission, which oversees the MMWA, issued regulations that provided that any dispute mechanism under the MMWA could not be binding, and it has opined that the use of a binding arbitration agreement is not permitted by the MMWA. Koons Ford argued that the Federal Arbitration Act trumped the MMWA, and that binding arbitration of MMWA claims was permissible.

Normally, the FTC's interpretation of the MMWA and its own regulation would be the end of the question. However, several courts have told the FTC that its interpretation of the MMWA is wrong. The 11th Circuit Court of Appeals (the only court any higher in the federal system than a U.S. Court of Appeals is the U.S. Supreme Court), the Fifth Circuit Court of Appeals, U.S. District Courts (federal trial courts) in Alabama, Arizona, and Michigan, and state courts in Alabama, Indiana, Illinois, Michigan, and Louisiana—all had addressed the issue and had concluded that the FTC got it wrong; rather, that the MMWA claims may be the subject of binding arbitration.

The Maryland Court of Appeals went in the opposite direction, resting its decision, in part, on the "plain language" of the MMWA. That sort of makes you wonder whether all those other federal and state trial court and appellate judges, who were unable to discern from the MMWA any prohibition of binding arbitration, need to sign up for remedial reading classes.

The decision by the Maryland high court was not unanimous. Two judges dissented, pointing out that the authorities supporting the majority's conclusion consisted of "only three federal courts, a handful of law journal articles, and a dissent by one judge in the Fifth Circuit case."

The funniest part of the court's opinion is its lip service to the U.S. Supreme Court. The Maryland court quoted, with apparent approval (and probably with a perfectly straight face), a statement from a U.S. Supreme Court opinion that said, "The [Federal] Arbitration Act establishes that, as a matter of federal law, any doubts concerning the scope of arbitral issues should be decided in favor of arbitration."

Why is that funny? Well, if you were one of these robed wonders, and you were looking at opinions from two federal appellate courts, three federal trial courts, and three state top courts, wouldn't you have some doubts about whether MMWA claims could be the subject of binding arbitration? I certainly would.

But not the Maryland Court of Appeals.

The court's opinion isn't a total loss for dealers, sales finance companies, and other financing sources, however. Lobach had filed a six-count complaint against Koons; Count I was the MMWA claim. The trial court denied Koons' motion to compel arbitration as to the MMWA claim, but granted its motion to compel arbitration on the remaining counts. On appeal, Lobach argued that the buyers order containing the arbitration agreement was a contract of adhesion that rendered the arbitration agreement unenforceable as to all six counts of his complaint. The appellate court rejected the broad-based attack on the arbitration provision itself, holding that Lobach was bound by the document he signed, and, further, Lobach would be bound by the document even if he didn't read it.

You know a court is having trouble justifying the result it has reached in a pretty simple case when it uses 27 pages to explain itself. The dissent, which is less than two pages, is much more persuasive. Probably because it's right.

What do you expect from a state that names its university's sports teams for a turtle?

The South Carolina case did not even involve a consumer making an MMWA claim. The arbitration agreement simply provided that "warranty" claims (the arbitration provision didn't mention MMWA claims expressly) were subject to arbitration, and the court seized on that fact as a reason to pronounce that the requirement to arbitrate warranty claims was unenforceable.

The court cited only an Alabama federal trial court decision and a 2001 11th Circuit decision *that did not even involve* an MMWA claim, but instead dealt with an oral warranty under state law that the court found not to be subject to the MMWA. Incredibly, the court ignored the later 2002 11th Circuit opinion in *Davis v. Southern Energy Homes*, 305 F. 3d 1268 (11th Cir. 2002), holding that MMWA claims are subject to binding arbitration, as well as the Fifth Circuit case, and all of the other contrary authority that the Maryland court at least had the intellectual honesty to recognize.

So, both the Terrapins and the Gamecocks got it wrong, in my humble opinion. The Maryland court at least looked at all the right authorities; it just came to the wrong conclusion. The South Carolina court got it sloppy wrong. I guess that they just aren't making law clerks like they used to.

Koons Ford of Baltimore, Inc. v. Lobach, Maryland Court of Appeals, No. 66, March 20, 2007. *Simpson v. MSA of Myrtle Beach, Inc.*, Opinion No. 26293 (March 26, 2007).

Put That Knife Away!

July 2007

By Thomas B. Hudson

Savvy dealers use arbitration agreements to reduce their exposure to class action lawsuits and large punitive damages awards. An arbitration agreement will accomplish those objectives—provided that a court will enforce it.

Consumer lawyers who encounter a dealer using an arbitration agreement will pour over the agreement looking for reasons to argue to the court that the arbitration agreement should not be enforced. Often, they argue that the terms of the agreement are "unconscionable" (if they hadn't paid a fortune for a law school education, they'd used a word like "unfair"). As we have reviewed court opinions over the years, we've seen many arguments that various provisions are unfair and should not be enforced. One of those arguments, raised frequently, relates to so-called "carve-outs."

If an arbitration agreement says that all disputes between the customer and the dealer or creditor will be subject to arbitration except for repossession, that's a carve-out. Over the years, we have seen a few courts hold that such a carve-out makes the arbitration agreement too one-sided, and those courts have refused to enforce the agreements.

I generally don't favor carve-outs for repossession. There's always a risk, albeit, I think, a small risk that a court will refuse to enforce the agreement, because it thinks the carve-out isn't fair. That risk might be worth taking, if there were a worthwhile benefit to be realized in return. I don't think there is, however, because the experience of our clients is that defaulting consumers almost never ask for arbitration. The last place on the planet they want to be is across the table from the creditor that they have failed to pay.

The operative word in that last sentence is "almost." There's always an exception, and this case illustrates one.

David and Pritam Hamilton bought a car and financed the purchase with Ford Motor Credit Company. The financing agreement included an arbitration provision. The Hamiltons missed their first payment on the car, and FMCC granted them a two-month extension. After that extension, the Hamiltons missed three more payments. At that time, FMCC determined that the Hamiltons' account was uncollectible and filed a replevin action seeking return of the vehicle.

After FMCC filed the replevin action, the Hamiltons

attempted to make payments on two occasions, but FMCC refunded those payments; instead, the credit company chose to accelerate the agreement, requiring payment of the full balance. The Hamiltons moved to dismiss FMCC's replevin action and to compel arbitration under the terms of the financing agreement's arbitration provision. The trial court granted FMCC's replevin request and denied the Hamiltons' motion to compel arbitration. The Hamiltons appealed.

The Arkansas Court of Appeals affirmed the trial court's ruling. The appellate court found that the arbitration provision clearly provided that FMCC did not surrender the right to enforce its security interest in the car, and that FMCC's replevin action was merely an attempt to enforce its security interest in the car. Thus, because FMCC exercised a right clearly reserved to it under the arbitration provision, the appellate court agreed that the Hamiltons were not entitled to compel arbitration.

In this instance, the creditor used a repossession carve-out and withstood the customer's challenge to arbitration. You can draw a couple of conclusions from the decision:

- The first possible conclusion is that I'm too cautious in suggesting that dealers and creditors not use repo carve-outs. This case illustrates that, at least in some instances, they work.
- Second, FMCC might have dodged a bullet here. Given a more consumer-oriented judge, the case might have gone the other way. But the worst case for FMCC would have been to arbitrate its replevin action.

Carve-out, and take your chances with enforcement. Or no carve-out, and in the very rare case, you arbitrate a replevin action.

For me, that's an easy call. I still say, "No carve-outs."

Hamilton v. Ford Motor Credit Co., 2007 WL 1490786 (Ark. App. May 23, 2007).

Courts Uphold Arbitration Agreements

September 2007

By Nicole F. Munro

Score two points for the good guys! Two recent arbitration decisions are keeping arbitration in its rightful place as an option for creditors to resolve their disputes with consumers. Arbitration is by no means a way of trying to take away from the consumer the right to assert a dispute or to take legal action. Rather, it is a more cost-effective and time-efficient manner of working through and resolving disputes—a resource savings to benefit ultimately the consumer, because it reduces a creditor's overall cost of doing business.

In one case, *Ritter v. Grady Automotive Group*, the merger clause in the purchase contract (i.e., buyers order) threatened to invalidate a contemporaneously signed arbitration agreement. Thankfully, the court didn't think so.

Jennifer Ritter bought a new 2003 BMW 745Li vehicle from Grady Buick, a dealership that is a subsidiary of the Grady Automotive Group. Her husband, Daryl, did not accompany her to buy the vehicle. Jennifer signed several documents, including a "Motor Vehicle Purchase Contract," a retail installment contract, a power of attorney, an arbitration agreement, and a title application. Jennifer alleged that the dealership represented to her that the BMW 745Li was the safest vehicle on the road, partly because it had front and side air bags. While driving the 745Li several months later, Jennifer was involved in an accident. None of the air bags deployed. Moreover, the seat belt allegedly failed to hold Jennifer in place, and she sustained injuries. Daryl was not in the vehicle.

Jennifer sued Grady Automotive Group, BMW, and other defendants, alleging misrepresentations, manufacturing defects, defective design, negligent and/or wanton installation of the air bag and seat belt systems, breach of contract, and breach of warranties. Daryl also sued the defendants, asserting a derivative loss-of-consortium claim.

Grady moved to compel arbitration of all of Jennifer's and Daryl's claims, based on the arbitration agreement signed by Jennifer. The trial court granted the motion. Both Jennifer and Daryl moved for the trial court to alter, amend, vacate, or reconsider its order compelling arbitration. The trial court refused, and Jennifer and Daryl appealed.

Jennifer and Daryl argued that the merger clause in the purchase contract rendered the separate arbitration agreement invalid. Daryl also argued that the arbitration agreement did not bind him, because he did not sign it.

The Alabama Supreme Court affirmed the trial court's decision. It found that the merger clause did not operate to render the contemporaneously and separately signed arbitration agreement invalid. It also found that Daryl's claims were subject to arbitration, because they were derived from Jennifer's contract with the dealership.

This decision is very helpful in situations when a spouse is not present when the transaction documents are signed. The next case, while not an auto finance case, is instructive regarding what disputes an arbitration agreement will cover.

In *Gardner v. Randall Mortgage Services, Inc.*, Randall Mortgage contacted Judy Gardner through a mail solicitation to refinance her mortgage. The solicitation contained information that could only be obtained from a credit report. Gardner had never given Randall Mortgage permission to obtain a copy of her credit report.

Gardner contacted Randall Mortgage and spoke to Eric Smith, a broker. Smith allegedly promised her a loan in the amount of $83,000 with a 2-year fixed rate of 8.99% and an adjustable rate thereafter, with payments not to be greater than $600 per month. An appraisal of Gardner's home, arranged by Smith, valued the home at $105,000. However, the actual value of Gardner's home was not more than $50,000. Smith then arranged for Mark Ferrar to close the loan. Ferrar visited Gardner at her place of employment. He presented her with several documents for execution, one of which was an arbitration agreement. Gardner noticed that the loan amount was for $89,000, with monthly payments of $695, and that a $6,000 broker fee was included. She did not protest these terms. Gardner claimed that she was too embarrassed to ask questions because her co-workers were within listening distance. In addition, she claimed that she did not have an opportunity to read the documents that she signed and that she did not receive copies of these documents.

Several years after closing the loan, Gardner attempted to refinance and learned that the appraisal of her home far exceeded the home's actual value. Gardner sued Randall Mortgage for violating the Fair Credit Reporting Act.

Randall Mortgage filed for a stay, pending arbitration. The U.S. District Court for the Southern District of Ohio granted the stay. Specifically, the court found that Gardner did not allege being deceived into signing the loan documents and that ignorance of the terms of the arbitration agreement was no defense to its enforcement. In addition, the court rejected Gardner's argument that some of her FCRA claims were not subject to the arbitration agreement, because they had occurred prior to the transaction with Randall Mortgage. The arbitration agreement, the court found, provided for arbitration of any dispute concerning the parties' relationship. Furthermore, Gardner did not limit the FCRA claims in her argument to those that occurred prior to the time period when she transacted business with Randall Mortgage. Rather, she asserted that the violations occurred throughout her transactions with Randall Mortgage—during the loan repayment period—and that they continued regularly.

Thankfully, arbitration was allowed to proceed in both cases, further reinforcing the right of parties to decide how to resolve their disputes. These cases reinforce the fact that careful drafting of the arbitration agreement is critical. In addition, to avoid some of the issues mentioned above, it's a good idea to have an established process for presenting and having consumers sign arbitration agreements.

In summary, it is critical to understand how all the transaction documents interplay. While this is evident when you're talking about a conditional delivery agreement (i.e., spot delivery agreement) and the retail installment contract, it is not always so evident when you're considering arbitration agreements and other transaction documents. Therefore, it's never a bad idea to have a qualified attorney review the language in your arbitration agreement and the process you use for having consumers sign it.

Ritter v. Grady Automotive Group, 2007 WL 1454458 (Ala. May 18, 2007). *Gardner v. Randall Mortgage Services, Inc.*, 2007 WL 1432047 (S.D. Ohio May 14, 2007).

Appendix 1

Auto Finance Lexicon

This book deals with the legal side of auto finance and leasing. In the articles, we sometimes use shorthand references to legal terms. Here are some of the terms you will see from time to time and a short description of what they mean.

AG: Stands for Attorney General. Every state has one, essentially he or she is the top legal officer in the state. AGs usually enforce consumer protection laws and regulations. When we are being cynical, we sometimes say the "AG" stands for "Aspiring Governor." We also sometimes say the same thing when we aren't being cynical.

CLA: The Consumer Leasing Act. The CLA governs disclosures in consumer lease transactions. The CLA is actually Chapter 5 of TILA, but is usually referred to as if it is a separate piece of legislation. The Federal Reserve Board's Regulation M deals with the Consumer Leasing Act.

ECOA: The Federal Equal Credit Opportunity Act. The ECOA prohibits credit discrimination on the basis of sex, race, marital status, etc. The Federal Reserve Board's Regulation B deals with the Equal Credit Opportunity Act.

F&I: The "finance and insurance" department of a dealership is called the F&I department. That's where financing terms are arranged, and various products like credit insurance and extended warranties are sold.

FRB: The Federal Reserve Board. The FRB authors a number of credit-related regulations that implement acts of Congress. These include Reg. B (The Equal Credit Opportunity Act), Reg. Z (The Truth in Lending Act), and Reg. M (The Consumer Leasing Act).

FTC: The Federal Trade Commission is a federal agency that enforces several federal laws and regulations with respect to car dealers, including the TILA, the ECOA, and Regs. Z and B). The FTC is the toughest, most consumer-friendly enforcement agency in Washington, and is the "federal cop" for car dealers.

Reg. B: A regulation of the FRB implementing the ECOA.

Reg. M: A regulation of the FRB implementing the CLA.

Reg. P: An FTC regulation implementing the Gramm-Leach-Bliley Act's privacy provisions.

Reg. Z: A regulation of the FRB implementing TILA.

RISA: Refers to a "retail installment sales act." Nearly every state has a RISA. Some states (about half) have a special version of a RISA for motor vehicle financing, and a separate RISA for other kinds of personal property financing. RISAs typically regulate finance charge rates, late charges, grace periods, bad check charges, disclosures, and the like in auto financing agreements between dealers and customers.

RISC: A retail installment sale contract. This document is used to document a credit sale from a dealer to a buyer. After the transaction between the dealer and the customer is completed, the dealer then usually sells the RISC to a finance company or bank. Buy here, pay here dealers hold RISCs and collect payments from buyers, unless they have created an affiliated finance company to which they assign them. If you call a RISC a "loan," Spot (the Dalmatian mascot for our legal newsletter, ***Spot Delivery***®), has instructions to bite you on the ankle.

TILA: The federal Truth in Lending Act. TILA governs disclosures in consumer credit transactions. This is the "granddaddy" of federal disclosure laws. The Federal Reserve Board's Regulation Z deals with the Truth in Lending Act.

Tort: A tort is a "civil wrong." The actions that comprise a tort can also comprise a crime, but a tort is not necessarily a crime. Examples of torts are negligence, fraud, and defamation.

UDAP: Refers to unfair and deceptive acts and practices. The FTC has UDAP provisions, and most states do, as well. Only the FTC can enforce the FTC's version; that is, a consumer cannot bring a private lawsuit to enforce it. This, however, is not necessarily so at the state level, since many state UDAP laws permit consumers to sue. UDAP laws are favorites of lawyers who sue dealers, because they are very general in their prohibitions and usually provide for a multiple (two or three times the consumer's actual damages), plus attorneys' fees.

Other terms you may see, and what they mean:

ADA: Americans With Disabilities Act

CLA: Consumer Leasing Act

FCRA: Fair Credit Reporting Act

FFI: Federally Insured Financial Institution

FinCEN: A unit of the U.S. Treasury Department

FMCC: Ford Motor Credit Corporation

GAP: GAP is an insurance, or an insurance-like product, which, in the event of a total loss of a vehicle, pays the difference between the consumer's insurance proceeds and the amount owed on the car.

GLB: Gramm-Leach-Bliley Act, the federal law dealing with privacy.

GMAC: General Motors Acceptance Corporation

HIDC: Holder-In-Due-Course

MMWA: Magnuson-Moss Warranty Act

NADA: National Automobile Dealers Association

NMAC: Nissan Motors Acceptance Corporation

OFAC: The Office of Foreign Assets Control, a Treasury Department Unit

RICO: Racketeer Influenced and Corrupt Organizations Act

SAR: Suspicious Activity Report, required under certain circumstances

SBCWA: Song-Beverly Consumer Warranty Act

SID: Starter Interrupt Device

UCC: Uniform Commercial Code

UCLA: Uniform Consumer Leasing Act

Appendix 2

A Quick Primer on Laws and Regulations

A word about laws and regulations: Laws are passed by legislatures. Congress passes federal laws, and state legislatures pass state laws. "Rules" (such as the FTC's Used Car Rule) and regulations are issued by agencies or other state or federal non-legislative bodies that have been given rule-making or regulatory authority by the legislative body.

An attempt to change a law requires having Congress or the state legislature pass a new law, a process that can be very difficult. Changing regulations can also be difficult, but not usually as difficult as changing a law. Sometimes regulatory authorities don't have the power to change regulations, because the laws they are administering won't permit the change. As an example, even *if* the Federal Reserve Board wanted to amend Reg. Z to apply to auto finance transactions in which the amount financed is over $25,000, it could *not* do so because TILA—an act of Congress—provides that such transactions are not subject to TILA's disclosure requirements.

Appendix 3

Index

E

M

N

U